339

Sacred Mountains

Adrian Cooper is a writer, traveller, painter and independent scholar. He obtained his Ph.D. in geography at Birkbeck College in the University of London. He is a frequent broadcaster and has woven his academic interests in sacred landscapes and ancient wisdom into a series of radio meditations and other programmes.

Sacred Mountains

Ancient Wisdom and Modern Meanings

Adrian Cooper

Floris Books

First published in 1997 by Floris Books

British Library CIP Data available

ISBN 0-86315-235-X

Printed in Great Britain
by The Bath Press, Bath.

Contents

To my parents, with all my love.

Acknowledgements

First and foremost, I must thank all the people who agreed to take part in the research interviews for this project. They gave their time, their experience, and their wisdom freely and eloquently. In doing so, they gave me one of the most stimulating and fulfilling opportunities in my life. I have learned so much from all those wonderful individuals. Ultimately, this book is both an analysis of their mountain experiences, as well as a celebration of the vitality and grace of their insights.

I am also profoundly grateful to my editor, Christopher Moore, without whose vision and patience this book could not have been developed. It has been a privilege to receive Christopher's advice and guidance, and to have worked with a man whose experience inspired me to keep writing.

Many other people have offered me their encouragement and assistance during the ten year development of this book. Among them, Dr John Davis, Birkbeck College, University of London, helped me form my early ideas and sense of direction as I began to navigate the vast potential of spiritual geography. Professor Surinder Bhardwaj, Kent State University, Ohio, and Dr Carol Prorok, Slippery Rock University, Pennsylvania, were also exceptionally generous to me as I took my first faltering steps in publishing and lecturing to a broader audience. At home, my lunch-time companions have also been more than generous. To Mr Malcolm Reay and Mr Bill MacGregor, I offer my warm thanks for the loan of books from their personal libraries. And to Mr Michael Wood, I am also grateful for having the opportunity to view his vast collection of mountain and architectural slides. (But Mike, I'll always say your work should have a much wider circulation!).

Finally, I must record the incalculable debt I owe to my parents for all their love, and their belief in my work. Without their support and encouragement, my writing would not have received the oxygen it needed. My imagination would not have been ignited. My curiosity would not have been aroused. And my life would not have been as richly stimulating as it is.

AC

Introduction

These mountains are our temples, our sanctuaries and our resting places. They are a place of hope, a place of vision, and a very special and holy place where the Great Spirit speaks with us. Therefore, these mountains are our sacred places.   (Snow 1977, 13)

Since the early dawn of human civilization, mountains have been held in absolute awe and sacred wonder. Their sheer size, their changing light, their often ferocious weather patterns and their constant ability to claim human lives have all forged, across every continent, a reverence for mountains and their unique, inspiring majesty. Visions, forces and events were encountered within these highest and most dramatic places which could not be explained without reference to divinities, eternal truths and ancient wisdom. Terror and the sense of inescapable supernatural power seemed to pervade and haunt the traveller at every peak, chasm, pinnacle and ledge. But in addition to these threatening interpretations, mountains also contributed to an awakening of human consciousness, creativity, enquiry and thought. Ways of seeing the entire cosmos developed through quests toward realities beyond the immediate, the ordinary and the everyday. Whether those philosophies were constructed around ideas of self, wilderness, the absolute, emptiness or the unconscious, mountains dominated and inspired the early millennia of human development. Within the great variety of these philosophies, there was often a significant association between mainstream human culture and mountain landscape. Indeed, 'the symbolic and religious significance of mountains is endless.' (Eliade 1974, 99)

For most people today however, those traditional ways of seeing mountains are far removed from their everyday lives. Mountains are now distant places: perhaps seen on vacation or possibly noticed as part of the scenery in a film or television programme. Certainly, such glimpses at mountain landscapes do not inspire the same universal reverence they used to in distant times and places. Indeed, within technological societies at least, we could be forgiven for developing a mistaken belief that mountains no longer have a significant part to play in our ways of understanding ourselves or our contemporary world.

But despite this deceptive impression, there remains a genuine and persistent thirst for the spiritual, for a sense of awe and wonder and for an encounter with mysteries beyond the attention of technology and rational science (Fox 1983). It is that persistence which lies at the foundation of this book. Whether it is from received religious doctrine or in varying reaction to that instruction, the 144 interviewed people who contributed to this book (see Appendix) have kept hold of their will to seek out and relish spiritual experiences from their visits to mountains. This research is a record of those people's spiritual experiences in mountains, their own stories in their own words. And where specific passages of literature have added further colour to those encounters, those passages too are quoted here.

Ultimately, this book is a barometer of the inspirational value which these 144 people place upon the time they spend in mountains. But this account comes unashamedly with a critical voice. It aims to inspire further thought and debate, to present a challenge and provoke change. Quite simply, for many Christians, Jews, Taoists, Buddhists and others, all over the world, not enough attention is paid by their religious leaders to the spiritual experiences which can be discovered from making such personal journeys.

Through their own personal search, these interviewees have found places, and distinctive ways of seeing, from where they can resist the mechanical, reductionist and rational philosophies with which they remain so disillusioned. In one sense, this resistance was the principal motivation for travelling to mountains: 'to escape the rat-race,' 'to get away from it all,' 'to take it all in,' 'to become alive again.' Yet, these modern experiences of mountain spirituality have also been influenced by the individuals' everyday lives away from the peaks. And in their turn, those everyday lives have also been significantly influenced by the mountains visited. An active, provocative and powerful exchange of meaning and inspiration between mountain spirituality and everyday life, has therefore distanced these people from the mundane, the hum-drum, and their received notions of personal ambition and material success.

Among the world's mountains, these 144 people, along with countless others, have encountered the unknowable mysteries of the sacred which lie far beyond our understanding, and yet still draw us toward them. Indeed, for many of the people who contributed to this book, the prospect of encountering their vision of the sacred acts as one of the most powerful magnets in their lives. Vacation and travel destinations are never a problem when the mountains call — a call of the unknown and the unknowable. Powerful forces which, even when they are seen and studied, sketched, painted, photographed and reflected upon, still remain fascinatingly 'other': always beyond our grasp of understanding and expression. By its very nature, the sacred will always remain elusive.

A way through the clouds

It was Rudyard Kipling's 'Explorer' who saw that the concealed mysteries of mountain landscapes can bring out the child-like and dream-like in all who are willing to search for the sacred:

> Something hidden. Go and find it.
> Go and look behind the Ranges —
> Something lost behind the Ranges.
> Lost and waiting for you. Go!

We are drawn on, surrounded and inspired by evidence of sacred treasure 'behind the mountain': ancient wisdom and eternal truths with which so many yearn to be at one. In each phrase and sentence of Kipling's 'The Explorer,' it is easy to imagine excited young hands fingering the sides of vast, towering walls of mountain rock. Excited eyes gazing upwards in awed, silent wonder. And at sun-set, or dawn, or after a violent thunder storm, when the effects of subtle light and shade are even more rare, this sense of encountering the marvellous and unknown has even greater emphasis.

Within the Brihadaranyaka Upanishad, a sense of encountering a higher realm of experience and beauty is concisely expressed:

> From the unreal, lead me to the real.
> From the darkness lead me to the light.
> From death, lead me to immortality.

Encountering the sacred in mountain landscapes is as much a pilgrimage as any other journey of devotion and quest. The ascent of a mountain face or path can symbolize a search for fresh insights and understanding of ourselves and of the world in which we live. The

struggles of any climb are only overcome when we are completely
focused on overcoming our own limitations: our doubts, our distractions and our dilemmas and other anxieties. All these limitations are
left behind, as if they were a tattered old coat which can now be discarded in favour of new clothes: new priorities, new criteria for personal success, and therefore new goals. Throughout this inspirational
discovery, many travellers find they uncover an energy which they
had never before experienced — a new energy, intensely exhilarating
and fresh as the mountain air, an energy which completely transcends
all the laborious rites and rituals of doctrinal, organized religion. In
part of the Hindu Manasakhanda scripture, this transcendence of rite
and ritual is captured perfectly:

> He who thinks of (the Himalayas), even if he does not see it,
> is greater than he who accomplishes all his devotions at
> Benares. He who thinks of (the Himalayas) will be freed from
> all his sins ... (Atkinson 1974, 307-8)

But of all possible pilgrimages, how many can inspire their modern
devotees with such visions of vastness, harmony and enlightenment?
Within Wordsworth's autobiographical poem 'The Prelude,' the sense
of a personal mountain pilgrimage of awed discovery is expressed
with astonishing clarity in his description of a night-time ascent on
Mount Snowdon, Wales:

> The Moon hung naked in a firmament
> Of azure without cloud, and at my feet
> Rested a silent sea of hoary mist.
> A hundred hills their dusky backs upheaved
> All over this still ocean; and beyond,
> Far, far beyond, the solid vapours stretched,
> In headlands, tongues and promontory shapes,
> Into the main Atlantic, that appeared
> To dwindle, and give up his majesty,
> Usurped upon far as the sight could reach.
> (Wordsworth 1850 14.39-49)

For Henry David Thoreau, his pilgrimages through mountain landscapes were a personal quest for 'wildness.' He sought out the wild
essence of mystery and grandeur which he only saw in mountains, but
which he found most convincingly celebrated in traditional, native
American cultures:

> At the same time that we are earnest to explore and learn
> all things, we require that all things be mysterious and
> unexplorable, that land and sea be infinitely wild,
> unsurveyed, and unfathomed by us because they are
> unfathomable. We can never have enough of nature. We
> must be refreshed by the sight of inexhaustible vigour, vast
> and titanic features ... (Thoreau 1971, 317-8)

In a very similar appreciation of these themes concerning physical exploration and spiritual quest for the sacred, the Chinese Ch'an meditations of the Tang Dynasty poet and mountain recluse Han-Shan express many of these resonances of quest and unknowability:

> Men these days search for a way through the clouds,
> But the cloud way is dark and without sign,
> The mountains are high and often steep and rocky;
> In the broadest valleys the sun seldom shines.
> Green crests before you and behind,
> White clouds to east and west —
> Do you want to know where the cloud way lies?
> There it is, in the midst of the Void!
> (Han-Shan 1970, 87)

In addition to recording these, and other, passages of literature which have inspired the 144 interviewees in their spiritual travels, this book also records extracts of their own words: personal stories and reflections, dilemmas, questions and expressions of insight, awe and wonder alongside the words of more familiar writers. Side by side, these voices support each other. For many of the contributors, the literature gave them the words which helped them express their own reaction to the often over-powering impressions of being in the mountains. And at the same time, the literature of Muir, Wordsworth, Han-Shan and others is only kept alive, and elaborated upon, through the ways in which it is read and re-read, discussed, re-interpreted and challenged today. In the following extract for example, Clare, an Administration Supervisor from San Bernardino, California, described some of the ways in which her experiences of the mountains in Zhejiang Province, China were heightened through the ways she found inspiration from Han-Shan's words:

> I need to keep Han-Shan's verse by me when I'm at work,
> and also in my bag when I'm out. So at a break-time I can

take them out and remember the great times we had down in Zhejiang (Province, China) and out in the T'ien-t'ai (mountain range). Just being with the other guys. Being there, really living in the moment, and finding what we need there ... But also, I know, you can never get fully inside those words (of Han-Shan) ... We live in completely different times, and we have different problems on our minds in the twentieth century ... And, for me, the mountains are my first, major inspiration. But then, after I've read Han-Shan's words, they help to form that inspiration into something I can relate to more fully, so I can use it within my life now.

This, then, is a book of many voices. Sometimes in agreement. Other times not. But at the heart of all these voices is a sense of having been profoundly awakened and inspired by mountains. Whether that awakening is directed toward a specific deity, a new sense of self, or a raw unfathomable nature, the meaning of mountains can inspire people to grow beyond the person they once were: beyond the burden of everyday anxieties. The Scottish mountaineer W.H. Murray captured this sense of finding new inspiration within himself, and in his transformed vision of the physical world, when he described the first time he saw the Himalayas from the north Indian plains:

> An Arctic continent of the heavens, far above the earth and its girdling clouds: divorced wholly from this planet. The idea of climbing over such distant and delicate tips, the very desire of it, never entered my heart or head. Had I been born among or in sight of them, I might have been led to worship the infinite beauty they symbolized, but not to set boot on their flanks, or axe on a crest.
>
> For a moment dazzled, we suddenly saw spread before us a world made new. All the senses of the soul were not so much refreshed as reborn, as though after death. We were free men once again, for the first time in months really able to live in the present moment. (Murray 1951, 28, 34)

John Ruskin's first sight of the Alps inspired a similar heightened appreciation for what he saw:

> There was no thought in any of us of their being mere clouds. They were as clear as crystal, sharp and pure horizon sky, and already tinged with rose by the sinking sun. Infinitely

beyond all that we had ever thought or dreamed — the seen
walls of lost Eden could not have been more beautiful to us;
not more awful, round heaven, the walls of sacred death.
(Ruskin 1885, 97)

Of all the 144 contributors to this book, thirty-seven identified themselves as mountaineers in contrast to others who preferred to walk or
ski. Throughout the interviews, those thirty-seven continually returned
to quote and discuss a small number of mountaineering authors whose
writing embraced the resonances of sacred meaning to be found
within mountain landscapes. Of all such authors, the Italian climber,
Guido Rey, was most frequently quoted. As the following extract illustrates, Rey's words bring an honesty and humanity to his extraordinary encounters with an unknowable sacredness on the Matterhorn:

> ... I tasted the fresh, ineffable joy of reaching the highest point
> — the summit; the spot where the mountain ceases to rise
> and man's soul to yearn. It is an almost perfect form of
> spiritual satisfaction, such as perhaps attained by the
> philosopher who has at last discovered a truth that contents
> and rests his mind. (Rey 1946, 126-7)

The raw, painful experience of finding inspiration which Rey
describes here makes his words very closely comparable to the cultures of traditional peoples for whom mountains have assumed the
aura of divine symbolism. Rey's view of heaven was often completely
unified with the way he saw the Alpine mountains themselves. The
two become one, as was often the case within traditional cultures.
Place and paradise as a single experience. A single vision. In 1865, the
Matterhorn provided Edward Whymper with just such an encounter.
Having suffered the loss of four climbing companions who had fallen
to their death on that expedition, Whymper described the following
encounter with completely unworldly visions:

> ... a mighty arch appeared, rising above the Lyskamm, high
> into the sky. Pale, colourless, and noiseless, but perfectly
> sharp and defined, except where it was lost in the clouds, this
> unearthly apparition seemed like a vision from another world;
> and, almost appalled, we watched with amazement the
> gradual development of two vast crosses, one on either side.
> If the Taugwalders (the local guides) had not been the first to
> perceive it, I should have doubted my senses. They thought it

had some connection with the accident, and I, after a while,
that it might bear some relation to ourselves. But our movements had no effect upon it. The spectral forms remained
motionless. It was a fearful and wonderful sight; unique in
my experience, and impressive beyond description, coming at
such a moment. (Whymper 1900, 387-8)

Whilst still gripped in the teeth of danger and anxiety, Whymper's
experience exemplifies the theological writing which mountaineers
have felt inspired to record. But perhaps no climber has sought to
reflect upon the spiritual aspects of mountaineering more than George
Mallory:

Have we vanquished an enemy? None but ourselves. Have
we gained success? That word means nothing here. Have we
won a kingdom? No ... and yes. We have achieved an
ultimate satisfaction ... (Mallory 1918, 162)

In Mallory's view, the climber can never completely conquer a
mountain. Even to consider that conquest is nothing but complete
vanity. Rather, only part of the self is overcome. As a Hindu yogi
conquers the arrogance of pride through self-transcendence, so can a
mountain climber achieve the realization that material success is at
most secondary to the more profoundly satisfying enlightenment
gained through his or her physical and spiritual struggle to reach a
summit. It is the ultimate and most complete of all challenges. On
occasions however, such challenges can be terrifyingly vivid and stark.
Whilst suffering from delirium on Annapurna for example, Maurice
Herzog saw a premonition of the mountain as his grave:

I looked death straight in the face, besought it with all my
strength. Then abruptly I had a vision of the life of men.
Those who are leaving it for ever are never alone. Resting
against the mountain, which was watching over me, I
discovered horizons I had never seen. There at my feet, on
those vast plains, millions of beings were following a destiny
they had not chosen.
    There is a supernatural power in those close to death.
Strange intuitions identify one with the whole world. The
mountain spoke with the wind as it whistled over the ridges
or ruffled the foliage. All would end well. I should remain
there, forever, beneath a few stones and a cross.

They had given me my ice axe. The breeze was gentle and
sweetly scented. My friends departed, knowing that I was
now safe. I watched them go their way with slow, sad steps.
The procession withdrew along the narrow path. They would
regain the plains and the wide horizons. For me, silence.
(Herzog 1952, 311)

Although the physical boundaries of mountains are clearly limited,
their influence beyond those limits is far more complex and varied.
Confronting their awesome height and massiveness is often the first
time we encounter a natural phenomenon which literally dwarfs us.
Contrasting forms of wilderness, such as deserts and tundra, can only
stretch away from a viewer toward the horizon. And although the
colours and temperature ranges of those wilderness landscapes may be
different from more familiar landscapes, it is almost impossible to
appreciate the vastness of such areas, even with the benefit of an
aircraft or helicopter. In contrast, standing at the foot of a towering
peak can have a profound, humbling immediacy not found elsewhere.
It can therefore change personal priorities, ambitions and criteria for
individual success. It can inspire people to tell members of their
family, as well as friends, and others, about those profoundly trans-
forming experiences. At work, the people with whom I developed this
book have often described how they found themselves dealing with
colleagues and customers with more understanding and tolerance:
ways of working which they find more consistent with the humility,
compassion and sensitivity inspired from their travels in the mountains. I have even been told by office staff of the ways they have
surrounded their computer screens with photographs of favourite
mountain scenery as a way of dealing with the monotonous routine
and attrition of their daily work.

In whatever way the inspiration of mountains is expressed — in the
need to have photographs in the office or home, or in other, more
profound ways — the power of mountains to shape and inspire
personal and shared spiritual experiences is undeniable. At a time
when organized religion is finding the challenge of adapting to new
ways of thinking and seeing to be so difficult, I hope that this book
and the voices of the people who helped make it, may contribute to
the exploration of new forms of religious gathering, worship, and
reflection, as well as to the finding of credible and personally satisfying responses to spiritual questions and quests.

For a mountain to play the role of Mount Analogue,

I concluded, its summit must be inaccessible, but its base accessible to human beings as nature has made them. It must be unique, and it must exist geographically. The door to the invisible must be visible. (Daumal 1974, 42)

CHAPTER 1

North America

In sorrow I am sending a voice, O six powers of the earth,
hear me in sorrow. With tears I am sending a voice. May
you behold me and hear me that my people may live again.
De Mallie (1984, 296)

Ancient wisdom

Sacred mountains have inspired awe, wonder, terror and tranquillity since the earliest development of native American spirituality.[1] Following the time when their ancestors crossed the Bering Straits from Siberia over 40000 years ago, native Americans have developed a rich, compelling and provocative collection of wisdom through which they maintained a profound reverence for the mountains they knew.

In the eastern woodland regions of the Appalachians, in modern-day Maine, the Passamaquoddy and Penobscot peoples shared stories about the spirit of the night wind which blew around the ice-shattered granite face of Mount Katahdin.[2] In fear of those ferocious rock-walls, the Passamaquoddy and Penobscot held the summit of Katahdin as a complete taboo: it was never approached, never climbed, always avoided. The risk of encountering the giants and other grotesque spirits who lived within the mountain always outweighed any sense of adventure which might attract the foolish climber to try and conquer these unimaginable horrors.

Further south, in New York state, the Iroquois held their own extraordinary visions of reverence for the Adirondack mountains. Among them, Mount Marcy was clothed with mystery and intense significance for every possible event which might occur: a rock-fall, a stream observed in the light of a full moon, evidence of decay among the woodland, and the shape of individual boulders, all carried with them stories and wisdom which held the Iroquois in an abiding state of unity with their mountain — a unity of reverence and respect for powers which lay beyond the vocabulary or the imaginations of those people. But above all else, an abiding source of inspiration, education and community spirituality.

However, whilst these mountains of the east were often shrouded in cloud and rain, the summits of the south-west were surrounded by a clear, dry air through which its inhabitants could gaze for mile upon mile of sharp rocky horizons. A panorama of the supernatural. As with the eastern peoples of the Appalachians and Adirondacks though, the tribes of the south-west, such as the Rio Grande Pueblos, the Tewa, Apache, Navaho, and the Hopi, kept away from the summits of their mountains.[3] They would approach, but they would never climb. They would perform ceremonial and medicinal rites, but they would never desecrate those mountains by walking on them as they would upon the dust of the arid desert. Within Hopi tradition, for example, an adventurous climb up a mountain might lead to a heart-stopping encounter with a katsinga spirit: an experience which would inevitably lead to supernatural punishment.[4] These mountains therefore defined limits to tribal territory. To challenge those boundaries often lead to exile, or even the ultimate terror of all: slaughter by unimaginable mountain spirits.

Despite the sacred power of these boundaries, none of them compared to the physical and spiritual barrier of the Rocky mountains: a monumental and towering range stretching from northern Canada for a distance of almost four thousand miles to the Mexican plateau in the south.[5] Many of the peoples who inhabited the eastern slopes of the Rocky mountains were there as migrants, driven from their homelands for reasons of drought and famine. From the Ohio valley, the woodlands of Minnesota, or the Great Plains, this experience of long-distance travel encouraged migrant peoples such as the Cheyenne or the Crow to develop more adventurous rituals and rites which drew them closer to the mountain spirits than their eastern or south-western counterparts. These people would climb their sacred slopes and remain for long periods near the summits in a test of endurance. They would dare to encounter the spirits who dwelt there. And once they had communed in that way with the natural and supernatural powers, their visions of life would be transformed forever. They would be mature, in overwhelming awe of the mountains. They would have visions of human existence in which the seeds of ancient wisdom could be sown and nurtured for the benefit of future generations. Such initiations would therefore publicly and privately mark the beginning of true adulthood.

Over the years, those experiences and insights could be enhanced through further sacred vision quests among the mountains. For the Crow people, the higher the altitude of a chosen site for contemplation, and the more impenetrable it was agreed to be, the more fulfilling was its meditative potential.[6] Solitude had to be earned and sweated over. It had to be conducted in a place far away from shelter or companionship, a place which would test the whole person in full measure. Even today, the Stoney people of Calgary, Alberta, maintain their adherence to these intense trials of physical, emotional and spiritual endurance among the peaks surrounding Lake Louise and Banff. Once they have purified themselves, they move off in search of fresh inspiration, new visions, further insights, and eventually greater unity with the power of the mountains.

Ultimately therefore, among the Crow people, development of their individuality, wisdom and community strength, was completely at one with their private experiences of mountains. Ancient wisdom was kept alive by new stories and new experiences. New legends would be told on hearing a bird take flight in the chill of a mountain dawn. Myths would be enhanced and maintained through insights found in the rustle of grasses, the song of a river, or the music of winds blowing across rock faces, above the highest summits, or toward the farthest horizon. This was a spirituality always alive to its surroundings, a sensitive wisdom of the sacred, an undeniable and indelible link between nature and supernature.

First visits

This prospect of intense spiritual discovery, challenge and insight drew many of the contributors to this book toward the Sierra Nevada, close to the west coast of the United States, as the area of their first visit to North American mountains.[7] But although they found the Sierra Nevada an easy travel destination, they all described their surprise and frustration at feeling 'ill-equipped' and 'unprepared' to encounter the often profound spiritual experiences they found there. While the physical journey of getting to the Sierras was no real problem, the spiritual journeys they made when they got there were altogether more traumatic. One of the clearest examples of this feeling of intense anxiety was described by Danny, a usually enthusiastic apprentice motor-mechanic from Los Angeles, California:

DANNY:

> *It was as if I was a beached whale out there. I had no education in looking at the sacredness you immediately feel there. And no way of dealing with any of what I found at first ... about all the sacredness I felt there.*

At the heart of Danny's frustration, as well as other people's descriptions of this same anxiety, was the fact that they had only been taught to look at landscapes in scientific terms: as ecosystems, as river basins, and as parts of the mechanical universe. More than with any other range of mountains, anywhere in the world, this point was most frequently introduced into our interview meetings concerning the Sierra Nevada mountains. For Jed, Danny's travelling companion in the Sierras, and a fellow apprentice mechanic, his experience in these mountains broke down this science/spirituality barrier for the first time in his life:

JED:

> *All my life, I'd been taught that, like my religious questions and all those kind of things were just in one kind of 'box.' And over here, was science. Totally different ... As if they both said 'Hands off, we're different from each other!' ... But out in the Sierras, wherever we went, all I felt was wow! ... But I felt so numb because I didn't even have the words to say what I was seeing.*

Throughout their search for 'new words' to express these overwhelming experiences of freedom from bounded concepts of spirituality, Danny and Jed found themselves re-thinking their rejection of 'regular' evangelical Christian worship in which they had been educated by their parents at the Crystal Cathedral in Garden Grove, Los Angeles:

JED:

> *For me, I guess the reason why I turned my back on that sort of brand of Christianity, was because it kind of claimed to have the right answers to everything. As soon as we got into Yosemite, I knew there are no right answers to look at this place either ... and I saw I was going to have to start from scratch again, with my whole religious assumptions.*

From this unexpected, powerful and disturbing association between experiences of mountain-landscape, religious meaning and individuality, both these men found 'new words' in the writings of John Muir, naturalist and environmental campaigner.[8] Subsequently, those words served as the foundation to a more satisfying and compelling relationship with the Sierra range. Whilst they had both read some of Muir's books before their visit to the Yosemite Park, it was not until they had 'both been through this "wall" of major and complete bafflement' (Danny) that they were able to re-read Muir with a revitalized interest and appreciation. Muir's writing gave them the words they had been searching for. These were the words which gave meaning to their own experiences. These words of Muir became their 'new words' which they wove into discussions of their new insights into what they were seeing in the Sierra Nevada.

The following extract was the most frequently quoted in describing the ways in which Danny and Jed gradually answered their new need to understand these mountains 'as a very spiritual and holy thing' (Danny):

> Brooding over some vast mountain landscape, or among the spiritual countenances of mountain flowers, our bodies disappear, our mortal coils come off without any shuffling, and we blend into the rest of Nature, utterly blind to the boundaries that measure human qualities into separate individuals. (Muir 1979, 7-8)

As Danny read this section aloud at the first small-group interview meeting he attended with Jed, it was clear that both men had found a form of words which they treated with the respect of a sacred text. Thus, within their own discussions and descriptions, they frequently referred back to single words from this extract such as 'brooding' and 'vast,' or phrases such as 'we blend into the rest of Nature.' In the same way, Georgia, a bubbly art lecturer, found Muir to be an inspiration to her on her first visit to Yosemite, which was made independently from Danny and Jed. And just as those men had discovered their most important 'Muir quote,' Georgia had hers, too:

> Should one faint by the way who gains the blessings of one mountain day. Whatever his fate, long life, short life, stormy or calm, he is rich forever. (Muir 1979, 61)

Clearly, Muir's words have provided these people with the right 'new words' with which they could read and interpret Yosemite, and other parts of the Sierra Nevada during subsequent visits in ways which truly satisfied them. These were words which cast out the redundant divisions between science and spiritual feeling: between insight and equations, and between mechanics and miracles. These were a set of 'new words' which emphasised a feeling of 'amazingly reverential awe' (Georgia) and wonder. Whilst their Christian upbringing had apparently encouraged them 'to say something as soon as anything happened' (Jed), Muir's words inspired a greater confidence in remaining silent: in 'letting it be' (Georgia) and to 'accept that time out there, as so precious that you just wanted to savour it, and not worry too much with saying anything for no reason' (Danny).

For other people, Muir's *Mountains of California* was employed in exactly the same way: as a form of words which linked mountain-landscape to a personally satisfying spiritual experience. In response to Danny and Jed's quotation of Muir (1979, 7-8), the other five members of that interview group, all of whom travel, climb and walk together, suggested the following extract as a further example of words creating the 'right meaning' (Josie) for the walls of Mount Ritter, also in the Sierra Nevada, in terms of that mountain range's inspiration of personal spiritual experience:

> How truly glorious the landscape circled around this noble
> summit! — giant mountains, valleys innumerable, glaciers and
> meadows, rivers and lakes, with the wide blue sky bent
> tenderly over them all. (Muir 1894, 51-52)

As with the descriptions of Danny and Jed, this, and similar extracts, were pored over at length by these people, with 'key words' and phrases being picked out for particular mention and elaboration using stories of personal inspiration drawn from specific memories of Ritter. The following illustrates this further use of Muir's writing as 'the key to really open up that place for me in terms of its holy meaning of being out there' (Simon):

SIMON:

I just love those two words: 'truly glorious.' Truly glorious. That's all you need isn't it ... And I can remember now, sitting out there (on Mount Ritter), and just waiting until it was totally dark, and running those two words through my mind. 'Truly glorious' ... and for me, I'm a practising Buddhist, those two words formed the moment for me. That was it. And it was totally perfect. Living in the now. It was 'truly glorious' ... Those words allowed me to concentrate on the moment. To focus. And to begin to describe that precious time for myself, so I could really, really, enter into it.

Simon's use of John Muir's words within his meditation was similar to other Buddhist, Jewish and Christian contributors, all of whom found that their experience of the Sierra Nevada, during their first visit there, helped make them feel more at ease to pray and meditate. With people for whom prayer is part of their daily routine, private, silent prayer was always described as being almost spontaneous and always 'more fluent' (Kyle) than at other times, away from those mountains. But, equally, among others, such as Danny and Jed, who had not prayed or meditated for a period of years before they visited the Sierra, and who had visited those mountains with no interest in resurrecting their attention to prayer, they found that landscape-experience, and Muir's words through which they found personal meaning in the mountains, to be a 'natural starting point to pray again' (Jed).

JED:

> *If there's one thing I took away from my first visit to the Sierras, it was a total relaxation when it came to prayer. For the first time in my life, I felt I could pray quietly and privately when I felt the mood take a grip of me. And it was so beautiful. It was incredibly moving for me. And it's something, I hope, will never go away, because it's too precious to me now to lose at all.*

Again and again, this overwhelming inspiration to pray and/or to meditate was returned to within our interview meetings. In particular, descriptions and stories of prayer/meditation experiences revealed that they were not simply in response to the mountain landscapes alone. Rather, it was only when these people had found the words with which they could create a satisfying interpretation of the mountains that they could begin to respond to it, prayerfully and meditatively, in ways which satisfied them. But having identified a need for the right words with which to pray, or the words with which to articulate meditation insights, many went through spiritual experiences of attempted prayer, and attempted meditation before they discovered 'new words.' The following contribution from Gene, a thoughtful and softly spoken military policeman from Washington, is typical of the thoughts of other contributors on the need for the right words to help productive prayer and meditation:

GENE:

> *It was just like being crushed by this awesome weight! I mean, where do you begin? This huge, vast, massive place. Nothing prepares you for*

it ... You see it on TV, but that's only on a small screen, and you're distanced from it. On the other side of the room ... But there, with it all around you. My mind was racing. And I knew I just wasn't enjoying it or getting anything from it because all the time, I was just looking for a 'handle' to it all ... And as soon as I'd found that 'handle,' those right words to express myself to myself, then it all began to happen for me.

When the right words had helped people like Gene begin to pray and meditate, those same words formed a first link with the multiple traditions of creation spirituality: an awe and wonder inspired from the divine wisdom embodied in the natural landscape. With the right 'new words,' the appreciation of creation as a divine wonder could begin:

> In the beginning was the Word,
> and the Word was with God
> and the Word was God.
> He was with God in the beginning.
> Through him all things were made;
> Without him nothing was made that has been made.
> (John 1:1–3)

In a similar way, the Taoist contributors to this book found value in the right words to structure their new insights in their first visits to the Sierra Nevada. For Chester, a middle-aged Texan with an ability to capture and express the thoughts of his interview-group in a single expression, his own Taoist beliefs found renewed energy during the first time he visited Yosemite:

CHESTER:
A couple of days into my time there (in Yosemite), I was reading that Richard Wilhelm book, The Secret of the Golden Flower, *and I found a section where he says we participate in all the cosmos (page 11). We participate. Fully. In every way. We participate in the cosmos. Inwardly and outwardly ... and as soon as I'd read those words, and with all I'd seen that day. That was it, for me. That was like someone dramatically taking away a cloth and saying 'Boy, that's your path right there. Follow it. Savour it. Treasure it.' ... Those words (from Wilhelm) triggered that insight for me. They were the key which unlocked that door.*

Later in that discussion group, and on other occasions as well, Chester described how his discovery of just a few words of inspiration unlocked his quest into the traditions of appreciating creation within his Taoist persuasion. And others too, within their own spiritual paths, also found a way into this long and multiple tradition of creation spirituality. In addition to inspiring these people to reach out, beyond the confines of the ways of thinking they had inherited from parents or from traditional, orthodox churches, synagogues and temples, they found more and more imaginative and creative ways of seeing, thinking and experiencing the mountain landscapes they encountered on these first visits. Specifically, through the discovery of these 'right words,' careful reflection on the mountain-landscapes, and a revitalized experience of prayer and meditation, it was a consistent theme within our conversations to hear anecdotes from people about the ways they had found themselves using more of their senses to fully empathize with the mountains: seeing with greater attention and appreciation, hearing the myriad sounds and songs, smelling more subtle fragrances, touching leaves, rocks, and tree bark, and tasting the wind on their lips and tongues.

Not only were the rich traditions of creation spirituality unlocked through these experiences of words and mountains together, but new connections and new concerns were formed among these interviewees. With Linda, a fast-talking and devastatingly witty librarian from Ipswich, England, new connections 'started popping' into her head as soon as she began to appreciate the awesome dimensions of the creation traditions within her Christian faith:

LINDA:
... so imagine the scene. Cross-legged and awe-struck on my first visit to the Cascades, and God was pelting me with all these ideas. Bang, bang, bang, bang one after another after another. Education and faith. Faith and news events. News events and buying a new shower curtain when I got home. Don't ask me where I got that one from! But out they poured. In the middle of such overwhelmingly powerful and beautiful and wonderful mountains. And at sunset, I was almost breathless and gasping. Ideas and ideas and ideas .... It was totally, totally wonderful and liberating, as if I was being taught to think and to connect in new ways all over again!

Whilst other flows of inspiration were experienced in other mountain ranges, in other parts of the world, two sets of connections were most frequently recalled in association with first visits to North

American mountains. First, there was a heightened seriousness regarding the 'ecological crisis' (Danny). More than elsewhere in the world, there appeared to these people to be a clearer contrast between the overwhelming beauty and inspirational value of North American mountains compared with the polluting industrialization of the northeast United States, for example. Acid rain, impoverished physical health, and compromised bio-diversity were all listed as being clear examples of the devastation 'which simply must be guarded against' (Mabel):

MABEL:

I'm what you might call a late arrival to mountain-walking, since I only started when I was sixty. But let me say one thing. Almost as soon as I'd got a chance to look around me, it became as clear as day. We all need to tell it. And keep on telling it. We need to stop the pollution. And those words kept coming back to me almost at every turn ... As I turned another corner, and, say, found another breathtaking waterfall, a voice inside me seemed to be saying, 'compare that to a river foaming with chemicals' ... And I don't think I've understood the urgency of anything else before or since my first time there (to the Cascade Mountains).

For Mabel and others, pollution was seen, for the first time in their lives, as a sin: an act of desecration against things of divine beauty and precious wisdom. Only when she had begun to wonder and marvel at the Cascade mountains as a sacred creation did Mabel find this new broadened insight into pollution, a problem in which previously, she freely admits, she had found 'next to no interest at all.'

Related to new insights into the problems of pollution, came fresh ways of thinking about macro-economic issues, such as how governments allocate public capital and other resources. In particular, many of our conversations contrasted the sense of sacred, created balance and harmony which these people found in their first visits to these mountains, to the 'crashing discord' (Gary) and fragmentation which they encountered in their everyday lives. The following illustrates how this alignment of mountain landscape-experience, spiritual insights and economics became impressed on three fun-loving students who travel and climb together. The conversation followed a very similar expression to that described by Linda above, on the ways new insights and ways of seeing can unexpectedly arise:

GARY:

It was almost exhausting, and just totally amazing. At one moment, all around us was this amazing calm of the mountains. I'm thinking about a time around sunset in particular. And then suddenly your minds go into overdrive! And your brain floods over with inspiration. Idea after idea after idea. And the whole, complete, contrast of what we saw (in the Cascades) really brought a whole new line of conversation to us, didn't it?

TREVOR:

Yeah. Well, as students, it's pretty likely that we'll be facing at least some time unemployed when we finish. And we were suddenly talking about that whole idea of unemployment. And even misemployment. You know, workers working on destructive enterprises while the earth needs caring for. Working on the wrong things, while the right things keep being neglected ...

ROY:

It's just a sign that most people's energies are being directed in ways which are so destructive and unproductive. And yet if only everyone had seen what we'd seen (in the Cascades) maybe they'd agree there are some really major changes needed. But no one listens ...

TREVOR:

Because they haven't seen what their works could be destroying ...

GARY:

It's madness, isn't it. And whether you want to call that a 'sin' or 'doing wrong,' or just plain stupidity, call it whatever you like, but it's important ... and it only really, really became important in that way for us when we'd been out there (in the Cascades) and we'd seen all the simplicity and the wonderful, wonderful colour and shapes and feeling to it all.

One of my most valued memories from attending these interview meetings is the way in which conversations like this with Gary, Trevor and Roy covered so much varied, valuable and stimulating ground in a matter of moments: from precious creation inspirations to the anxieties of everyday life. From mountain waterfalls at sunset to the injustices of unemployment and the lack of equal opportunity. From the peaks of insight, imagination and soaring inspiration to the depths of individual despair, dismay and overwhelming responsibilities. None of these spiritual insights which became inspired by these mountains ever remained completely detached from everyday life for long. Mountain spirituality and 'street spirituality' in mutually challenging, and mutually inspiring union. And with the breathtaking zest of spiritual insight, came the often crushing sense of obligation to carry these messages to others, to help organize change, to inspire and show others how it is possible to find an overwhelming integrity in one's spiritual path within contemporary society. In this way, they found a new confidence on their spiritual path in stark contrast to the introverted embarrassment which had accompanied their faith before visiting the mountains. More than with any other series of mountain-experiences in this book, the ranges of North America provoked this child-like awakening toward the need to learn more, experience more, tell more, and share more of these insights.

Although our interview-meetings ranged over so many familiar and unfamiliar facts, opinions and argument, it was frequently the case that conversations concerning everyday life and 'the spirituality of the street' preceded further discussions on the ways a first visit to these North American mountains re-formed individuals' views on education. In a very real sense though, these opinions drew from the need to discover and savour 'new words,' and 'the right words' which triggered these insights. In the following illustration, Gene describes how he found a 'completely' satisfying form of words with which he could 'enter into' the Sierra landscape, 'to find a real sacred and holy well-being there.' He found it an inescapable conclusion that others should also be told of, and fully educated in, these words:

GENE:
> ... but without the right words, from Muir, or any of those other writers, you can't even start. You don't know what it is you're looking at. So it might as well not be there ... and certainly may not become important to you, even if it kind of draws your attention. You always need words and structures to inspire you. To capture the moment for you ... But where do you find that in the schools and colleges? They only seem to teach facts. And that's all they're giving out in those places ... Why don't they take courage one-time and start teaching (native American) Indian wisdom? There's a real need. And I really appreciated it out there (on Mount Ritter) as I just sat, and thought and admired the feeling and sense of latent wisdom I got there.

For others, such as Eric, a genuine radical thinker, who describes himself as an 'intellectual terrorist,' there was a major problem with people thinking they could understand that native poetry when they had not received the 'correct' education in its interpretation. Eric elaborated upon this important point with reference to the first time he walked around Moraine Lake and the Valley of the Ten Peaks, in the Canadian Rockies. The following discussion was part of Eric's recollections of Moraine Lake, and the Valley of the Ten Peaks, alongside other contributors who had first visited Pike's Peak, in the Colorado Rockies, and who had all found the work of Black Elk to be directly informative to their adherence with Zen.[9] The source quoted here for Black Elk's words is De Mallie (1984):

ERIC:

... but you just said you haven't been taught to understand any of that (Black Elk) stuff, so what makes you think you've got a real and believable understanding of it all?

DAVEY:

Well, I'm not saying I have the ultimate and definitive understanding of this literature at all. That's not what I meant. All I'm saying is that I, or we, have discovered something of real value in those words ... And maybe we wouldn't have found that meaning if we'd received a formal education in these (Black Elk's) ideas.

ERIC:

Yeah, but I get a kind of picture that you might be putting a whole new meaning on those words which Black Elk and his people never wanted to be there. And I'm just interested in how you think you've got a real handle on those words if you haven't been taught their background and history.

MARY:

... You make it happen for yourself. And I don't think it matters if you don't measure up to Black Elk's way of looking at the mountains. If his teaching is on your 'path,' you can pick it up. It's become yours. And that's the key to it all.

JOSEPH:

That's right. It's part of the meditation of being there. Just way out in the Peak. Totally alone, or with your friends.

Within this and other discussion-groups, the contentious questions of empathizing with the sacred words and ideas of the Amer-indians were frequently resurrected, repeated, and added to from personal anecdotes. They almost always returned to the need to educate the young, and adults too, in creation-centred ways of thinking, and their related ways of seeing mountain landscapes. As was so often the case, Chester was able to express the thoughts of many others on this subject:

CHESTER:

What happens is you find yourself out in the evening, say, and your mind is calm and then suddenly whoosh! You're filled with this question and that thought, and this dilemma and that problem. And your mind races and races. But most of the time you're kind of swimming around because you just have not received the right background to deal with that most amazing of experiences ... It often seems to me, having now travelled all over the world to other mountain areas, that young people, which eventually means all of us, are educated only for slots. You become a peg in a slot, surrounded by other pegs filled, you've guessed, by other slots. And as soon as you really, really feel that, it hurts. And you want others (young people) to be taught differently ... to use their imaginations more, to learn to be overwhelmed and inspired and touched by greatness. And I'm not an idealist because it's a practical necessity, I think, for dealing with problems from boredom to domestic strife. It's needed. And it can work!

Alongside the need for schools, colleges and universities to accommodate these creation-centred subjects, such as story-telling, wisdom literature, art, meditation, and dance, everyone who contributed to this book agreed that religious leaders and media managers also had a responsibility to address these subjects. With Tye for example, a self-confessed 'sceptic' of all faiths, there is now very little difference between the required agenda of education on these creation-centred subjects in the mass-media or among religious leaders:

TYE:

The one big thing I remember from my first ever visit out there (to the Black Hills), way back now, was the way I felt things become a lot more simple for me. I saw things, I think, more clearly. And so, for me, I guess I see churches, and other religious leaders, alongside TV documentary makers, and magazine writers, and all kinds of broadcasters as having a primary responsibility to bring us out of the everyday. They have this duty to show us other things. To take us to where we can't go. Because we're all at work all day! And yet they don't do that! We aren't always taken out of the ordinary. We aren't always shown new ways of looking at things, because they (religious leaders and media managers) themselves haven't been taught these things (creation-spirituality). So everybody, everybody needs to learn. But they more than the rest of us, have a responsibility which comes with their territory.

One of the benefits of a transformed education agenda, along with similarly enhanced religious and media agendas, would be the development of a clearer, and simplified vision, or 'wisdom' as many contributors called it, for the future of humankind. Certainly, Tye was not alone in recalling the single most important experience he remembered from the first time he visited the North American mountains as a 'stripping away of the unnecessary, and a cherishing of what is right, and precious, and simple, and true.' Some interviewees cited the following extract of Carl Jung's discussion on the need to 'reach out for new levels of consciousness' (Jane). Jane's explanation of this idea follows an extract from Jung that the major problems facing humankind can only be resolved by 'outgrowing' them, and developing new ways of thinking:

> This 'outgrowing' proved on further investigation to require a new level of consciousness. Some higher or wider interest appeared to the patient's horizon, and through this broadening of his or her outlook, the insoluble problem lost its urgency. (Quoted in Jacobi 1978, 304)

JANE:
> *I'm always reminded of this quote from Jung, because it confirms my own little theory that my visits to the mountains have been like a stepladder in my inspirational journey. The first visit takes you so far, and then other visits take you further, and further ... And eventually, as Jung says, you outgrow your previous concerns and worries, and maybe even help others, from whatever background, to outgrow theirs.*

If there was a common theme to the inspiration found in all these first visits to the mountains of North America, which was distinctive from first visits elsewhere, it was a strong sympathy with the need for ecumenism: a profound appreciation of the eternal truths and ancient wisdom within all the world's varied religious groups. For Lucy, a kitchen assistant, originally from Florida, her first mountain experiences emerged over a two week tour in the Rockies, and firmly established her ecumenical ideals:

LUCY:

> ... *travelling with a couple of girl friends in this old camper-van we'd borrowed. And I was a practising Buddhist by that time in my life ... but as we drove around and sat around our fires in the evening, and you know how your mind puts things together, and casts other things away ... I think I saw a lot of common links in world spiritualities which bridge the divides between Buddhism, and say, Christianity, or Judaism or Islam and Hinduism ... it was a feeling for life, and a feeling for what can be precious: a holding on to those precious sacred things. We all share those things ... And I kind of pieced that insight together for myself over that tour way, way, away in the Rockies and it's stayed with me today as probably my firmest memory of those mountains, and how they helped shape that ecumenical idea for me.*

Within times spent together, conversing with her friends, as well as time walking in the many camping stops across the Rocky mountains, Lucy described how she felt 'led on by a spirit in those mountains towards this feeling of unity among religions.' As the insight emerged, Lucy found a 'real, real thrill which I could never contain. I really knew I was onto something important: knowing we can learn from each other. And there's a need to start listening to others with other experiences to help us work through our problems.'

Independently from Lucy, Charles had travelled alone on his first visit to the Rockies on an equally varied and extended route. But from his impressive knowledge of literature, he captured the essence of this shared appreciation of ecumenical unity. The following quotation is taken from the work of Gerhard von Rad, theologian and specialist in wisdom literature:

> Wisdom requires surrender, verging on the mystical, of a person to the glory of existence. (von Rad 1974, 165)

In discussing the importance of this quotation from von Rad's work, Charles suggested that ecumenism is a 'surrender of your pride that you and your faith-group think you have the one and only right answer to religious searching.' Consequently, Charles suggested, the 'full richness' of von Rad's 'glory of existence' can only be achieved 'by giving up the barriers, and keeping hold of the parts which you can share around':

CHARLES:

I can remember exactly when all those ideas hit me. Not just at the words-level, but really and truly in my heart. I'd been riding my (motor) bike really hard all day out there (in the Rocky mountains) and I reached a point when I was just dead-beat, and I pulled up just on the side on this old road. I didn't know where I was. But as I packed everything up for the night, I suddenly became aware of the stillness. Total quiet. But it wasn't eerie at all. And it just came upon me like a gentle wave: gently at first and then really stronger, that I felt so much at one with the night, and the stars, and the isolation with the mountain tops silhouetted on the horizon. Everything seemed together. And anything that wasn't really a part of that togetherness had, like, got it wrong. And I remember, that was a good, good feeling, I tell you.

In a very similar anecdote to Charles, Arnie, a quietly spoken Texan truck driver, recalled the single sentence from John Muir which captures his approach to ecumenism from his background as a Christian inspired by creation-theology:

No particle is ever wasted or worn out, but eternally flowing from use to use. (Quoted in Wolfe 1951, 123)

ARNIE:

Whenever I'm looking for the words to sum up what I've seen in my mountain trips, it's always John Muir I turn to. But why I like that sentence is because as you drive through the mountains, or you walk along the paths, most people's eyes are looking up, at the glories. But if it wasn't for the strength of the paths, made up of dust, mostly, they couldn't ride those ways. So it's the dust which holds people up. Dust. You know, the humble people. The quiet folks. They're the ones who tend to accept others, and spread out kindness. Not only the lofty peaks. And the dust is never worn out. It's always there as a strength for others to stand up and live.

Subsequent visits

In only the fourth week of our interview meetings, Chester identified the major difference between the spiritual experiences encountered in further visits to North American mountains, and subsequent visits to other mountains, elsewhere in the world:

CHESTER:

> *I've been listening to what we've all been saying here, and I guess
> there's a word which sums up this difference. And that word is dabhar.
> Some folks have used it here, as they've talked. And others haven't
> known of it, but they've shown they felt it just the same.*

In other interview groups, other contributors agreed with Chester's
suggestion. Although Chester is a practising Taoist, he was familiar
with the Hebrew word *dabhar*, meaning the creative energy of Divinity. Within his Taoist belief, he admitted that he 'perhaps stretches
the original Hebrew to mean the creative energy of the Way, or
the Tao.' *Dabhar*, in this context, therefore describes the way in which
the mountains of North America were found to have been truly
brought to life as these people anticipated and encountered their subsequent travels. For three American Jewish college students, Rachel,
Ben and Elizabeth, their knowledge of *dabhar* captures the essence of
their expectations and experience of their more recent mountain
travels:

RACHEL:

> *I don't want to sound too pretentious here, because that's not my aim.
> But, I guess, the only words I can find to explain my use of dabhar, is
> that I find being out there (in the mountains) is a cleansing from all
> the cynicism and greed I find from living in the United States.*

BEN:

> *You mean the intensity of that cynicism here compared to other coun-
> tries.*

RACHEL:

> *Yes. I mean I've travelled and lived other places. But you can't deny
> that American values and ways of being are probably the most manipu-
> lative ... So yes, it is dabhar I feel being there. That purity and real
> wisdom which the United States has almost completely lost. That's
> what I see. And those mountains are examples of that ... they help
> restore the balance between what's wrong there (in American society)
> and what we should be focused on (creation spirituality).*

For Rachel, her climbs on Katahdin, in the State of Maine, exemplified her use of *dabhar* and its precious value to her which 'set alight'
all her mountain experiences, after her first climbs in the Sierras:

RACHEL:

> *I always climb Katahdin with my friends whenever we're up there (in Maine) ... but always, and I mean always, when you get up to the top it's always this amazing 'yes!' This incredible oneness with all that's been. And all that will come after us. And dabhar is the word which keeps tumbling back to me: that unimaginable vastness of creative wisdom which you feel there.*

From another interview-group, and with no direct knowledge of the word *dabhar*, the following discussions between Gene and Simon show a clear affinity with the idea of Katahdin as an example of God's creative energy and wisdom. In describing this way of seeing Katahdin as an expression of the universal creative power, both men also drew from their knowledge and admiration of Henry David Thoreau's book *The Maine Woods* in which he recalls his own experience of the mountain:

GENE:

> *I guess I'd been climbing for about four years when I (first) made it up Katahdin. But, man, the first time I looked out from the summit there, I knew that was going to be one of the real big ones! ... I instantly felt aware of this awesome and huge creative force which God had brought to bear here ...*

SIMON:

> *I thought there was a purity about being there which I hadn't found before that.*

SIMON:

> *Maybe it's because Katahdin isn't like one of these real well-known mountains. You know, like the Sierras are.*

GENE:

> *It's all a lot greener too, which kind of brings off that feeling of being surrounded by bountiful creation and really precious beauty.*

SIMON:

> *And we'd both been reading the Thoreau before we climbed it first time out. And, like we were saying about the Sierra Nevada, words keep coming back to you and give the experience meaning. And that was the book which certainly did it for me. And I saw it (Katahdin) as something much much bigger spiritually I mean, than I'd seen in the Sierra on my first visit there.*

The words from Thoreau which both these men had in mind when they provided this contribution are the following:

> Some part of the beholder, even some vital part, seems to escape through the loose gratings of his ribs as he ascends ... Vast, Titanic and inhuman Nature has got him at disadvantage, caught him alone, and pilfers him of some of his Divine faculty ... She seems to say sternly, why came ye before your time? This ground is not prepared for you. Is it not enough that I smile in the valleys? I have never made this soil for thy feet, this air for thy breathing ... (Thoreau 1950, 271)

When Simon first read this passage at a one-to-one interview meeting, I asked him why he thought Thoreau appeared to be describing 'Nature' in the Maine mountains as being unwelcoming, exclusive, and perhaps even forbidding. Simon's reply, however, showed a further empathy with the Hebrew notion of *dabhar* in these mountains as a cleansing experience: a feeling that the wisdom and creative power manifest in these mountains is not necessarily impatient or intolerant toward these climbers as individuals, but rather toward the secular, 'consumer-oriented' (Simon) values of everyday life. Simon continued:

SIMON:

> *I felt it (being on Katahdin) was like being purged. And Henry David Thoreau seems to be saying, well the way I read him he does, that all the vanity and ambition which you're supposed to go for in your life away from the mountains just isn't good enough there (on Katahdin). It has no place among this pure and special kind of creativity and wisdom which put the place together.*

This intense appreciation of divine creative wisdom, which blossomed on subsequent visits to North American mountains, was described in another way by other Buddhist contributors here. In particular, they responded to the meditative qualities of the changing colours of light in the mountains they visited and re-visited. This alignment between interpretations of mountain light and a personal Buddhist spirituality was exemplified in the interviews devoted to interpretations of Mount Shasta in northern California, near the Oregon border.[10] Since it is located relatively close to the Pacific coast, Shasta is the focal point for violent storms which, for those who witness them, can awaken a vivid awareness of the mountain's inspirational power. In the following illustration for example, two pan-pipe musicians from Los Angeles, Davey and Joseph, describe their attendance at the Harmonic Convergence event in 1987, where thousands gathered in an attempt to focus the mystical energy of Shasta to induce a dawn of universal harmony and peace:

DAVEY:

There was a complete vastness there at Shasta standing before us, almost like a pyramid ... And the more I looked at it, throughout each day we were there, the changing light seemed to bring a new wave of wisdom, and this kind of cleansing creativity, to the crowds there.

JOSEPH:

It was the best example I've ever been at where nature and humankind come together with a single purpose. You know, for the benefit of all. But the light was the thing maybe which captured it for me too. Every colour, from blues and mauves right through the spectrum to perfect snow-capped white. Pinks. All the colours and all aspects of that eternal wisdom we should all be a part of.

As the colours on the mountain changed from dawn toward evening, and as different weather patterns moved above Shasta, Davey and Joseph described feeling 'part of a very, very privileged audience' before an exhibition 'of omnipresent wisdom' (Joseph).

Even among those who have visited Shasta with no sustained spiritual commitment, their experiences there have inspired an appreciation which accords to the idea of *dabhar:* a sense of being in the presence of a divine creative wisdom, a force of harmony, and a power from which we may learn according to our needs, questions and anxieties. One of the English contributors, Bill, a thoughtful but lively man 'in (his) second or third adolescence,' summed up this sense perfectly:

BILL:

Something really hit me there (at Shasta) which, I knew, felt sort of spiritual, but which I also felt really good about. All my life, I've really been put off religion, certainly Christianity, because it always puts forward such narrow, and trite answers ... But there, I caught sight of maybe what the world's great theologians have been struggling to get a grip of. Something that's probably too simple for them to understand. But also something, you know, a power and a real sharp wisdom which can touch everyone ... And it really made me feel good, you know. It actually made me scrap the rest of my holiday plans because I wanted to stay there and see more (of Shasta's changing light).

One of the ways in which experienced travellers in the mountains of North America showed their maturity of spiritual experiences was in the ways they were able to describe savouring and relishing their meditations on divine creativity in those places. Descriptions from a personal knowledge of the 'blessing' of being able to pray and meditate, discuss and walk, in awed silence, were all distinctive elements to the conversations of these spiritually experienced travellers. The following illustration from Tom, a middle aged Technical Sergeant in the United States Air Force, shows how he has noticed this developing awareness of the blessing and quiet pleasure of 'dwelling in the divine creativity' manifest in North American mountains:

TOM:

Well, I think if I tell you about Mount Rainier (Washington State), that should explain it pretty well. The first time I was there, it was just overwhelming. It knocked me out. But now that I've been there well over a dozen years, I feel more able to take it all in. I can relax there. I can appreciate what God's hand really has done there. And I think with the time I've spent away from Rainier, back at work some-place, it stays with me. And as you think about it, it prepares you for your next visit. And gradually, you notice it in yourself. You look out for things. You know what the mountain can offer and you're there ready to receive, and to cherish it. Whether it's the light and cloud effects, or the glaciers, ... and then when we've driven back along the Cascades, you'll look up and continue this kind of dialogue, as you look out for things you know were there the last time you passed through. And then you see them, and you praise God. And your journey goes on and on like that. The longer you keep going back, the more you're able to look out for, and expect, and pray and praise at being there ... And that whole experience of being blessed so directly like that grows and grows in you.

But as with the first visits to these mountains, described earlier, Tom confirmed that he still has 'special writers' who are able to capture his appreciation of Rainier. These writers' words subsequently became a part of Tom's prayers of thanksgiving at this personal sense of 'blessing.' The writer from whom Tom quoted most frequently, was the naturalist Theodore Winthrop. The following section is 'without doubt the most special of Winthrop's words' for Tom:

... studying the light and majesty of Tacoma (a native name
for Rainier), there passed from it and entered into my being,
to dwell there evermore by the side of many such, a thought
and an image of solemn beauty, which I could thenceforth
evoke whenever in the world I must have peace or die. For
such emotion, years of pilgrimage were worthily spent.
(Winthrop 1916, 38-9)

Among a group of English post-graduate science students, the
words of the creation-centred theologian, Annie Dillard, were often
quoted in the same way as Tom quoted from Winthrop, as a source of
continued inspiration to pray and to receive the 'blessings which
divine hands make available' on Rainier:

The extravagant gesture is the very stuff of creation. After the
one extravagant gesture of creation in the first place, the
universe has continued to deal exclusively in extravagances,
flinging intricacies and colossi down aeons of emptiness,
heaping profusions on profligacies with ever more vigour.
The whole show has been on fire from the word go! (Dillard
1975, 9)

SALLY:
*Those words sum everything up about all the mountains I've ever been
to in the States. The colours. The light. The ways it's big and wonderful and overpowering. And more than that, that sense of really feeling
blessed there ...*

GRACE:
*The words are so precise and so 'American' aren't they. 'The extrava-
gant gesture,' could only be America. But at the same time, there isn't
the ugly brashness of, say New York or Las Vegas. It's extravagance
from God's hands being distinctive in that particular continent ... and I
use those (Dillard's) words all the time when I'm there (on Rainier) to
pray.*

In addition to this inspiration to pray, the blessings encountered in
these mountains have inspired others to make it a personal priority to
tell family, friends and fellow church and temple-goers about these
most private of experiences. Among many of the Christians who
described their maturing experiences in these mountains, the first three
verses of the twelfth chapter in the Book of Genesis were often quoted

as the scriptural source which confirmed this conviction to 'spread the word of these mountain blessings' (Geoff):

GEOFF:

> *This passage speaks to me because I first came across it on about my fifth time in the Cascades and it just seemed to say 'tell everyone you meet about what you have seen.' And I have this mental image in my head of thousands of people, like a whole nation perhaps, of people who God has spoken to in this way:*
>
> > *I will make you into a great nation*
> > *and I will bless you;*
> > *I will make your name great,*
> > *and you will be a blessing.*
> > *I will bless those who bless you ...*
> > *(Genesis 12, 1-3)*

A further set of experiences which were distinctive to these people's descriptions of subsequent visits to North American mountains was their particular way of feeling 'humble' when faced with these mountain landscapes. But whilst humility is often thought of as a form of passivity and obsequiousness, the humility described by the people who contributed to this section was a willingness to feel at one with the inspiring wisdom which they found manifest in these mountains. It was a humility which remained true to the Latin roots of the word: *humus* or earth. An appreciation of humility as a receptiveness to learn more of the earth's rhythms, its lessons, its violence, its limits, and its sources of continuing inspiration. Humility as an alignment with Chief Seattle's words: 'this earth is precious to the Creator and to harm the earth is to heap contempt upon its Creator' (quoted in Rich, 1947, 40). For Phillip, a young, quietly spoken military policemen, each of his ten visits to different areas in Yosemite Park have inspired this same response to humility:

PHILLIP:

> *Each time I go back there, either alone or with friends or my parents, I keep wanting to get closer to the whole feeling of harmony I feel there (in Yosemite). And even in the Valley, where they're at last getting on with the meadow-projects, building those up, you get a feeling of getting back to the harmony with nature which the Indians had. It will take time. Probably, a lot of years. But there's a lesson in that. We've seen we went wrong. We took time to put it right. And we're seeing it*

slowly come back together. And I think that lesson should be sent around the world. Getting back to a being-at-one with the land, whether it's in that Valley, or anywhere ... there's a wisdom there that you can take away with you.

Among the Zen Buddhist contributors, their knowledge of Japanese haiku poetry became applied in ways which echoed Phillip's belief in the simplicity of this humble oneness with the mountains. Agnes for example, an enthusiastic school teacher from Baltimore, Maryland, found a 'thrilling, tingling, humbling harmony' between some of her favourite haiku verses, and her spiritual experiences and insights found in her travels to Mount Marcy, the highest summit in the Adirondack Mountains of New York State:

AGNES:
They're (the haiku poems) like jewels which spring into my mind while I might be walking or climbing out there ... I like the one by Issa:

> *A frog!*
> *Quietly and serenely*
> *He gazes at the mountains.*

That's it! That's the moment, isn't it! Completely perfect. And absolutely nothing else has to be said: 'Quietly and serenely, He gazes at the mountain.' I love it. It's so simple and calm. There's just enough there. But never, ever too much. But there's another I love too, by Basho:

> *The fragrance!*
> *Though I know not*
> *Whence it comes.*

Do you see? Only just enough, but enough to completely capture all I need on Marcy. It's always been a special place for me, with all the memories of taking friends there. But as I meditate, these haikus are the words I need. They form a perfect harmony ... and I have to say, I find it exhilarating and profoundly humbling all at the same time.

Turning points

For four of the sixty-two people who contributed to this chapter, their spiritual experiences of one specific North American mountain have persuaded them to radically re-appraise, and change, their life-styles. These four people, all from England, and all mature theology students at an English university, were experienced climbers the first time they visited Mount McKinley, in Alaska. However, whilst other interviewees here experienced profound insights which have shaped the ways they continue to live their everyday lives, these four men can be considered separately in this section not only because their descriptions of their mountain experiences were consistently different from other contributors, but also because they changed the direction of their lives as a consequence of their experiences at McKinley.

As the following illustration shows, none of these individuals anticipated the major effect which their encounter with McKinley would inspire:

CLIVE:

... we had just successfully negotiated our first year exams and had visited McKinley as a highlight of the summer holidays. That was the plan. It was a climbing holiday, pure and simple.

ALAN:

... even within the first two or three days there, I don't think any of us imagined that anything extraordinary was about to happen to us. In terms of a profound religious experience, I mean.

At dawn on the fourth day in Alaska: the start of the first full day of climbing, two of the group woke in their separate tents and independently experienced 'the most profound sense of awe-inspired remorse, and sense of wasted effort' (Malcolm) they had felt:

MALCOLM:

I remember it so clearly. I woke up. And suddenly I felt really wide awake. No drowsiness at all. And I knew I had to get out of the tent and see the face (of McKinley). I had to do it. Why, I didn't know. But even as I shuffled out of the tent, before I'd even taken my first look at it, I just broke down. I could not contain myself. And I cried and cried and cried. I couldn't stop. And it physically drained me. I moved, but only very, wearily slow. Crying all the time. Really sobbing.

TIM:

... and, to put it simply, I was doing the same ... It was like being squeezed by a hand which was wringing me dry like a dish cloth ...

This spontaneous and profound expression of tearful 'sorrow' (Tim) was simultaneously encountered by Clive and Alan. At first, the experience of these four men sobbing together beside their tents caused them 'utter bewilderment' (Malcolm) and an 'all embracing fear' (Alan). After a few hours of continued tears, each of them independently felt their 'minds gradually clear' (Alan) and focus on a single short passage from theologian Claus Westermann's *Blessing in the Bible and the Life of the Church:*

ALAN:

We'd all read it as part of the university course we'd all been on. But it certainly hadn't changed any of our lives (hesitation) then, at any rate ... But it was a combination of that utter purity, beside McKinley, and Westermann's lines, you know, where he says 'it would be a perversion of the biblical data to reduce God's dealings with his people to the one concept of 'salvation'' (Westermann 1978, 28) *... And it was that combination ... that vast, enormous, ultimately overwhelming immensity of Mount McKinley, along with those words, which squeezed and pushed into those tears and that realization that we all had some complete changes to make from that point on.*

Following that emotionally and spiritually traumatic morning, the climb of McKinley was abandoned, with the remaining time of that holiday in Alaska being devoted to 'soul-searching in its most literal form' (Tim) which developed through group discussion among the four men, as well as through private reflection. This continued for the next two weeks with each individual 'feeling bombarded with these juxtapositions of the mountain as a great teaching metaphor and our tiny awareness of the right texts and things to think about' (Malcolm).

ALAN:

But what I found so incredible was the way my mind had been cleared, and things I'd only very briefly thought about or looked at, even years before, all came back to me with astonishing clarity.

The central theme of this subsequent reflection on McKinley 'as a great teaching metaphor' was an interpretation of being 'blessed.' That is, within the context of their transformed relationship with God, each of these men described an experience of receiving a 'blessing' of new insights into that transformed relationship, regarding the priorities of that new relationship, and the elements of their former understanding of God which they now felt able to abandon.

MALCOLM:

It was like (Claus) Westermann says, 'salvation,' in the narrow, fundamentalist evangelical sense, is only a small part of our relationship with God. And I think, with hindsight, being on McKinley and being so totally and crushingly aware of that vastness, maybe even with God-given eyes, I don't know, this transformation took place.

Even when Malcolm and the other three men were reflecting on their spiritual experience at McKinley, their open and frequent discussion of the mountain's vastness was particularly important. Significantly though, Nelson (1983, 45) notes that part of the Koyukon people's way of holding McKinley to be sacred was to refrain strictly from talking about the size of the mountain whilst standing on its slopes. However, in encountering and developing their own experience of the sacred powers on those same slopes, Malcolm, Clive, Alan, and Tim knew of no such taboo. Indeed, they felt the need to talk freely, 'for hours on end' about their experiences and insights, and about the ways in which those encounters were to change their lives:

TIM:

To cut a long story short, we all knew that our lives had changed for ever. That much was clear. But I think it was a few days before we felt able to piece together and discover the need to drop out of the university and to all live there (in Alaska), independently, and to teach. And that's what's happened.

CLIVE:

So you can imagine, I hope, that when we sprung this idea on assorted friends, lecturers and parents, they were disappointed.

TIM:

Or perhaps mildly devastated?

CLIVE:

It took quite a while for most people to accept what we'd been through. And I think some parents and families still think we're completely barmy ... But we really had no choice. All our assumptions and priorities had been ripped to shreds on McKinley. So we had to do what we had to do!

At the time of writing, all four men live and teach in different parts of Alaska, 'within driving distance of McKinley' (Clive). At 'irregular intervals' they visit the mountain, either individually or as a group to walk, climb and reflect upon the way the place contributed to their current response to Christian faith.

MALCOLM:

In a nutshell, and I know I can speak for the others here, our appreciation of God is now vastly larger than when we were being taught at university from the books on salvation alone ... Our faith now, I think, is more accommodating ... There remains an important place for the ideas of salvation. Of course there must be. It has to be that way. But in addition, there is so much more. And perhaps what's surprised me is the way I find myself willing to learn from other faiths and to weave those lessons into my own Christianity. Ideas of meditation for example, and forms of yogic breathing have all come into the way I teach (as part of an alcohol rehabilitation programme) and think about my faith for me.

Conclusions

The most striking and distinctive theme in this chapter has been the ways in which the purity and simplicity of these people's recollections and descriptions of their experiences among these sacred mountains has been variously aligned with issues and concerns from their everyday lives. Problems of education, pollution, politics and the social concerns of unemployment and even misemployment have all been woven into these experiences of the sacred among North American mountains:

BEN:

There's always a danger of retreating to these mountains, to just use them as a sanctuary away from the rest of the world.

RACHEL:

That's right. And I've been guilty of that. There have been times when I've just taken off and 'hidden.' And that's the only word I now use for those times. I thought I could hide from problems I once had with various people around me by doing that, by taking off and hoping that when I got back everything was all cleared up ... and of course, it never was.

ELIZABETH:

Oh, but to be fair to yourself, you haven't done that in a long, long time.

RACHEL:

Sure. Because now I think that the challenge of being out in the mountains is an opportunity to put the two together: the spiritual and the ordinary. And make the value of both work for each other. And that's where I'm at right now. It's hard. But that's the goal. To draw from the harmonies you find there (in the mountains) and use them and apply them in your everyday life ... It's essential to do that.

Alongside the inspiration of these mountains, lie important undercurrents of personal concern and dilemma about the ways in which that relative spiritual simplicity can contrast with, and yet support, other concerns and problems.

CLIVE:

It's an impossible balance isn't it. It will always be there. Always gnawing at your conscience. And I think with these mountains in particular, they're all so comparatively easy to get to, and to get lost in. Spiritually and inspirationally, it's the easiest thing in the world to use them to shut yourself off from the rest of life, rather than to use the mountains to open yourself up to the everyday, and to let the two complement each other, ... something which is always a lot easier said than done.

Clive's point, regarding this problematic balance, was developed in a particularly clear way among the more experienced mountain-travellers who have the benefit of comparing their own various experiences and inspirational encounters in those ranges, with the experiences and encounters of other people they have met, and with whom they have conversed on these questions:

JANE:

... over the last thirty years or so, I've visited all the main mountain ranges of the world ... And where I'd put people's experiences of these mountains is at the level of 'discovery.' People I talk to, in helping with this book, and in my travels, see American mountains as a sort of 'first-level' of their inspirational journey. Like 'Lesson 1'! ... But in other mountains, they tend to explore other, more powerful, more inspirational and more challenging problems. It's not always like that, because with some other mountains, some folks just find the challenge of what they represent too overwhelming to deal with at any level.

This generalized recognition, by Jane, and many other experienced mountain-travellers was in no sense intended as a criticism of the ways these mountains can inspire their visitors. Rather, such inspirations were unanimously agreed to be 'foundational' for other spiritual experiences in mountains, elsewhere in the world. In addition, it was agreed that, following such broader travels, North American mountains may also be invested with more mature spiritual questions and thoughts, dilemmas and inspirations.

Within these conversations, it was also agreed that if others are to accept the challenge of this book and explore experiences and questions of mountain spirituality, it is with the mountains of North America where their initial attentions may focus. The following illustration by Keith, for example, a communications engineer with five years experience in television in the United States, exemplifies the feelings of many contributors here:

KEITH:

It's right to group religious leaders and TV and newspaper people here. They're all in the business of informing people, and giving them information to inspire them. And in the States, and Canada, people know of those mountains. Even if you haven't been there, you'll have heard of Yosemite Park, and Alaska, and maybe even the mountains of the south- west. So religious teachers and the media have a handle on their audience already. And if they really thought about it, they could take this amazing hunger in a lot of people right now for this sort of spiritual inspiration and mould their own teaching and programmes to deal with that hunger. And they could always refer to fairly familiar terri-

tory in the Americas. That would be where they'd probably be best off in starting.

For Suzannah, a thoughtful and well-travelled school-teacher, and her friend Mabel, a retired accounts clerk, Keith's point was accepted, but then elaborated-upon:

SUZANNAH:

I enjoy watching a lot of the nature programmes on the television, because the chances are that I've been to those places, so I like to see how they've changed ... But sooner or later, the audiences are going to demand more. Different programme-formats. And the same with the churches. I agree with Keith, church-goers will inevitably drift away if they're told the same old story week in week out.

MABEL:

That's right. You can address the same truths of spiritual inspiration but using new stories (of creation spirituality). Or, really, most of them aren't so new, are they? They're probably a lot older than the Bible! But what I'm saying is the Church and television people can use a broader set of stories to tell people about life and its full richness than just the narrow selection they currently choose from ...

CHAPTER 2

Latin America

*It would be illusory, useless, and even blasphemous to
claim to bear witness to God without engaging in practical
activities to repair creation. Faced with the basic needs
evident within our continent, all experience of God and all
witnessing by the Church must logically start there.*
Sobrino (1981, 165)

Ancient wisdom

It is impossible to understand either the land or the people of Latin
America without first understanding its mountains. From the ice-
encrusted fjords surrounding Tierra del Fuego on Argentina's southern
tip, northward across barren lands of soaring Andean rock spires,
vertical walls and sheer, wind-scarred granite, toward the heat and
humidity of the Caribbean, this is a continent abounding in natural
superlatives. At 4500 miles, the Andean mountains form the longest
range in the world. To their west, they are bordered for almost 2000
miles by the world's driest desert: the Atacama. The world's largest
area of jungle surrounds the Amazon river and traces its western
border along those same mountains. Even within the Andean mountain range, natural superlatives continue. For here are the highest
summits outside Asia. Further north, the Andes finally abate, and the
sub-tropical highlands of Central America and Mexico soar and surround the highest volcanoes on this planet. Across the breadth of
Mexico, mountains dominate almost every natural panorama. To the
west, there lies the Sierra Madre Occidental. To the east there is the
Sierra Madre Oriental. Where these ranges meet is the site of the Aztec
capital, Tenochtitlan. Today, it is covered with the urban sprawl of
Mexico City: a symbol of the ways in which modern arrogance has
virtually destroyed the ancient learning of pre-Columbian civilizations

which inhabited these mountain landscapes from 1000 BC to a time less than five hundred years ago. But even before those civilizations ascended the heights of understanding and empathy with their mountains, smaller groups of villagers had revered these peaks ever since they migrated south from North America 20000 years ago.

Of all the Andean forms of wisdom, the Inca empire came closest to perfecting a way of life which worked in sympathy with the rhythms and constraints of these mountains.[1] Theirs was a wisdom of reverence and adaptation, worship and everyday practicality as an interdependent whole. A wisdom in harmony with the physical adversity of their dry, high-altitude and vertiginous environment. And an everyday pragmatism which was applied from the empire's most northern point, in modern day Ecuador, south over 2500 miles to central Chile. A remarkable combination of belief and practice which pervaded all levels of Inca society and culture. But nowhere within that empire were these combined virtues of reverence and practicality expressed more clearly than at Machu Picchu: a profoundly sacred site of worship located on a narrow ridge high in the Peruvian Andes between snow-capped mountains and Amazonian jungle.[2] Encircling the collection of houses, temples and terraces on Machu Picchu are other mountains situated at each of the four compass points: Huayna Picchu, and the three snow-capped mountains of Salcantay, Veronica and Pumasillo. At the heart of the Machu Picchu complex is the Intihuatana rock: shaped in striking similarity to the summit of Huayna Picchu. Today, mystery still surrounds the Intihuatana rock. Perhaps it represents a mountain spirit. It may even represent a long-forgotten Inca god whose power was invoked during ceremonial rites.

Immediately adjacent to Machu Picchu, the city of Cusichaca was erected to act as a storehouse and support facility for the temple complex, a practical response to the everyday requirements of priests and pilgrims. With a population of over 1800 people, Cusichaca's economy became so prosperous that it was able to export crops of potatoes, maize and other vegetables to any part of the empire. But that astonishing export potential was only made possible by an ingenious network of roads. Even over the most challenging terrain, the Inca road system developed in size to exceed other systems built by the Roman, Chinese or ancient African civilizations. The Incas were therefore able to use their road network to transport food and armies anywhere they wished. Even today, travellers find sections of Inca roads and river bridges which have stood firm through the centuries.

Other forms of communication were also conducted along the Inca roads with astonishing speed. Any message could be sent the full length of the empire in only one week. By positioning a series of messengers at waystations along those roads, they could run an allocated distance before passing the message onto their next colleague. Thus, in a matter of days, thousands of miles were covered in reliability and accuracy. Even on horseback, the same distance cannot be travelled over these treacherous landscapes in such a short time. It was a fast, efficient system which emphasises again the way in which Inca society worked within the constraints of these mountains.

In response to the unpredictability of the mountain climate, the Incas also applied their roads as a network to receive and distribute supplies from their vast storehouses. According to Spanish chronicles, some Inca city stores were able to accommodate up to one million bushels of potatoes and maize. Consequently, each year, new crops of grain and vegetables were delivered in from the broad terraces of agricultural land which had been carved and irrigated on the surrounding peaks. Where those terraces became narrow, the Inca footplough was particularly useful for cultivating every corner of available soil. Nothing was wasted. Indeed, no civilization has subsequently been able to draw from this land in such an efficient and continually harmonious manner: another testament to the adaptive wisdom and understanding which the Incas maintained. However, within that system, everyone was required to complete their shift of work in the fields. No one was considered too rich, or too powerful to be excluded from those requirements. And anyone who refused to work in that prescribed way did not receive a share of the crop.

At the heart of the Inca cities, a vast central square was almost invariably constructed. This provided a space for civic hospitality, an opportunity to receive travellers and offer them meals and assistance, fresh provisions and advice on trade or directions to continue their journey — a civic expression of wisdom and compassion which remains lost to all cities today. But it was through this emphasis on bonding communities together, that the Incas were able to maintain their empire until it was destroyed by Spanish invaders in the sixteenth century.

The Spanish appetite for power, gold and wealth, along with their superior firepower and military strategy, also saw the end of the Aztec, or Mexica people, as they called themselves. As with the Incas to the south, the death of Aztec traditions was also the end to a profound reverence for their mountains. It was the end to a pattern of worship in which the veneration of local summits and their surrounding rainclouds bonded communities together. A bond between all Aztec people, their mountains, and the unimaginable forces of life and death which lay within and beyond those peaks. Today, that intense awe and fear of mountain gods is no longer fully understood. In the late twentieth century for example, the volcano of Popocatepetl, near Mexico City, lies virtually silent. At the height of the Aztec empire however, it shot flames and smoke hundreds of feet into the sky, two or three times each day. Within that terrifying environment, Aztec worship saw a demand for the ultimate invocation to the deities: human sacrifice. A ceremonial arrangement with the gods in which a relatively few lives were offered in exchange for the safety of the many. A trade-off with breathtaking divine powers over life and death which became ingrained into the everyday life and expectations among Aztec people. On many of the Aztec feast days therefore, this most profound reverence for these mountains saw the lives of men, women and even young children offered to the Mexican gods. Practices which may appear incomprehensibly barbaric to modern ways of thinking, were nothing more than a wisdom of survival and protection for the Aztecs against the wrath of their gods. A wisdom which combined spiritual aspirations with the simple requirements of everyday life.

But whilst the brutality of those human sacrifices was also consistent with other aspects of the Aztecs' warlike culture, their reverence for mountains cannot be isolated from the impact which earlier civilizations made on that worship and wisdom. The influence of the Mayan people in particular inspired the design of Aztec temples and altars. From the Mayan style of building mountaintop pyramids, the Aztecs built their own places of worship among their own summits. On top of the 13615 foot Mount Tlaloc, north of present-day Mexico City, architects and priests constructed a temple to the god Tlaloc: one of the most powerful deities within the Aztec pantheon. Tlaloc was not only the god of life; through his ability to bring forth rain, he was also the god of lightning: a terrifying and deadly force which was directly associated to the power of Tlaloc's mountain. For the Spanish chronicler, Diego Duran, the painted image of Tlaloc which he found in the god's temple in Tenochtitlan, the site of present day Mexico City, was incomparably hideous:

> Its horrendous face was like that of a serpent with huge
> fangs; it was bright and red like a flaming fire. This was a
> symbol of the brilliance of the lightning and rays cast from
> the heavens when he sent tempests and thunderbolts ...
> (Duran 1975, 155)

Alongside the astonishing natural beauty of Latin American mountains there has also been ferocious brutality. But as modern travellers to these countries frequently discover, the alignment between beauty and brutality is an abiding theme throughout Latin American life. Within Chile for example, a country whose natural landscapes are dominated by the Andean mountain chain, government priorities are focused more on generating export revenue and foreign investment than they are on developing social policies for the rural and urban poor. Further north, in Peru, it is the poor who suffer most with annual inflation figures averaging 20%. In Ecuador and Colombia, annual inflation averages 28% and 24% respectively.[3] Consequently, it is the poor whose lives have become a living sacrifice to the priorities of their governments. The mountains which modern travellers discover are therefore a strong, provocative and contrasting inspiration which can never be ignored alongside these contemporary expressions of social brutality and political power.

First visits

All the new travellers who contributed to this chapter knew of the contrasts between ancient forms of worship in these mountains. They had learned of the human sacrifices practised by Aztec priests. They knew also of the more mystical and reflective rituals held by the Incas. But this knowledge was of far greater significance than an academic understanding. It coloured these travellers' ability to draw spiritual inspiration from these mountains. It even prevented some of them from drawing any constructive, personally helpful, experiences from the Mexican volcanoes on which human blood had been spilt during the Aztec reign. A contemporary interpretation was placed on those blood sacrifices which acted as a barrier between modern visitors and the sacred power of the mountains. In the case of three merchant bank managers from New York, William, Bret and Bethany, the Mexican volcanoes of Popocatepetl and Iztaccihuatl were only ever regarded as being forbidding, tainted and 'empty of their original beauty.'

WILLIAM:
I'd been looking forward to seeing Popocatepetl and Iztaccihuatl years before my first visit to Mexico City because I wanted to feel the power

of those volcanoes which had always been such a threat to the Aztec.
But as we drove out to them, and especially Popocatepetl, I've got to
tell you that my stomach started to tighten and my mouth became dry,
and I became profoundly, profoundly nervous and tense almost at the
first sight of the thing.

BRET:

But for all of us, it was strange, we all started to tense up.

BETHANY:

That's right. We all acted in the same way. First we got tense. Then we
felt our minds were almost locked solid. I mean, we couldn't even ratio-
nalize ... And I instantly got this awareness that it was my knowledge
of those Aztec human sacrifices, which have always really appalled me.
And I've never been able to understand them on their terms.

Three travellers sharing a glimpse of the dark horrors which they
imagined surrounding Popocatepetl during rituals such as the Tepeil-
huitl Feast of the Mountains: the major ritual in the thirteenth month
of the Aztec calendar.[4]

BRET:

They had a ritual called the Nicteocua, which was a meal meaning
'I eat God.' And what they were eating was the remains of their
human sacrifices and little bread figures representing the spirit of
the mountain ... And I really struggle to understand the need to
destroy life like that. I mean, it wasn't just adults they sacrificed
there. But children too.

The conclusion drawn by each of these three travellers was to
recognize a need to understand the profound fear and reverence
which maintained the Aztec tradition of blood sacrifices. Although
they were repelled at the thought of human lives being slaughtered in
the name of spiritual ritual, each of them left Mexico with an ambition
to try and understand 'the emotional and psychological value which
those ceremonies had for those people.'

BETHANY:

Maybe it's impossible. But as soon as I got home to New York, I wan-
ted to meditate on what I'd seen. And to take time to let those feelings I
had there speak to me in a clearer way ... I wanted to get away from the
shock I felt when I first saw mountains like Iztaccihuatl, and move in

my mind, and through my reading, to a greater empathy with that amazing power and force which those people felt in the mountains ... because these days, I just find we've lost a lot of that feeling.

From her initial perception of the 'barbarism' within Aztec ritual, Bethany is therefore trying to discern an ancient wisdom. She is trying to repair the void of misunderstanding between modern morality and historical fears and expressions of a people whose lives have been lost, but whose fundamental lessons on reverence for nature, Bethany believes, can still have a powerful and important contemporary relevance.

In a very similar way, travellers to mountains revered by the Incas also emphasised their potential educational value which combines sublime spiritual experience with the Incas' ability to work out a harmony with their mountains. But that harmony was never easily won. It always demanded continuous attention and raw, hard work before it would bear its magnificent reward. The example of this very brittle harmony which all these travellers quoted was the enigmatic temple of Machu Picchu. Located on a narrow ridge descending from the 20574 foot Mount Salcantay in Peru, Machu Picchu lies at the heart of the most sacred mountains within Inca belief. The most holy of holy places, the focus of pilgrimage and inspiration then and now. Indeed, for Gillian, an archaeologist from London University, it was possible to reflect upon the Inca rituals held in this place and then draw personal value from them within her Buddhist consciousness:

GILLIAN:

I definitely believe you can be in a place and still pick up its feeling. Even if it became abandoned for worship centuries ago, like Machu Picchu. There's always an aura to these places ... But I also think it's important not to romanticize that sense of harmony which the Inca had with these mountains. Because it was always a struggle for them. And it was a very precarious balance ... But, I think, if you put that powerful aura of the place together with that sense of harmony which needs working at, you find yourself learning so much (from Machu Picchu) in terms of its relevance for us today ... So although we always say it's been abandoned, it doesn't have to be obsolescent. And I remember on my first visit there, being reduced to tears by the clarity of vision I received from thinking about that harmony which needed constant attention ... It's definitely a lesson for our times!

The contrasting elements of Machu Picchu have been interpreted by Gillian as a form of jigsaw, the pieces of which can be re-connected, and re-assembled to form a new modern shape, a late-twentieth century shape from the remnants of five hundred year old architecture. And similar spiritual shapes and meanings were drawn from Machu Picchu by two American students from New Orleans, Gregory and Pete, whose first journey through Latin America also included Mount Ausangate, in the Cuzco region of Peru near Machu Picchu.[5] For these two travellers however, the two places formed a seamless continuum of mystical inspiration and contemporary relevance:

GREGORY:

First, Ausangate and Machu Picchu are pretty much in the same region of Peru, so you go from one to the other pretty quickly. And the inspiration you get from one, carries on soon after to the other ...

PETE:

But the key to both mountains was the word 'interdependence.' Because if the Inca didn't have their amazing road system, then not so many of them could have made the pilgrimage to these mountains. And if they didn't have the agricultural expertise to carve out fields as terraces from the side of those mountains, and store their food, they couldn't have sustained the pilgrims.

GREGORY:

So the whole of Inca traditions in finding spiritual inspiration in mountains are made up from the practicalities of engineering and agriculture, as well as an emotional and imaginary openness to the impression the mountains made on their minds. And if they'd lost just one part of that jigsaw, the whole set-up would have collapsed.

Without roads, there could not be the volume of Inca pilgrimages. Without food, their stay in these mountains would have been brief and superficial. Without their sensitivity, awe and wonder, there would have been no reason to build roads at these altitudes, over such apparently impossible mountain terrain. Through all these interconnecting elements, Gregory and Pete suggested there are more opportunities for modern travellers to find inspiration from these mountains within their own terms. Engineers may find wonder from the Inca technology in building roads leading up to Machu Picchu. Agriculturalists and ecologists may discover the astonishing ability of Inca farmers and store managers to grow and keep food in these mountains for months at a time. Many paths to an enduring inspiration which can still amaze their visitors, and change their lives.

GILLIAN:

> *I think I was lucky when I first visited Machu Picchu because I was able to stay there for three months. So I could sit quietly for long periods of time and take it all in, without the need to rush and cram it all in in a couple of hours ... But when it finally hits you that the Inca reverence for that place, and for the other mountains around Cuzco, was so multi-faceted, I couldn't help finding myself looking at my (archaeological) work, as well as the rest of my life as a whole, as well as a part of a greater whole. I mean, I think I'd probably thought that way occasionally, before that visit, but now I think it's become far more ingrained in me. It's a part of the way I naturally think about things now, instead of a way of thinking which I was just aware of, and which I may choose to apply now and then.*

Whilst this more unified way of seeing and thinking also became apparent for Gregory and Pete, they found a further benefit from having such a breadth of themes with which to describe their travel experiences to others.

PETE:

> *I think I'm a fairly broad minded Christian. But when I tell people about my spiritual experiences, I also try and tailor what I say to the interests of those people, so they don't think I'm being completely irrelevant ... But unlike other parts of the world I've been through, there are so many ways of describing how you became inspired when you talk about the mountains within the Inca empire because they had so many facets to their reverence for those places ... Whether it was through art, pure spirituality, road making, bridge building, farming, city building, administration. The list is a long one!*

Subsequent visits

The more experienced travellers in these mountains found the same bewildering collection of interconnecting elements within Inca sacred meaning. However, from their greater experience of mountains, along with other aspects of Latin American society such as rural and urban poverty, these travellers were able to identify even broader spiritual networks of meaning which surround the Andean and other peaks. They discussed broader collections of ancient teaching as well as a greater breadth of modern inspiration and concern. A clear example of this expanded consciousness which was inspired by repeated visits to several Latin American mountains arose in the following contribution by Brian, a civil engineer from Savannah, Georgia:

BRIAN:
> *When I visit those mountains, throughout Latin America, I'm always left with the thought that if only politicians down there would look at those amazing scenes, they wouldn't allow all the ethnic discrimination to continue ... Because whenever I go to those mountains, I always feel angry at some form of injustice I've just seen back in the city some place. Or which I've read about in a (news) paper. So with those thoughts of anger and frustration in my mind, I go to the mountains down there and always find the complete opposite ... Standing in front of those mountains, I feel humbled by what I see, but I never feel my dignity is overwhelmed ... In fact, sometimes, I feel that the mountains are the only places in Latin America where human dignity is never crushed in any way.*

For Brian, the towering purity of these mountains stands in stark contrast to the social injustice which he finds in Latin American society. Among the many examples which Brian quoted to illustrate that contrast was the devastation suffered in 1995 by 139 families after a gas explosion had destroyed their homes in Mexico City's Membrillo shanty-community. Brian had followed that story through newspaper and magazine coverage, and was appalled at the lack of government assistance to those families. More generally, Brian also described the escalating trend, throughout Latin America, where families are being evicted from their squalid homes, and forced to live on the streets, by unregulated landlords who demand excessive property rents. From Chile, Brian also described his memories of visiting the coastal resort of Vina del Mar in 1994, and witnessing 'the blatant contrast between all the glamour on the beach, and the shanty housing, unemployment, drug addiction and alcoholism going on only a few minutes' drive away.' But in describing these facts, memories and feelings, Brian also emphasised his belief that the notions of social justice which the mountains inspire in his imagination are consistently timeless. They are immediately modern, and yet deeply rooted in the ancient past. That clear sense of social justice is therefore as relevant to Brian's Christian response to the modern tower blocks of Mexico City, Quito, Bogotá or Caracas, as it is to the mountain rocks whose ages are counted in millions of years:

BRIAN:
There are lines in the Book of Jeremiah which always come to mind when I'm comparing mankind's social sickness, with the spiritual inspiration I find in those mountains. And if you want to know what message I find in those mountains for our times it's this:

> *He defended the cause of the poor and needy, and so all went well. Is that not what it means to know me, declares the Lord. But your eyes and your heart are set only on dishonest gain, on shedding innocent blood and on oppression and extortion. (Jeremiah 22:16–17)*

I actually first read those words back home in Savannah. But as soon as I did, my mind was catapulted back to Latin America.

Other experienced travellers also described passages of literature which captured 'the full voice of these mountains' (Jake). In his capacity as a computing lecturer, Jake is a frequent visitor to Latin America from his home in Chicago, Illinois:

JAKE:
There are a lot of wonderful writers from those countries who've written books over the last thirty or forty years which will become the wisdom literature of generations in the future. And those writers have become more and more important to me because they all highlight the contrast between a spiritual order to life which I find in the mountains down there, and the absolute disastrous obscenity of life in some of those (Latin American) cities and farm areas.

In elaborating upon this comparison between critical social commentary and mountain experience, Jake drew from a host of contemporary literature. From the work of liberation theologian Gustavo Gutierrez for example, Jake suggested that his own sustained experience of finding spiritual and creative inspiration in mountains, rests in a clear and uneasy contrast with Gutierrez's observations on the subordination, prejudice and hatred which still remains the norm within Latin American city and rural communities.[6] For Jake, and for Gutierrez, this contrast will only be resolved by a form of education which teaches people living in those conditions to challenge the status quo:

JAKE:

> *I remember one time a group of us climbed right up Llullaillaco (in northern Chile). It was a beautiful day. And you saw miles out to the horizon. And I'd just got into what Gutierrez was writing, and in a moment I had this amazing sense of understanding the Inca reasoning for building their shrine up there. But also in that moment, a oneness with what Gutierrez was saying about the need to find an inspiration to challenge conformity. Everything in my mind, and in my sight, was saying 'freedom to think.' 'Freedom to live.' 'Freedom to be.' It was like a crowd of people shouting those slogans in my mind, like at some sort of political convention.*

For Jake, as well as other experienced travellers, the Latin American theologian, Jon Sobrino was also unanimously regarded as a powerful voice who identifies the unnecessary contrast between personal inspirations found within mountain journeys, and these travellers' other journeys through Latin American cities, towns and villages.[7] Sobrino's work particularly appealed to Jake through its emphasis on the need to be creative with Christian social concern. Sobrino is therefore not afraid to confront past failures of Christian involvement in Latin American society, and to identify bold new options for challenging current political priorities which almost invariably fail to accommodate the needs of the poor and disadvantaged. During the following conversation with Gordon, a marketing executive from London, Jake suggested that Sobrino's words emphasise the contemporary relevance of Latin American mountains:

JAKE:

> *From a spiritual viewpoint, none of those mountains have ever just been pretty. They've always been used by people to awaken their awareness of the world around them, beyond the mountains. And although*

Jon Sobrino doesn't focus exclusively on mountain spirituality, I always think that, when I'm down there in the real wilds of the Andes, I always feel this discrepancy between the freedom which you feel there, and the oppression in the cities which Sobrino protests about.

GORDON:

I think you're right. But what's interesting is the fact that even when people haven't discovered writers like Jon Sobrino, they often feel intuitively that that contrast exists. Between the modern cities and the modern meaning of those mountains ... And then when they do discover those writers, there's an empathy between reader and writer straightaway ... And I've met a lot of people, who spend a lot of time travelling throughout Latin American countries, who've all told me about that type of experience.

Alongside the voices of modern theologians such as Jon Sobrino and Gustavo Gutierrez, Latin American mountains are consistently regarded by these experienced travellers as a symbol of liberation, freedom and magnificent inspiration. They are places of spiritual enlightenment in a continent darkened by exploitation and intolerance.

GORDON:

When ever I'm lucky enough to travel through the Andean chain I'm often reminded of a passage from the Gospel of Luke, which is often subtitled 'Mary's Song.' And I like to imagine that one day, people will travel through these mountains, and they'll find such inspiration within their souls that they'll be able to change the way those countries work ... And oppressive regimes do get overturned. Communism. Eastern Europe. It's happened before, and it will definitely happen again ... But I often think Mary could have been singing about Christ's divine spirit of reconciliation within those mountains:

> *My soul praises the Lord*
> *and my spirit rejoices in God my Saviour,*
> *for he has been mindful*
> *of the humble state of his servant*
> *... His mercy extends to those who fear him,*
> *from generation to generation.*
> *He has performed mighty deeds with his arm;*
> *he has scattered those*
> *who are proud in their inmost thoughts.*
> *He has brought down rulers from their thrones*

> *but has lifted up the humble.*
> *He has filled the hungry with good things*
> *but has sent the rich away empty.*
>   *(Luke 1:46–53)*

Gordon's Christian response to the mountains leaves him with a clear and powerful reminder that social oppression does not last for ever. The mighty can be scattered in confusion. And the humble can find peace and dignity. But whilst this conclusion was reached from a foundation of Christian understanding, the same truth was reached, independently, by a Scottish writer and photographer, Teresa, from her Buddhist background:

TERESA:

> *I spend a lot of my time in and around Mexico City because I think some of the images going on there really are at the cutting edge of what's happening to modern society ... in terms of the huge divide between peoples. And I find those stark contrasts to be a real challenge to my Buddhist spirituality because I always like having my beliefs challenged and tested by what I see ... But, for me, that contrast is always most powerfully embodied in one mountain in particular, Tlaloc, north of the Popocatepetl and Iztaccihuatl volcanoes in Mexico. And just about anyone else I travel with always feels the same way too.*

Within Aztec mythology, Tlaloc was the source of rain: the means by which fields could be watered, crops could grow, and human life could continue.[8] For Teresa, this symbolism of sustained life combines with her knowledge of the Hindu notion of Daridranarayan where God is seen to be manifest within the lives of the poor, the victims, the oppressed and the neglected:[9]

Opposite top:
North Cascade Range with Mount Baker in the distance, Washington State.
(Image Bank)

Below:
The moon and Venus over the Rocky Mountains, Colorado.
(Steve Satushek/ Image Bank)

TERESA:

> *In my mind, I put the ancient mythology of Tlaloc's life-giving qualities together with my studies of Daridranarayan where God is a life-sustaining force in the lives of the victims of society ... and I find Tlaloc represents, for me, a hope for Mexico. I look at that mountain and there's a contemporary life-giving force which comes from it. And certainly it brings me a lot of strength. And I know that's also how a lot of my Mexican friends feel too ... But I think we all reached that conclusion from different spiritual paths. Me, with my Buddhism and studies in Hinduism. And them from a Christian background.*

Above: Snowy peaks reflected in Saddlebag Lake, Sierra Nevada, California.
(A & L Sinibaldi/Tony Stone)

Left: Snow and forest-covered mountains, Sierra Nevada, California. (Baron Wolman/Tony Stone)

Opposite top: Mount McKinley, Alaska.
(Image Colour Library)

Right: Yosemite National Park, California.
(Image Colour Library)

Opposite top: Mount Rainier & Gig Harbour, Washington State.
(Image Colour Library)

Left: Mount Shasta, California.
(Baron Wolman/Tony Stone)

Above: Machu Picchu, Peru.
(Image Colour Library)

Right: Inca Inti Rami festival, Peru.
(Image Colour Library)

Left: Tlahuizcalpantecuhtli Temple, Tula, Hidalgo, Mexico. (Image Colour Library)

Below: Torres de Paine and Lago Pehoe, Chile. (Image Colour Library)

Right: Mount Popocatepetl with Cholula Church in foreground, Mexico. (Robert Frerck/Tony Stone)

Teresa has discovered that not only does the sacred meaning of Tlaloc completely transcend the boundaries of religious doctrine, but it also speaks to many of its visitors with a single message. The message that a life of dignity will return to the poor of Mexico. The prophecy that social life within Mexico will only begin to consistently improve when the unnecessary exploitation of farm labourers, factory workers, women, ethnic minorities and the uneducated is brought to a halt.

TERESA:

Even when I'm away from Tlaloc, or the other Mexican mountains which inspire me, I often see things which remind me of what that mountain stands for. And it might be a family meal in the rural areas where I listen to the angry voices of farmers. Or when I listen to women who've had enough of being beaten, and who want more for themselves and for their children. I mean, I've listened to loads and loads of stories which convince me that some day, very soon, the life-giving spirit of Mexico, which is clearly within its people, will be realized in revolution. You only have to spend a few days listening to people to work that out, because it's so clear ... And then Tlaloc will see the fulfilment of its prophecy. And life will return to a blossoming, creative, open, free, liberated way of being.

This extraordinarily prophetic and insightful reading of specific mountains was also echoed from yet another spiritual direction. Ralph is a Zen teacher from Los Angeles, California who leads groups of meditation students high into the Andean mountains of southern Chile. In particular, Ralph always tries to take these students to camp, walk and climb near to the Towers of Paine in that southern part of the Andes:

RALPH:

Almost always we do make it down there (to the Towers of Paine). And the first thing I ask my students to do is to sit as comfortably as possible in silence for two hours. And what we do is to look. And see. And really study the physical shapes and the spiritual force being offered by those Towers ... We're there to receive and accept new inspiration.

Ralph's students have ranged from teenagers to grandparents. They have come from almost every conceivable profession and social background. And yet one theme becomes inspired by these southern mountains more than any other.

Opposite top left: Lava flowing into ocean, Volcanoes National Park, Hawaii. (G Brad Lewis/ Tony Stone)

Top right: Kilauea Volcano erupting, Hawaii. (G Brad Lewis/ Tony Stone)

Below: Kilauea lava explosion, Hawaii. (Paul Berger/Tony Stone)

RALPH:

> *Anger. That's what people first feel when they really learn to see these mountains. This awe-inspiring beauty and force in exactly the same continent, and even the same country, where the societies are anything but beautiful.*

Alongside their studies in silence, Ralph's students also discuss the haiku poems which capture the essence, simplicity and wealth of Zen wisdom. But from a personal point of view, Ralph finds that two verses by the Japanese poet Matsuo Basho return continually to his imagination. In doing so, both verses always inspire more insight which Ralph tries to pass on to his students:

> The sea darkening
> Oh, voices of the wild birds
> Crying, whirling, white.

* * *

> Lightning flashing:
> Beyond the darkness darts
> A night heron's scream.

RALPH:

> *They're two poems written to describe crying voices. But those voices are perfectly at one with their environment. They're in complete harmony with natural rhythms and the flow of physical and spiritual life. But the amazing thing is that when you take those words down through the west coast of Chile, and then you ask students to react to those poems after they've seen those mountains, and after they've seen the cities of other places in Latin America, if only on TV, we always get the most amazing reactions.*

Ralph described how some of his students simply react with tears. Others need to immediately turn away from the discussion and walk alone in order to deal with their anger and frustration. In contrast to the poems and the mountains, human society in Chile and other Latin American countries remains 'crass and unsustainable' (Ralph). And in contrast to those cities, the mountains inspire 'wisdom, compassion, creativity, openness, oneness, harmony and equality' (Ralph). The contrast between Latin American society and Latin American mountains therefore remains as clear, vivid, powerful and enduring for

Ralph from his Zen background as it does for Teresa from her more eclectic Buddhist path, and for Gordon from his Christian perspective. These travellers have all found a single form of truth and wisdom from a vast range of mountains, from an equally contrasting series of starting points. They have been travellers from many paths who have reached a single prophetic conclusion. That prophecy is one of complete social change which will sweep right across Latin America. From oppression, there will become liberation. From subordination there will be freedom and creativity. From those victims, there will be a whirl-wind of future inspiration.

Turning points

In November 1989, three botanists from San Francisco, California travelled to the world's highest altitude forest at Cajas, near Cuenca, in southern Ecuador. At over 13000 feet, Cajas is an area of primary rainforest in an Andean landscape which is continually under threat from encroaching deforestation. The main goal of these botanists' project was to study the habitat of a designated number of endangered plant species with specific reference to the forest's epiphytic orchids. But although the scientific results of this project fully satisfied their terms of reference, it was the spiritual upheaval arising from that journey which left a more dramatic impact on each of them.

During the second week of their assignment in the Cajas forest, Jessica, Neil and Steve began an analytical programme which involved spending several days at a time camping within the rainforest. Each day, the three scientists would move their equipment to a fresh site where they would photograph and catalogue the plant species in which they were interested. At dusk on the fourth day of this programme, they were walking toward their next camp site when Neil stumbled and hit his face against a fallen tree trunk. With the weight of his thirty pound backpack on his shoulders, Neil's face was pushed against the trunk with considerable force. The impact caught him directly on the bridge of his nose and he began to bleed profusely. In the few moments it took Jessica and Steve to be at his side with a first aid box, Neil's nose was streaming with blood. At first, they thought he was still conscious. Jessica quickly found some swabs and gripped

Neil's nose according to standard emergency aid procedure. But when Steve noticed that Neil had lost consciousness and that blood continued to flow from his nose, the seriousness of his injury finally became clear.

Without any other medical support, Jessica and Steve were simply obliged to persist with their basic first aid procedures. They had no idea whether the techniques would work whilst the blood continued to flow from Neil's nose, covering his face and neck.

But for Neil, the experience was dramatically different:

NEIL:

As soon as the blood started pouring out of my nose I lost consciousness immediately. I guess that was a combination of tripping up, and smacking my face fully against the tree, as well as the sudden loss of blood ... And, like a second later, I was looking down on the other guys as they started their emergency aid on me. And for a moment there, I couldn't work out what was going on. But there I was, just floating above the two of them, and I could see my body pouring with blood ...

For several seconds, Neil continued to look down from what he describes as his 'near-death experience.' During that experience he felt no pain from his injury. Nor did he feel the grip of Jessica's fingers as she gripped his nose to try and stop the bleeding.

NEIL:

And I guess I watched what was going on for a couple of minutes. But then I wanted to look around me, because, obviously, I'd never done any floating around before! ... And as I looked around, at the trees, and the whole scene, I began to feel a fantastic kind of love. And it was so relaxing. And kind. And gentle. And it was at that point that it occurred to me that I had actually died and that this was a sort of prelude to heaven.

Prior to that moment, Neil had adhered to no spiritual interests whatsoever. Indeed, he described himself as a 'rational scientist ... and a complete atheist' who was fully persuaded by the impersonal 'logic of evolution' to account for the development of life on earth. But with this first encounter with the 'prelude to heaven,' Neil felt neither fear, regret nor any other anxiety:

NEIL:

The only way I can describe it was that I felt understood. You know, my reasons for not having pursued any religious interests or enquiries seemed to have been accepted by the source of this love ... This awesome force which was holding me above my friends ... And again, I looked down, and saw them both, clearly, trying to raise me up, and gripping my nose, and doing what they had to do.

By that stage, Neil had fully worked out the decision which lay before him. He had reached a turning point in his life. He had the opportunity to leave his companions in the Cajas forest, die more fully, and pursue the loving light which surrounded and supported him as he floated above the forest floor. Alternatively, Neil knew he had the chance to return to Jessica and Steve, and continue with their expedition.

NEIL:

At first it was a real dilemma. I wanted to continue to float and swim in this amazing feeling of being loved. But I also desperately wanted to carry on with the research. And the more I thought about the science, I realized I had to go back ... And as soon as I took that decision, I regained consciousness.

Neil's first sensations were of a searing and stinging pain right across his face and neck. He felt nauseous and dizzy, sweaty and exhausted.

Over the subsequent years, Neil's experience in the Cajas forest has led him to pursue three extended meditation courses in Buddhism. In doing so, he suggested that of all the world's spiritual paths, Buddhism is the only one where its teachers have been sufficiently sensitive to accept his former atheism, his current questions and dilemmas, and his developing enthusiasm for wishing to account for his near-death experience.

NEIL:

Right now, I feel the circumstances are leading me away from a complete atheism onto something more open and inspired. But a lot of that inspiration really transcends the limits to any religion, because what I'm learning is more fundamental, and more common to human wisdom than any specific doctrine ... And I'm always able to check whether an idea is good for me because I just think back to the light I felt, or saw, in the forest. And I get the feeling of whether an idea is precisely right. Or if it's right for now, but later it'll be changed a little.

Although Neil's enthusiasm for Buddhist meditation and instruction arose from personal experience, Jessica and Steve have also felt cautiously drawn to that form of wisdom. However, whilst they do not attend any class or meditation group, they have read widely on the subject, and have individually begun to meditate in private.

JESSICA:
When a good friend who you trust, like (Neil), tells you this stuff, I think you listen. I mean, the guy's definitely not a nutcase or anything. He's been through something different and unusual. And it's something which he wanted to share with us, and, in our way, we're checking it out.

STEVE:
And I think we're both finding it opens up a lot of doors for us ... For a start, it widens out the way we all look at science now. I mean, there's a whole lot more here than just logic. That much is clear ...

JESSICA:
But we've also talked about this a lot, as you can imagine! And I think we're both a lot more aware of the morality of our actions now. We're more careful and caring with people. And I think that's a big difference. That constant awareness to try and love, and show compassion.

Whether or not Neil's love-light can be identified as God, within the Judeo-Christian tradition, remains an open question for each of these three scientists. It also remains a largely irrelevant question for them. The name of the love-light is less important than its inspiration. To name it would be to limit it. And Neil's early experience of that inspiration is that it can, and must, transcend boundaries. It transcends the boundaries between religions as well as the boundaries between science, morality and spirituality. It is an inspiration which shows that all boundaries are at best transient, and at worst deceiving, confusing and erroneous. Instead, there is a unity emphasising the virtues of wisdom and compassion, reverence for nature and reverence for others. Simple eternal truths which became manifest within ancient wisdom, and which pervade modern life as well.

Conclusions

Although the mountains of Latin America have provoked discussion among these travellers on a vast range of sacred and secular subjects, those discussions have almost always been confined in their content to the countries immediately adjacent to those mountains. The key to understanding that simultaneous breadth and concentration of themes lies in two sources. First, all these travellers had spent time in the cities, towns and villages of Mexico and the countries immediately adjacent to the Andean chain. During that time, even if it was only for a few days, they became angry at the sustained evidence of social inequality and injustice. Second, the auras of wisdom and ritual which continue to linger among these mountains are powerful and intensely provocative. Whether it is the remaining spirit of Aztec sacrifices or the more sublime spectre of Inca ceremonial among the Andes, all these travellers suggested that these mountains had a 'very peculiar depth of meaning to them' (Gillian).

GILLIAN:

Mountains are never just heaps of rock. And the more I talk to other people who've travelled a lot further than I have, it seems that ranges of mountains, or even individual mountains definitely have a personality of their own ... And it seems to me that in that stretch of countries from Mexico, down through central America, and then through the Andes, you have a very distinctive combination between continual social struggle and astonishing beauty.

Brian's conclusions on these mountains matched Gillian's in almost every detail:

BRIAN:

You can't travel to those mountains without first landing in one of the cities down there, and seeing the contrast between the squalor and the wealth. And I've never met anyone who hasn't been deeply moved by that experience ... But then you move up into the mountains. And although you physically leave those sights behind, they're so intense, that you wouldn't be human if you completely left them ... So by the time you're 15000 feet up somewhere, you're struck by the amazing freedom and beauty of those mountains, and the equally astonishing confinement and intolerance beneath you in the cities. It's a powerful

discrepancy ... and I think the reason why people compare the meaning
of those mountains with almost every aspect of Latin American society,
but nowhere else, is precisely because both the society down there, and
the mountains, bore such an indelible impression into your mind, you're
hypnotized by those specific memories and experiences, and those alone.

The second conclusion which these travellers drew from their experiences in Latin American mountains exposed the false and misleading contrast between human physical and spiritual requirements. With particular reference to the Inca empire, all these people variously discussed their knowledge of the hard-won harmony which the Inca rulers, and their subjects, maintained with the physical environment of the Andean mountains. It was always an unstable harmony. It always had to be managed. And it always had to be prayed for. Consequently, there was a seamless union between agriculture and worship, food storage and prayer, road building and pilgrimage.

PETE:
The Inca really inspire me because there was such a hard-working unity
to their life. Spirituality and everyday life were just one thing. And
there was no separation between religion and city building, or any
other part of their life ...

For other travellers, this interdependence between the secular and sacred activities of society returned their discussion to the ways in which spiritual and social interdependence has yet to persuade political and industrial leaders in those countries to exercise more compassion toward the people for whom they are responsible:

BETHANY:
You can't be romantic about Mexico, or, I guess, most other countries
in Latin America. Because when you look beyond the beauty which you
always see down there, there's an amazing amount of cruelty and bru-
tality. Sometimes it's hidden. But I've worked with too many people
down there to be fooled by the gloss ... Out in the mountains, there's a
simple, strong inspiration to be creative and cooperative and compas-
sionate and to get the best out of life as a community. That's the only
way you can survive up there. I mean, just think about the Inca. That
shows it's true. But then you travel down, back to the cities, and all
that inspiration is trodden on and crushed ... But I tell you. One day,
very soon, that inspiration will become so powerful that that whole con-
tinent will be turned upside down. And then everything will change.

CHAPTER 3

Australasia

*The creative Wisdom of all things has established
marvellous and ineffable harmonies by which all things
come together in a concord or friendship or peace or love or
however else the union of all things can be designated.*
John the Scot (1976, 137)

Ancient wisdom

From its northern point among the volcanic islands of Hawaii to the
southern coast of New Zealand, and from the western beaches of
Australia to the scattered profusion of south Pacific islands in the east,
Australasia is one of the most diverse and compelling regions on
earth.[1] Within that huge area, and with an area of over sixty-four
million square miles, the Pacific is the world's largest ocean. Breaking
its surface are thousands of islands and atolls. Most of them rise to
only a few feet above sea level. However, there are breathtaking
exceptions to these low-lying panoramas. Among them is the world's
highest mountain if total height is measured from base to summit.
From its own base on the ocean floor, the Hawaiian volcano Mauna
Kea measures 32 000 feet, over two thousand feet higher than Everest.[2]
From sea level to summit, Mauna Kea towers an inspiring 13 796 feet.
Further south, the highest summit in Australasia is the 16 500 feet
Mount Jaya, a dominating mass over the tropical jungles of New
Guinea.

Among the mountains of Australia, every feature is a precious
source of Aboriginal wisdom and tradition. Every rock, every curve of
the landscape and every gully has been read and re-read, treasured
and contemplated by different tribal groups since these ancient peoples arrived from Asia between 13 000 and 30 000 years ago. Within the
Northern Territory for example, the world's largest isolated rock
monolith, Ayers Rock, lies in the baking sun.[3] With a height of 1 100

feet, a length of almost 2.5 miles and a width nearly 1.5 miles, Ayers Rock abruptly punctuates the flat surrounding landscape, and continues to astonish modern travellers by its size and spiritual grandeur. For the local Pitjantjatjara and Yankuntjatjara tribes however, the Rock will always be called by its ancient name, Uluru, a name and a presence which have been unchanged for thousands of years. And since Uluru is composed of impermeable rock, its minimal rainfall either evaporates in the burning sun, or alternatively drains to the base where it waters the surrounding grassland and trees. It is therefore within this timeless grace that Uluru has inspired a rich tapestry of legend which maintains its place as a sacred heart of Aboriginal wisdom.

Regarding Uluru's south face for example, stories have been told about the invading Snake warriors who travelled in from the west to ambush the peace loving Carpet Snake people. The battling forces fought in an area near the Mutijilda water hole at the foot of Uluru. At the height of battle, a Carpet Snake mother was surrounded by invaders. With her little son at her side, the mother's eyes were wide with terror. She stood before the invaders bravely, ready to fight. And as the Snake warriors came upon her, she fought with speed and agility to save her son from the ferocious violence of battle. But the mother was overwhelmed. Fighting to protect her precious son's life, she glimpsed a moment of victory only to see the boy snatched from her side, lifted high in the air, and mutilated by a Snake warrior's stone knife. In blind fury, the mother whirled her sharpened wooden stick high over her head and caught the murderous Snake warrior a deadly blow on his face, severing his nose completely, and causing it to spin away from the fight to a point marked today by a pointed boulder. Yards away, the Carpet Snake son lay motionless, slowly bleeding to death. All his mother could do was watch helplessly, and to weep as his young blood flowed into the burnt desert sand before being miraculously transformed into the clear water of Mutijilda Spring. Today, on the open plain adjacent to Uluru, the evil Snake warriors continue to menace the landscape in their current manifestation as dried oak trees.

Another sacred story was woven around the features on Uluru's northern face. It described the circumcision rites of initiation which elders in the Hare Wallaby tribe performed on their younger males. During one initiation, a bird flew among the ceremonial assembly and delivered an invitation from the Mulga Seed people. But since the Hare Wallabies were still busy with their initiations, they declined, and sent the bird away without apology. When the bird delivered the blatant refusal, the Mulga Seed people sought hideous revenge. Each of them arranged their wooden staves on the ground to form the outline of a demonic dingo. With the hair from their women, the Mulga formed the dingo's fur. Its teeth were drawn from a mole, and its tail was that of a bandicoot. When the composition was complete, all the Mulga joined with their medicine man and chanted the evil animal to life. Its first victims were the Hare Wallaby women and children. All that remains of their shredded flesh and broken skeletons are a pile of boulders and smaller rocks. Seeing the horrifying carnage before them, the men realized they could do nothing to save their families. Their only hope was to run and save the ceremonial pole which they used in their initiation rites. Where they dragged the pole across Uluru, there remain a series of deep furrows in the monolith, all of which lead to the pole's current resting place as a rock slab leaning against Uluru's northern side.

These, and many other legends of Uluru return the Aboriginals' imagination to the dawn of creation: a prehistorical era they call the Dreamtime. It was a time during which their ancestors journeyed across the earth, creating natural landscape features which can still be observed today. During that Dreamtime, Uluru was formed by two ancestral children from a simple ball of mud. Later, Kandju the red lizard lost his boomerang on Uluru, and in his desperation to recover it, Kandju dug the numerous holes and depressions seen across the monolith's sides. Simple stories capable of inspiring the youngest child and the most thoughtful adult to appreciate Uluru as being a special place, a sacred place which must be approached with reverence if it is to continue to offer shelter in its caves, water from its gullies and springs, and food from its surrounding areas of trees and scrub.

To the east, a distinctive form of spiritual wisdom also developed among the mountainous islands of New Zealand.[4] When the Maori settlers first saw the huge volcanic summits of North Island, and the Alpine peaks of South Island twelve hundred years ago, they were reminded immediately of the extinct Raiatea volcano, west of Tahiti, which had originally inspired so many of their creation myths and legends. But these enormous new islands seemed to grow out of those legends. Aorangi, the highest mountain in New Zealand, was regarded as the sacred remains of a legendary hero carrying a young boy to safety. The hidden caves of Te Aroha were identified as an appropriate final sanctuary for the bones of dead Maori. During their preparations for battle, the spirits of these dead bones, and the wondrous aura of Te Aroha were all remembered by the warriors as a divine source of inspiration. In a very similar way, a volcanic crevice named Tatau o te rangi on Mount Edgecumbe received the bones of Maori dead. As a Door of the Sky, the crevice was a sacred gateway between the worlds of mortality and immortality. A joining together of present time and the timeless world of spirits, ancestors and the foundation of ancient Maori wisdom. Even within the twentieth century, this close spiritual empathy inspires those who observe it with a need to learn more of its instructive power and healing potential.

Whilst one group of Maori ancestors left Polynesia in about 800 AD, another group of settlers had already sailed to Hawaii seven hundred years earlier. Amid Hawaii's enormous volcanoes, the new arrivals believed immediately that they had discovered the legendary paradise of Havai'i in which the Polynesian gods originally made their home. At 4000 feet above sea level, the imposing craters of Kilauea on the colossal grandeur of Mauna Loa were revered with stories of an ancient Polynesian fire god, Aila'au, whose insatiable tongue of fire earned him the name Eater of Trees. Higher up in the Hawaiian mountains, the goddess Poliahu was believed to reside within an enormous palace of snow on the summit of Mauna Kea. Even within the dense tropical highlands of the main island, deities commanded attention and ritual. One of the most highly regarded of those gods was Kane, the inspiration to magnificent prayers:

> O Kane of the great lightning,
> O Kane of the great proclaiming voice,
> O Kane of the small proclaiming voice,
> Silently listening in the mountains — In the great mountains.
> (Quoted in Beckwith 1940, 54-55)

But within so many volcanic islands, one goddess alone, the goddess of all volcanoes, soared above these other deities in the richness of legend and myth which she inspired. Her name was Pele. A wild, blazing and tempestuous spirit, merciless, unpredictable, completely fearless and untamed. Pele's fiery reputation has kept each of Hawaii's volcanoes sacred for almost two thousand years, ever since she was believed to have sailed from Tahiti in her miraculous canoe. However, Pele's departure had followed a time of tense, bitter jealousy and intrigue within her family. Even when she arrived in Hawaii, Pele learned that she was being closely pursued by her vengeful sister. Soon, the two goddesses met in a titanic fight. Far from home, Pele only wanted peace and sanctuary. In her desperation to find that tranquillity, she dug out huge craters in each Hawaiian volcano. From Big Island in the south to Kaua'i in the north, Pele's tormented search for simple, quiet solitude found no peace. At each new mountain, her sister caught up and sought terrible revenge. Finally, on the 10023 foot volcano of Haleakala, the sister grabbed Pele's exhausted body and tore it to shreds, scattering the pieces of ragged flesh and crushed bone far out into the Pacific Ocean.

In the stillness which followed, the battle seemed complete. The dust settled slowly, and no movement appeared from any part of the horizon. Pele's sister proudly surveyed the bloody carnage, laughed derisively at her triumph, and prepared to return to Tahiti believing that victory had been won. In those first silent moments, it looked as if the sister was right. It appeared that Pele had finally been conquered. Humiliated. Broken beyond the ability to retaliate. But then, almost imperceptibly, from the smoking ashes of defeat, Pele's spirit stirred once more. At first, gently, hesitantly, groaning with intense pain. Then, with more purpose. Then with more strength. Then suddenly with a shrieking and unquenchable sheet of fire which engulfed the entire Pacific sky, Pele screamed and roared out her resurrection above the peaks of Mauna Kea and Mauna Loa on Hawaii's Big Island. Where was her foolish sister? Where had she run to? Had she thought Pele could ever be defeated? Pele's snarling glare impatiently searched the islands and ocean, but to no avail. Pele was alone on the field of battle. She was alone to claim final victory and complete, timeless sovereignty over these wondrous tropical islands. For her palace, Pele selected the Kilauea craters beside Mauna Loa. A seat of supreme majesty from which Pele could survey and command every part of her new dominion.

In the countless generations since that final victory, Pele's spirit has remained strong and undefeated across the whole of Hawaii. Even in the late twentieth century, television and newspaper stories are still told of tourists naively dismissing the legends of Pele as mere non-sense, and choosing to take home rock fragments from one of the island volcanos. However, almost all of them subsequently suffer so much misfortune that they feel obliged to return the rocks to the hotels where they stayed, imploring the management to take the souvenirs back to their rightful place, and their rightful owner. Among the spiritually aware Hawaiians, their prayers continue to offer profound respect to the goddess whose name and spirit are not to be dismissed lightly:

> O Pele, god Pele!
> O Pele, god Pele!
> Burst forth now! Burst forth!

Launch a bolt from the sky!
Let thy lightnings fly!
(Quoted in Emerson 1909, 201)

First visits

Pele's charismatic and eternal spirit also acted as a powerful magnet
for the first time visitors to Australasia who contributed to this chapter. Particularly among the Buddhist travellers, the myths and legends
which incorporated Pele into Hawaii's precious, sacred volcanoes have
inspired and confirmed their individual spiritual paths. For Duncan
and Rosamund, two musicians from San Diego, California, their
Buddhist meditations were inspired by a completely new set of themes
which they had never previously considered. Starting on Hawaii's Big
Island, their tour started on the vast Mauna Kea and then took them
to the craters of Kilauea and Mauna Loa:

DUNCAN:
*After we'd first seen those mountains and we'd learned a little about
the stories of the goddess Pele, that combination of mountain and
mythology really opened a whole new way of seeing mountains to us ...
and we found there's something really sinister about those (mountain)
areas ...*

ROSAMUND:
*But it's a sinister feeling which is right and good, because it keeps the
mountains sacred. And from that sacred status those stories should keep
them special.*

DUNCAN:
*... what we found was quite a strange spiritual experience for us there.
It was a mixture of an unsettling and challenging kind of sacredness,
and an uneasy feeling about being in those mountains.*

Before they travelled to Hawaii, Duncan and Rosamund engaged in
their usual period of pre-vacation research into the mountains they
would visit. They had studied photographs and videos of surging

volcanic lava flows which cover new land and consume entire trees in a single moment of intense, disintegrating heat. These were the over-whelming pictures they had in their minds as they stood on the sides of Hawaii's volcanic mountains. Landscapes which appeared so breathtakingly inspiring and yet which are capable of taking on a nightmare appearance from the fires of hell.

ROSAMUND:

> *But the interesting thing was, when we drew that contrast between beauty and hellish images into our meditations out there, as well as when we got home, we quickly moved on from just concentrating on those mountains to a completely new discovery of the whole, tightly woven and interdependent way that life is ... mythology and threatening stories and mountains, and our experiences, all piled on top of each other, but somehow finding a way of communicating with each element of that composition.*

One of the most persistent themes to emerge from these new meditations was the way in which sacred places and deities can be the guardians of justice, a sacred justice such as that imposed by Pele, which promises unimaginable retribution against anyone arrogant enough to threaten Hawaii's volcanoes. A sacred justice which towers over these mountains, their mythology, and even over the modern planning proposals which threaten the inspiring and tranquil beauty of the volcanic landscapes. Mountains, myths and sacred justice: many threads within the simple truths of ancient wisdom and eternal harmony.

DUNCAN:

> *... and from this meditation about the justice which Pele promises to keep hold of around her mountains, you can go off in all kinds of amazing spiritual directions ... but the one which I found to be the most challenging was this idea of sacred mountains still representing justice over their land, like a sort of guardian spirit. Something which has always protected the mountains, and which, hopefully always will.*

In a very similar way, Hariette, a first time Christian visitor to these mountains, reached the same meditative conclusion about this sacred justice embodied within the spiritual reality of Pele's mountains. But although this same insight was concluded, it was initially developed from a distinctively Christian perspective. As a well-travelled, London-based journalist, Hariette was able to draw from first-hand observations regarding this link between sacred justice and mountain spirituality in other parts of the world.

HARIETTE:

When I went to Hawaii, I'd been reading the Gospel of Luke all that year. So a lot of that teaching was still going through my mind when I first began to think about what I was seeing ... and the thing which triggered off my ideas about God's justice out there was the first time I saw the raw, solidified volcanic lava ... In other places I'd seen molten lava flow down hills and mountains at tremendous speed, but I'd never had a chance to examine it, cold, really close up ... And from those wild, barren areas of land, it just reminded me of the parable of the Good Samaritan: the guy who didn't bother where he was, or how rough the road was. He was just concerned with a fellow human being ... And the more I thought about that association, between the wild terrain and the need for justice, the more I think I understood why the stories of Pele are so important to Hawaiian believers. Because Pele is a kind of spirit of justice who stands by to guard over her mountains.

In continuing to think about the modern meaning of Pele's reputation as guardian to Hawaii's volcanic mountains, and the association of that legend with other themes of sacred justice, Hariette found the following passage from the Old Testament Book of Isaiah to be a salutary reminder that where the need to maintain sacred justice is ignored, as with the need to conserve Hawaii's inspiring volcanic peaks, those landscapes may become little more than bland, obsolescent and silent wastelands. In the absence of sacred justice, only darkness and isolation will prevail:

> The new wine dries up and the vine withers;
> all the merrymakers groan.
> The gaiety of the tambourines is stilled,
> the noise of the revellers has stopped,
> the joyful harp is silent.
> No longer do they drink wine with a song;
> the beer is bitter to its drinkers.
> The ruined city lies desolate;
> the entrance to every house is barred.
> In the streets they cry out for wine;
> all joy turns to gloom,
> all gaiety is banished from the earth.
> The city is left in ruins,

its gate is battered to pieces.
So it will be on earth
and among all nations ...
(Isaiah 24:7–13)

HARIETTE:

If you think about the wine in that passage as being God's justice, then I think it all becomes clear. Basically, what it says is 'ignore divine justice at your peril!.' And just as that truth applies in Isaiah, I think it's interesting that traditional Hawaiian culture had almost exactly the same idea. An idea like, 'Upset Pele at your peril' ... but when I'd seen that connection between Pele and Isaiah, it made it very personal, because not only did it arise from somewhere I'd visited, but it's a connection that's not always talked about in the Church these days.

Within her own Church in London, Hariette suggested that a 'disproportionate amount of time' is spent discussing the ideas of salvation in the Gospels with a 'minimum of time' devoted to a Christian response about the questions of social justice and sacred justice:

HARIETTE:

... but if someone could tell me how you can develop a faith these days without having a strong link with social issues and justice, then I'd love to learn because, for me, the two go hand in hand ... And that's really what Pele's mythology is all about. On the one hand, you've got the godly power of that divine figure, but at the same time, you've got the very keen awareness that Pele stands for real justice ... a form of justice which seeks to preserve those mountains for all time.

Among other first time visitors to Australasia, Ayers Rock (Uluru) not only attracted their enthusiastic attention but it also inspired a very similar understanding of sacred justice to that which surrounds Pele's volcanoes on Hawaii. However, whilst Pele inspired an interpretation of sacred justice which is general and worldwide, Ayers Rock proved to be a more sharply focused inspiration, given its direct association with problems of Aboriginal land rights and their social disadvantages. With Gabbi for example, a feminist journalist, campaigner and 'progressive Jew' from London, the specific inspiration of Ayers Rock was immediate, and profoundly humbling. Out of respect for the Rock, Gabbi chose to call it by the Aboriginal name, Uluru:

GABBI:

> *My first visit to Uluru was one of those very, very rare experiences
> when I felt completely knocked back on my heels. I was speechless with
> awe. With thanksgiving. With humility ... And I cried. I don't mind
> admitting it because, immediately, I got this overwhelming sense of
> sublime, calm graceful beauty.*
>
> *But you also realize that this absolutely unique monolith has
> literally been stolen from its rightful relationship with the Aboriginal
> people.*

Gabbi's immediate response to Uluru was to walk slowly up to it,
reach out her arms, and press the side of her face and body as close to
the rock as possible. In recalling the moment however, she confirmed
that it was a purely spontaneous action. Gabbi had not planned to act
that way. And she wasn't aware how her travelling companions were
reacting. Gabbi simply felt drawn. Drawn to the timeless power of
Uluru. Drawn to its strength, its spiritual magnetism. And drawn to
the Rock's ability to create and inspire:

GABBI:

> *There are only a very few places left in the world which you can hon-
> estly say are a cosmic womb. But Uluru's definitely one of them ...
> What I mean is that that Rock can give birth to an enormous volume of
> oral wisdom. It inspires the creation of that wisdom ... and just by
> standing at its base, and feeling that womb against my face and body
> really was an amazing experience.*

The language with which Gabbi described her further experiences
on Uluru continued to bear a strong creative, sensual and erotic
theme:

GABBI:

> *For me, being near Uluru was an erotic experience because it inspired
> an overwhelming passion for the moment ... I loved being there ... But I
> also have to say that that passion always felt tainted and spoiled be-
> cause you always knew, Uluru is in the wrong hands ... The right
> people, the Aboriginal people, only have, at most, a token role to play in
> its management. And that's so blatantly wrong, it acts as a barrier, a
> wall, between you and the full power of the place.*

Gabbi's intuitive and erotic spiritual response to Uluru was made
even more personal when she found herself remembering a favourite

passage from the Old Testament Book of Isaiah which had originally inspired her to pursue her feminist campaigning and journalism:

> Is not this the kind of fasting I have chosen:
> to loose the chains of injustice
> and untie the cords of the yoke,
> to set the oppressed free
> and break every yoke?
> (Isaiah 58:6)

GABBI:

> *I've always had that verse as an inspiration for my work because it describes the real truth of what I'm trying to do with my life. But it so closely mirrored my immediate feelings at Uluru that, if anything, it re-emphasised the meaning of those words to me .... The kind of fasting I've chosen obviously refers to the fact that, what I do, in terms of my writing and campaigning, won't make me a millionaire. So it's a kind of a fast. It's a struggle ... But against that, there's always a need for people to work to loose the chains of injustice, and untie the cords of the yoke, to set the oppressed free and break every yoke. I mean, that's it. It couldn't be clearer. That's what needs to happen in freeing Aboriginal people to have greater access and privacy to live at Uluru. But at the same time, the injustice at Uluru reflects so much more arrogance the world over.*

Subsequent visits

With more experienced travellers, these associations between sacred mountains, social justice and sacred justice were located within a broader context of personal insight and spiritual inspiration as well as a provocative set of unresolved questions and dilemmas, doubts and anxieties. Regarding the towering summits of New Zealand for example, the mountaineers who contributed to this chapter all suggested that their interpretations of those mountains had gone through a series of learning stages which had begun with an experience of 'pure escape' (Robert) from the everyday world of work and routine, and which eventually reached a point where the aesthetic appreciation of these peaks was no longer enough to satisfy their spiritual quests.

They had reached a point at which there was a need to look beyond the beauty. A stage in their spiritual development when they needed to consider that beauty more deeply, and to discover the lessons it holds more fully. Among these experienced mountaineers, Robert, an insurance underwriter from London, exemplified this gradual transformation from joyous encounter with New Zealand's mountains to a more serious, reflective and concerned appreciation of the wisdom they offer travellers in the late twentieth century. In the following illustration, Robert is recalling his first climb in New Zealand, on Aorangi, that country's highest summit:

ROBERT:

As I look back on my first climb there, all I could think about was a complete sense of escape. It was a liberation, and even before we'd reached the summit, I knew I was hooked (on New Zealand's mountains) ... I felt I'd come closer to knowing God, because as I climbed I prayed ... I prayed for help on the tough sections, but I also found myself praying prayers of thanksgiving which I'd never really been able to do before, on a spontaneous level ...

But then came Robert's return to London. He found himself back among the mundane pressures of insurance work and the harsh logic of day-to-day survival in a capital city:

ROBERT:

I think the point when I moved from a purely receiving kind of spiritual relationship with those mountains to something more constructive and aware was when I realized what a tremendous opportunity I had in visiting these mountains on a regular basis ... I think I'd heard someone on the radio talking about their opportunities, and that word just triggered me into thinking more deeply ... So then, I was able to put more and more elements onto that awareness about contrasting opportunities. Along with the opportunities I have, are opportunities denied to other people. Why? Well, many reasons. But among them are a whole set of problems which those people can do nothing about. Poor education. Poor advice. Poor leadership. You know, the list can be endless.

Subsequent visits to New Zealand's mountains, further studies into these questions of contrasting social opportunities, and deeper thinking about the full meaning of spiritual inspiration have all led Robert to completely re-read these mountains:

ROBERT:

> *By the time I did my second and third year of climbing down there, I
> noticed that my views were changing all the time. Whereas my first
> trip gave me a very simple, powerful feel-good kind of experience, I
> think I've brought more difficult questions to my climbs in the more
> recent years ... And although my climbing has been more confident, my
> ways of relating to the mountains on a spiritual level have been pro-
> gressively unsettling ... because against that purity and inspiring envi-
> ronment, I'm much more aware of the discrepancy between all that and
> the realities of life which, apart from anything else, prevent a lot of
> other people from going to those mountains and seeing them for them-
> selves ...*

During Robert's contributions to this chapter, it was interesting to
listen to the many questions and dilemmas which continue to haunt
him. Robert's climbing experiences have therefore persuaded him to
see himself more as a pilgrim whose life inevitably borrows from, and
brings value to others. He consequently has an agenda of unanswered
questions regarding the oneness between sacred and social meaning,
spiritual inspiration and everyday experience. In pursuing these questions, Robert wants to learn more of the Maori wisdom which elevated
mountains to a sacred status among their ancestors. He also wants to
learn more of the creation wisdom within Christian literature. Finally,
Robert wants to try and put those first two elements together. The
love of mountains described within Maori wisdom, and the love of
creation expressed within the Old Testament books of Genesis, Exodus, Numbers, Deuteronomy, the Psalms, Proverbs and Ecclesiastes.
Equally, in the New Testament, Robert wants to learn more of that
unique discussion on creation: within the gospels as well as St Paul's
letters. In all therefore, Robert's continuing mountain experiences all
serve to challenge and inspire his faith. They serve to open that faith
up to a progressively rich series of inspirations and insights. Some of
those inspirations come directly from the mountains. Others arise
through his prayers, and his recently acquired interest in Christian
meditation. More insights and challenges develop from newspaper and
television stories on social inequality and injustice, on unjustified
exploitation and violence, cynicism and despair.

ROBERT:

> *I think my faith is a lot fuller now than it was before I started to climb
> in New Zealand. But at the same time, I'd also have to say that I have
> a lot more questions about my faith now than I did then. But then*

again, I do see that as a plus, and definitely not a weakness, because I find that those questions bring my awareness of life as a Christian into something that's a lot more realistic and valid as opposed to something that's inward looking and out of touch.

This personal development toward fresh spiritual inspirations and challenging social questions was also discussed by Joshua regarding his extensive mountaineering and hill-walking experience throughout Australasia. However, as a Buddhist, Joshua approached these questions of a faith which remains challenged and enriched from a contrasting perspective to that described by Robert:

JOSHUA:

I don't know whether it's because I'm a pianist or a native of California or whether I'm a Buddhist, but I like having my spiritual experiences probed and threatened by uncertainties and dilemmas ... I'd feel uncomfortable about a spirituality which felt overly comfortable and neat, with all the answers tidily ordered in a row.

The irony of Joshua's remark is important. For a spiritual experience to be mature, responsible, insightful, and inspirational to others, it cannot be overly certain in a world which is inherently uncertain. There must always be uncertainties, questions, dilemmas, unknowns. An absence of complete answers where only faith can lead the way. A dark, silent void in which believers are obliged to continue their exploration for further clues about sacred questions without any guarantees of finding coherent answers. The faithful must be prepared to follow their spiritual path into the darkest room where only their instincts can reassure them that the results, however beguiling, will justify the risk:

JOSHUA:

I've been up mountains all over the States, and pretty much all over Australia and New Zealand and New Guinea too, and I've found that to have a climb where you work by instinct, and where the moves are free and flowing is a beautiful experience ... You might look back on those moments and think, 'why did I move like that,' or 'why did I go up that route and not the other one' ... There are no answers other than to say it's instinct or faith or intuition, or call it what you will ... And to have a faith which also moves along on that knife edge between uncertainty and certainty has got to be healthy too ... It keeps you on the look out for more inspiration into where you are with your life ... and you never become complacent or jaded.

Since Robert was able to attend the interview meeting at which Joshua made these observations, he was able to offer his reactions:

ROBERT:

> *... to have that strength of faith which can welcome a lot of difficult questions is, I think, a wonderful virtue. And also, to be able to climb that freely is wonderful. But for me, I'd have to say that I'm still at the stage where I feel uncomfortable with major challenges to my faith ... and I'd also have to say that that's substantially due to the way I find the Church still works ... I find we (Christians) are almost told what to believe, and given the so-called right answers ... so when you come across an issue which directly confronts your faith, then that rocks the boat ... so maybe we (Christians) need to listen more to Buddhist teachers and learn to accept these difficulties more ...*

Among all the experienced mountain travellers who contributed to this chapter, there was a continued understanding and empathy with the open-ended spiritual experiences described by Robert and Joshua. For some, these unanswered questions have caused major personal crises requiring extended counselling meetings with their ministers and spiritual teachers. For others, there was a closer alignment with Joshua's ability to accept this flow of impermanence and uncertainty. But common to them all was a personal struggle to reconcile the sacred with the social. Spiritual inspiration with a profound concern with social injustice and inequality. A private quest which, whilst often remaining painful and deeply unsettling, is all part of their maturing commitment, and the struggle of their faith, experience, insights and integrity with which they are able to teach and advise others.

Turning points

As with the other contributors to this book, the travellers whose experiences are discussed in this chapter all found distinctive characteristics within the mountains of Australasia which contributed to their spiritual enrichment. For Hugo and Glen however, two design consultants from Vancouver, British Columbia, their first visit to Hawaii was made under the belief that all such inspiration and enrichment is merely 'self-delusion,' 'pure fantasy' and 'completely meaningless' (Glen).

HUGO:

If you were looking for a couple of guys who were completely non-spiritual, non-religious, non-aware, then that was us ...

GLEN:

... but it wasn't that we were anti-spiritual. We just didn't find anything in that whole set of ideas which spoke to us at that time.

When these men flew to Hawaii in 1989, to work on an engineering contract, they were not aware of the mythology and ancient wisdom surrounding Pele. Even at the end of their assignment, the goddess meant nothing to Glen or Hugo when they took a three day vacation to explore Mauna Loa and Kilauea on Big Island.

GLEN:

We're both into mountain walking, and that was our first time in Hawaii, so it made sense ... But then the big turning point for us began when we decided to collect a few rock samples from those volcanoes to take home ...

Almost immediately, misfortune seemed to descend on Glen and Hugo. Whilst driving down from the mountains, their car tyre burst, causing the vehicle to slew violently to the side of the road. Their flight home was delayed by three hours. When they arrived in Vancouver, one member of each man's family was suffering with sudden and serious illness. Upon their return to work, they were told that, due to a reduction in the project's budget, they would have to re-work three major elements of the design. The deadline given for those revisions was only seven days.

HUGO:

And that was how life was for us. One disaster after another. There wasn't a single day after we'd got back when at least one big thing didn't go wrong for us ... And eventually, over the period of about four months, that began to have big implications on our families, with a lot of major arguments ...

At the end of the fourth month after his return, Glen described this continuing series of problems to a friend who had frequently travelled to Hawaii.

GLEN:

> *... that was when I first got told about Pele. And of course, me being me, when I heard about it, I laughed. I thought it was ridiculous ... But then the guy I knew told me about all these other stories he'd heard of people taking samples of rock home from those volcanoes and instantly getting bad luck from this goddess's curse ... So I eventually said OK, I'll pack up my own rocks and send them to the company in Hawaii I'd been working for, and ask them to return them to the volcanoes ... I felt pretty stupid about it all, but at least my friend felt happy.*

Glen also approached Hugo and apprehensively explained his actions. At first, Hugo laughed and reacted in the same way as Glen when he first heard about Pele's curse. But in good humour he consented to return his souvenirs as well.

HUGO:

> *But the spooky thing was that almost as soon as those packages were in the post, all the bad luck stopped happening to us. In fact, work and home life took a major swing to the good. And I'm not boasting about that, because I thought it was frightening. And it really got me to thinking about that mystical side of life in a big way.*

At first, Hugo approached his local Roman Catholic priest and asked for guidance. The advice he received was less than sympathetic. After a period of private study, Hugo eventually began to practise Zen meditation.

HUGO:

> *I was looking for something that would let me understand the mystical and spiritual side to life without feeling bowled over with strict doctrines or too many rules. So I guess my meditation was a kind of search. Trying to figure out how I could reconcile those stories of Pele with my previous completely non-religious philosophy.*

Although Hugo pursued this course of meditation, and eventually joined a Zen class, Glen was still unconvinced, and dismissed their episode of misfortune as 'nothing more than an unfortunate coincidence.'

GLEN:

> *I thought the guy'd gone nuts! I mean, he's my friend so I tried to respect what he was doing, but it meant nothing to me at all. For me,*

the stories of Pele and her curses and such, were just folk tales, and nothing more.

One of the unexpected benefits of Hugo's meditation taught him to work better under stress. Two years after their return from Hawaii, Glen was eventually persuaded to join Hugo's Zen class 'purely to help me handle my own stress. That was all' (Glen).

GLEN:

And I was hooked! What that class gave me was one hour when I could completely relax. And, at that time in my life, I just didn't have that time or space to myself. And it was slowly killing me ... But I think after a couple of months, we did an exercise when we were asked to think of something we feared, and to focus on that ... And even without giving the subject a second thought, into my mind popped Pele. And I pictured all the bad luck which had happened to the both of us, and our families too, before we'd sent the rocks back ... And ultimately, you can only say two things. One is that it all happened. You can't deny that. And second, and I guess no one will ever know the full answers to that, but there's something other-worldly about those volcanoes which makes them special.

From a common experience of Pele's reputation, Glen and Hugo began their appreciation of Zen Buddhism with contrasting perspectives. One came in search of spiritual answers. The other arrived looking for a way to deal with stress. But both men have subsequently developed a genuine awareness of the spiritual aspects of human life and natural landscapes, along with the ways in which those sacred lessons can frequently be specific to a particular region, or range of mountains:

GLEN:

Looking back on the time we've been into Zen, I'd definitely say that the inspiration you get from Hawaiian mountains will be in big contrast to, say, continental North America, or some other place ... First off, whether you want to call it a psychic imprint, or a spirit, or a divine presence, that will always be different for a particular place. Then, second, you've got the social history of the people who've settled around that mountain, or who've travelled there, and built temples there ... All those generations of human activity and spiritual activity will always make a difference. And so, for me, that's why all those places will inspire and teach you something different and special.

Conclusions

Within the diverse mountain landscapes which stretch across the vast area of Australasia, three themes were woven together by the people who contributed to this chapter. First, they encountered the awe-inspiring wonder of these mountains. Second, they wove into those wondrous experiences a realization that, in order to fully experience the distinctive character of these summits, along with the mythology and wisdom which clothe them, these travellers have needed to let go of some prejudices and uncertainties. Within powerful, sacred landscapes, intolerant and inflexible ideas and doctrines are not always sufficiently persuasive to fully accommodate the inspirational quality of these mountains. The third theme within this distinctive Australasian tapestry of sacred experience was a realization that it is not sufficient simply to receive inspiration. Nor is it sufficient simply to let go of previously held beliefs in order to accommodate these new experiences. Consequently this third element demanded a radical transformation from these travellers in the ways they regard their spiritual life as a whole.

ROBERT:

I think the thing which stands out about Australasia as a collection of sacred mountains is the way it demands a real change in your ways of thinking if you're going to get the most from being there ... I mean, if you wish, you can simply accept the beauty of the mountains there. But you can go a lot further than that. Or, you can try and strip away at your prejudices and really test your thinking. Talk to people. Listen to them. Read. And try and let go of the walls I think we all put up between our inner selves and life's experiences ... But finally, I really think that unless you're going to make that third and final step into actually making some changes in your thinking, and doing something about the way those mountains act in your life, you're still stopping yourself from getting everything you can from being there ...

In a separate series of interview meetings, Gabbi also identified this three-part inspirational weave which she found distinctive to her experience of Australasian mountains.

GABBI:

Every country and every area of mountains has its own feeling to it.

They have their own history, their own literature and their own spiritual aura to them ... And what I find about that whole area around the south Pacific, including of course Australia, is that those mountains challenge you to re-appraise your whole outlook on life ... It's as if there's something menacing and threatening about those mountains, but it's a menace which is really a strong statement of justice, whether it's from the Aboriginal legends, or the Hawaiian stories about Pele. These places are special in a unique way, and those spirits are around to see that justice is done in keeping them special ... They threaten to remind people about the fact that sacred justice is an eternal fact of life.

Alongside the mythology of Pele, Gabbi continued to describe her profound appreciation of the legends surrounding Uluru, or Ayers Rock, in Australia's Northern Territory. Equally she felt awed by the Maori legends inspired from their mountains: Tongariro, Aorangi, Te Aroha-a-uta and Hikurangi:

GABBI:

There seems to be particularly fierce brutality about those stories ... they seem to grind you down and make you think. Really think. And the amazing thing for me is they all have a contemporary relevance. There's nothing out of date about them ... They all emphasise and re-emphasise that these places (the mountains) are special. They should be thought about and talked about. They should be allowed to change your life. And they should make you want to tell people about them ...

CHAPTER 4

Japan

From time immemorial the mountains have been the
dwelling place of the great sages; wise men and sages have
all made the mountains their own chambers, their own
body and mind. Dogen (1979, 47)

Ancient wisdom

The natural and spiritual landscapes of Japan are dominated by
mountains. Even among the prehistoric hunters and farmers who lived
over 10000 years ago, mountains were revered as the dwelling place of
gods and kami-spirits. And when the Shinto faith developed in the
sixth century AD, it was able to draw from a rich treasury of wisdom
and myth, art and ceremony, much of which drew its original inspiration from sacred mountains.

Most writers agree there are a total of 354 major sacred mountains
scattered throughout the islands which make up modern-day Japan.[1]
But even that impressive figure fails to take into account the many
hundreds of other, less well known, hills and peaks, all of which have
their part to play within Japan's spiritual history, geography, philo-
sophy and literature. Within one of the earliest forms of Japanese
poetry, the waka style, consisting of only thirty-one syllables, mountains were an abiding source of wisdom and inspiration. The following
lines show the simple elegance of waka, from the pen of Oshikochi-no-
Mitsune:

> How is it that I hear
> The noise of creaking oars
> In the deepest mountains?

In just a few lines, there is absolute delight in this simplest of
pleasures. A wisdom which draws the imagination to single moments,

and individual sounds. The gentle creaking of oars on a still mountain lake, whilst all around is silent. Other waka poetry painted similar mountain pictures. Snow-covered valleys. Isolated trees. Babbling streams. Each verse inspired by ancient wisdom, and each one presenting readers with the absolute heart and soul of that deceptively simple way of seeing.

Toward the end of the twelfth century, a further discipline was added to waka verse which captured its full sublimity and grace. Instead of thirty-one syllables, there became only seventeen. Arranged in three elements of five-seven-five, the haiku poem was to eventually become recognized as one of the most powerful and subtle expressions of Japanese spirituality. The haiku was therefore a more concentrated, and more considered, form of highly-developed writing. It shone the light of a writer's imagination toward the purity and intensity of ancient Japanese wisdom. Pearls of joy at feeling at one with a mountain view — an isolated mountain shrine — cloudscapes — the gentle swirl of dawn mists. Certainly, for the fifteenth century writer, Sogi, mountains remained an abiding source of delight:

> Snow-capped as they are,
> The gentle slopes of the mountains
> Fade into the hazy mist
> At twilight on a spring day.

Two hundred years later, the poet and traveller, Matsuo Basho, fuelled his genius for haiku verse from the profound personal meaning he found in all Japan's mountains.[2] The son of a samurai warrior, his early life was spent as a pupil within the aristocratic Todo family, where he developed a love of words and mountain landscapes with the young heir, Yoshitada. Years later, in the summer of 1676, Basho showed that among his most precious memories continued to be those drawn from mountains:

> My souvenir from Edo
> Is the refreshingly cold wind
> Of Mount Fuji
> I brought home on my fan.

Even during his years of intense personal suffering, the wisdom of meditation, alongside Basho's love of mountain landscapes, significantly aided his recovery. And toward the end of his prolific life, during his final journeys, mountains remained as a vital part of Basho's link with the primordial past, as well as the future of his disciples and other readers. In the spring of 1689 for example, Basho began a journey lasting two and a half years. Significantly, he travelled north, to a region which was regarded by his contemporaries as an untamed, unexplored wilderness. A mountainous area which symbolized all the darker and horrifying mysteries of the spiritual universe. Basho's route through those mountains was therefore as much of an inner journey as it was a physical pilgrimage. On the first day of April that year, he climbed Mount Nikko, about seventy miles north of modern-day Tokyo. The name Nikko means 'bright beams of the sun.' There, he paid homage to the holiest of Nikko's shrines: a sacred place whose benevolent power Basho had felt miles before he actually set eyes upon it. From this state of spiritual rapture, standing before that exquisite mountain shrine, Basho was inspired to write these lines:

> It was with awe
> That I beheld
> Fresh leaves, green leaves,
> Bright in the sun.

In the misty distance, another mountain beckoned Basho's curiosity and sense of wonder. Snow-covered Mount Kurokami shone and dazzled brilliantly white, and inspired Basho's travelling companion, Kawai Sogoro, to capture the moment:

> Rid of my hair,
> I came to Mount Kurokami,
> On the day we put on
> Clean summer clothes.

Kawai Sogoro had desperately wanted to travel with Matsuo Basho through the northern mountains. The line, 'rid of my hair' records the ritual shaving of Sogoro's head, in the form of a tonsure, prior to his donning the black robe of an itinerant priest which he wore as he accompanied Basho. But after only two hundred yards on Mount Kurokami, the travellers came upon a waterfall tumbling out of a hollow in a ridge, cascading hundreds of feet into a deep pool beneath. From the shelter of a cave, Sogoro stood transfixed, whilst Basho began to form the words of another haiku verse:

> Silent a while in a cave,
> I watched a waterfall,

For the first of
The summer observations.

Basho's experiences on these astonishing journeys were later to be recorded through other poetry, and prose, in the pinnacle of his achievement: a book which would eventually be translated into almost every language known to humankind: *The Narrow Road to the Deep North*. But having led a life so close to nature, and in particular to the inspiration of mountains, Basho chose to devote much of his remaining years to an almost continual meditation whilst he lived in a simple house outside Edo (now Tokyo). Contemplation and wonder, travel and wisdom, all continued to inspire Basho until his final days. Today, we are the heirs to his unique collected works of sublime inspiration and insight.

First visits

All the contributors to this research who visited Japanese mountains described their first visit as a form of 'pilgrimage' and 'journey' in much the same way that Matsuo Basho would have understood those words. Nothing should ever lie outside the pilgrimage of one's life-journey. All pilgrimage should be a personal quest for spiritual wealth. A continually rich life is only achieved through continual inspiration, continual searching, and continual discovery of new riches of real, lasting value. Consequently, those modern-day pilgrimages should not be regarded as being isolated from the resonances and rhythms of everyday life and mundane concerns. Rather, all these journeys are composed of spiritual quests as well as secular quests: journeys of the sublime, balanced with ordinary contingencies, concerns, dilemmas and anxieties. Surrounded too, by an unfamiliar and often baffling Japanese culture, these travellers still found a satisfying way of penetrating new truths on their individual journeys by drawing from a uniquely Japanese form of wisdom and expression: the haiku poem.

A sense of pilgrimage as a broad and open-ended experience of Japanese mountains is clearly illustrated in the following extract of discussion between three young software designers from Birmingham, England. Their conversation describes their first visit to Mount Ontake, near Tokyo:[3]

JENNIFER:

> ... as a Zen believer, I felt I had to visit Japan to really see for myself the sort of shrines and mountains where Zen began ... but that feeling was only partly down to my fascination with Zen because I'd reached a stage in my Zen studies where I wanted an experience which would push me into a realization that there is nothing weird or absurd about following the Zen path ... Because, sometimes, I did feel a bit of a freak, when I told other people what my beliefs were ...

CAROL:

> That was the same for me. I went to Japan, and in particular to On-take, because I felt half drawn and half pushed from where my Zen-life was, to where I knew I wanted it to be.

MARSHA:

> Yes, but don't you also agree that even when we were on Ontake and all the other mountains there, the whole way we reacted to those emotions and feelings was never wholly divorced from the more 'Monday-to-Friday' type of feelings too?

CAROL:

> But that's just being honest, and real to yourself, isn't it. Don't you remember that haiku poem by Buson? You know the one:

> > In the silent dusk
> > Nightingales begin their song:
> > Good! The dinner gong!

> What can I say? From the absolute sublime down to the stomach. In just three lines!

Each of these women enjoy painting and sketching. They were therefore excited to be 'adopted' by a group of Japanese artists just as they were about to set out on their first trek up Ontake.

MARSHA:

> It was almost too good to be true. We were at breakfast, and I think you (looking at Carol) had taken out a sketch book, or something, and all of a sudden these three other Japanese students came to ask if they could see your work ... and a few hours later, we were together, walking and talking up Ontake.

JENNIFER:

And to feel that sense of shared interest and love of Zen and art and mountains, between us all. It's that combination of factors why Ontake will be so important for me for as long as I live.

Whilst the three Englishwomen sketched, painted, talked, and meditated, each of them felt a new sense of their Zen experience emerge. In England, their Zen meetings had produced a mental picture of enlightenment as a 'goal' (Carol), and 'a far-off light, like a distant prospect' (Jennifer). But having shared nine days with their newly found Japanese friends, first on Ontake, and then on Fuji, and finally Mount Koya, the sacred nature of Zen became understood in an altogether more complete and immediate manner: [4/5]

CAROL:

... for all of us, I think, we learned that insight, or enlightenment, clothes you. It surrounds you. It supports you. It sustains you. It keeps you going. It's the wisdom that keeps insanity at bay. But. And there is a big 'but.' There's also a sense where you, yourself, nurture the form of enlightenment which you need. The enlightenment which grows inside you. Waiting to get out, and develop, and grow stronger.

MARSHA:

And, as usual, I like to quote a haiku poem! You know, my favourite, by Boncho, which just says everything that needs to be said about this new way of understanding Zen enlightenment.

> *The heavy leaf*
> *Falls of its own will*
> *On this silent windless day*

Perfect, isn't it. 'The heavy leaf.' This picture of something that's really beautiful, but maybe a little light-weight. Not quite as substantial and persuasive as it might be. 'Falls of its own will.' At the right time for each of us, we met that group of students just as we were going out to Ontake. And by being with them, and talking and learning and sharing with each other, this lightweight idea of enlightenment fell away on a 'silent windless day,' to be replaced with a really powerful, clear, shining and infinitely persuasive and beautiful vision of Zen, and what it can mean.

CAROL:

Which we learned together. In Japan. Among mountains. While we were painting together. All the elements. Everything which makes it so perfect, and irreplaceable!

In a separate interview group, David, a recently retired landscape-architect from Colchester, England, described a very similar sense of his own Christian spirituality developing into an experience of being 'enveloped by God ... but also feeling God inside me, as well.'

DAVID:

I know the theologians call it panentheism, don't they. But I have to say, I was so struck by Mount Fuji, by its great wondrous vastness. And I could feel these new insights coming to mind, being clarified there, as if they were on a screen within my imagination. And I did, honestly, feel that God became bigger for me there, on Fuji. Not only did I feel Him around me, more closely, like a really warm hug, but also as a guiding voice from within.

From David's studies into panentheism — the experience of finding sacredness within everything, and surrounding everything — he was able to bring a beautiful collection of literary quotations to our one-to-one and small group discussions, which perfectly complemented the haiku quotations introduced by Carol, Jennifer and Marsha.[6] In particular, David identified part of the 'Spiritual Canticle' by the mystic writer John of the Cross, which expresses so much of this combined encounter with mountain spirituality, and the profound enlargement in his understanding of God:

> My Beloved is the mountains,
> And lonely wooded valleys,
> Strange islands,
> And resounding rivers,
> And whistling of love-stirring breezes,
> The tranquil night
> At the time of rising dawn,
> Silent music,
> Sounding solitude,
> The supper that refreshes and deepens love.
> (Quoted in Kavanaugh 1973, 714)

Whilst Marsha was able to relate every line of Boncho's haiku to her personal experience of Ontake, David was similarly able to relate each line of this extract by John of the Cross to his first encounter with Fuji:

DAVID:

Those lines are a list, aren't they. They list out so many beautiful things which all helped me reach this understanding of who God came to be for me. So, if you look at the first line, His spirit is in the mountains. And you think of that extraordinary beauty. That, in itself, knocks you back, doesn't it. But then he (John of the Cross) goes on, because God's beauty is even greater than that of the mountains. And, don't forget, all these pictures, in all these lines are things which helped me see this idea of us in God, and God in us, more and more clearly. Wooded valleys. Strange islands. Resounding rivers. Different breezes. The tranquil night. And so on. Each line is so personal, it might have been written with me in mind.

Coincidentally, the Biblical quotation which David cited as being the one which most closely relates this sense of living in God, whilst God also surrounds and sustains His believers, was quoted by Suzannah, 'a forty year-old teenage mathematics teacher,' originally from New Hampshire, USA:

> Father, may they be one in us,
> as you are in me and I am in you;
> I have given them the glory you gave to me,
> that they may be one as we are one.
> With me in them and you in me.
>   (John 17:21–22)

SUZANNAH:

I'll tell you exactly where and when I finally got that feeling of complete unity with God figured out for myself. Because that's what we're talking about here. God in us and us in God. It's unity. It's a complete relationship. It's intimately personal. So it's intimately unique. It's a unique unity. A real, real sense of the whole experience of being with God ...

I was climbing late one afternoon, on my first time just getting close to the summit of (mount) Tateyama, in the Japanese Alps. And the colours in the sky perfectly matched my emerging understanding of this unity. Light yellows and oranges. They all formed my first sense of this complete unity with God. Because up until then, I think I'd had this idea that union with God, Him in us, and us in Him, would be very ascetic and monastic-like. Really removed from reality and everyday life. And incredibly narrow, impoverished and sterile. And absolutely no fun at all. But then, on Tateyama, ironically known as the mountain of hell in Japanese mythology, I found this heavenly, enriching, profoundly satisfying and incredible understanding of this real unity we can all have with Him.

Like many of the travellers who contributed to this chapter, Suzannah and David independently found, and memorized, a short selection of haiku poems which expressed the distinctive spiritual discoveries they had made about their faith during their first visit to Japanese mountains. For its personal and symbolic meaning, Suzannah frequently cited the following verse by Gyodai as being the most significant for her:

> In the cold sky of dawn
> Only a single pine tree
> On the peak.

SUZANNAH:

Gyodai's words are purely symbolic. It's a picture. But each line takes me back to that moment on Tateyama, when I was approaching the summit and 'zap,' I saw at last this almighty, precious truth of humankind in God and God in humankind. So that's the dawn. My dawning, in the first line. And it's a single, bold, long-lasting ever-green sort of a truth, like the single pine tree, standing up boldly and rightly 'on the peak.'

For David, as with many of the contributors to this chapter, his 'most special haikus' were discovered during conversations with other travellers on his first, and subsequent visits to Japanese mountains:

DAVID:

Well it was a total delight. Because we'd started to walk, and talk, with this other couple from Kyoto, and suddenly the gentleman stopped. And he looked at me with a mischievous grin, and I thought 'Hello! What's he going to do now.' But he just took out this tiny little note book. And translated this poem, which I actually copied out from his translation as we stood there (on a path by Mount Fuji). And those lines absolutely and completely capture that time for me out there, on our first visit. Slightly nervous and hesitant. But having just had this wonderful,

*wonderful truth of unity with the God I'd been struggling for years
and years to understand.*

The author of this haiku is Onitsura:

> I follow thee
> A noiseless flower
> In my inmost ears.

Alongside the discovery of this inspiring unity with the divine, many first-time visitors to these mountains described how they also felt moved to reflect upon the 'darker side of sacredness' and 'the anger within spirituality' (Martina). With all the people who discovered this insight, it was provoked by the experience of walking upon the sides of a volcano for the first time in their lives. A feeling of risk and uncertainty. A knowledge that there can be no form of order or absolute certainty when such an incalculable power is unleashed. Within the following description by Martina, a pollution controller from Montana, USA, this experience of uncertain risk and danger acted as the provocation to think deeply about this 'darker side of sacredness':

MARTINA:
I was very, very nervous, my first time on Fuji. I was travelling alone, which didn't help. Although it may have helped me to concentrate and figure out my thinking there. But on each step, I could imagine this towering edifice of a mountain, suddenly blowing its stack, and shaking violently ... This 'other side' of God, if that's who you worship. Or Krishna. Or other gods. Their names don't matter. Because they all have that anger in common. Especially the Christian God, in the Old Testament. But there's a raw, natural cruelty which comes to the surface in volcanic eruptions, or earthquakes. And it's then, when we see a fully complete sacredness, which we're all used to thinking about as lovely and peaceful, suddenly wells up and tears down whole cities!

As a practising Taoist, Martina is familiar with meditation exercises set by her teacher on living by trust. Trusting the integrity of sacredness and wisdom. Trusting the strength of her faith to help transcend fear, doubt and dilemma. Trusting in the healing power of confidence in one's chosen path. But whilst Martina, and others, had all meditated on these universal truths using an eclectic range of different mental images, it was not until she began to draw connections between her walk up Fuji, and this 'Way of Trust,' that those truths began to 'get a hold' of her curiosity, and to provoke new, and frequently unsettling questions. In this next illustration, Martina was in conversation with two other American women with whom she was comparing spiritual experiences about their respective first visits to Japanese mountains:

MARTINA:

I was really into meditating on Trust, right? The things I could trust: the wisdom, the teachings. That really worked for me. But then, there I was walking on this massive volcano in Japan! And my ideas of what I really was able to trust were taking a real pounding. And it was majorly traumatic!

CYBIL:

This sounds like an exact echo of my own experience! But go on. Because, did you find that frightening? I know I certainly did, when it was happening to me out there, the first time.

MARTINA:

Well it was bizarre. And like I said, this was a walk I took on my own. But it was a slow, really, really intense time for me there. It was like having some blinkers suddenly put on me, because all these questions and worries suddenly poured in on me. And I'm not sure whether I was ready for them.

NANCY:

I'm kind of familiar with these Taoist ideas of Trusting, and the Way, and the Right Path. But this is so interesting to listen to, because it exactly matches my first time, and my first thoughts on Mount Fuji. But the way I got to deal with this whole deluge of worry and intense spiritual upheaval, like a spiritual earthquake going off inside me, was to turn to the haikus. Because they always work for me. I mean, often they're just hauled out because they're beautiful. But they have another purpose. For me, anyway. And that is, they're great for crises. They make for wonderful first-aid material for bruised sensitivities!

And what you find when you're in situations like that are pockets of emptiness which cause you to doubt and wonder. You feel empty, because the moment one dark, empty void opens up inside your mind, another fifteen start to open up too. And suddenly you feel powerless. So I always find this haiku by the poet Buson such a beautiful picture:

A camellia dropped down
Into the water
Of a still, dark well.

Do you see the picture there? Into all our feelings of emptiness, and inability, comes a small sudden truth. And this mental picture of a camellia falls immediately into place. The camellia is what we need to stop the anxiety. So what I'm talking about here are the timeless truths, which can withstand the battering of walking up mountains and feeling hollow inside. Either literal mountains or metaphorical ones! But timeless truths are what we need. I mean, there's another haiku I often bring to mind, by Daio:

New Year's Day:
What I feel goes
Beyond words.

Among the Christians who visited Japanese mountains, their encounters with unfamiliar, vast, volcanic landscapes also inspired very pragmatic questions of trust: what to trust, why trust at all, and how and when to trust? For those Christian travellers who had not been taught about any other form of Christianity beyond the confines of fall-redemption doctrine, questions of sacred trust were a profound revelation. The following illustration by Derek, an engineering company director from Reading, England, exemplifies this sense of discovery, and the use of haiku verse to develop the meaning of those newly-found insights:

DEREK:
We were doing some mildly difficult climbing in the (Japanese) Alps, not far from (Mount) Tateyama when, yes, I actually found this sort of revelation come upon me. Now, that might sound terribly Biblical and pious, but that's the only word to use for it. Revelation. A revelation that there is this theology of trust. We need to find a way of trusting our faith in all conditions. But I'd never before felt new truths come to me so vividly like that. All of a sudden. A realization. Like a seed planted in my mind.

Whilst he was reflecting upon these feelings of revelation, and intense spiritual immediacy, Derek's walking companions introduced him to the following verse by Sokan which captured his feelings perfectly:

> Emerging from a perfect sphere;
> Yet how long it is:
> A spring day.

DEREK:

> *For me, Christianity can be the perfect way of life. Not always. But it can be. So that was the 'perfect sphere.' But what suddenly hit me about trust was there's so much more to my faith than I'd been told about. And as we climbed that afternoon, I felt my faith had been rejuvenated. It was a spring day, like in the poem. And the Sokan poem is a very Japanese, and appealing, way of expressing this new dawn to my Christianity.*

A spirituality of trust immediately confronts the spectre of fear. Fear of falling; fear of pain; fear of uncertainty. And particularly, on the more challenging climbs in the Alps, or elsewhere in Japan, this fusion of western faith, and westernized versions of eastern wisdom, merged powerfully for many of these people as they learned more of their faith by drawing from a haiku literature in translation. For Pamela, a 'wife, mother, secretary and eternal pilgrim' from Ipswich, England, her own fundamentalist Christian faith 'which, when I got to Japan, was in a bit of a trough,' was re-energized by discovering the need to develop a spirituality of trust as part of her Christianity:

PAMELA:

> *I was climbing with friends and my husband on Mount Tateyama, when this amazing insight of the need to trust, and reach out, and lose all fear, came to me. I'll always remember the moment that happened, and the haiku which captures it best for me is that one by Matsuo Basho:*

> > *A child of a poor family*
> > *Stopped grinding rice*
> > *To look at the moon.*

> *When that poem was first read to me, I cried. Because I knew that child was me. And grinding the rice was the way my faith had ground on in a fairly mundane and uninteresting routine. Then suddenly, I really and truly learned to trust. I learned to trust my faith. And to know my faith would work on the mountain; at the end of the rope. You know? I had learned to trust. And it was liberating!*

But neither Derek nor Pamela, nor any of the other travellers who discovered this spirituality of trust, ever suggested it is a simple or blind virtue. Rather, trust, for these people, was a source of questioning — questions which lead them to engage more fully in their faith. Guy, a Buddhist, and self-employed carpenter and cabinet-maker from Glasgow, Scotland, drew from a rich list of haikus to illustrate the ways in which the theme of trust had provoked 'question upon question upon question' about the integrity of his Buddhist beliefs:

GUY:

I love haikus, because I think they capture specific moments and questions so well. But there's one I adore. And I'm always quoting it because it sums up how I see myself, and the way I related to those (Japanese Alpine) mountains as I grew to know them when I lectured out there:

> *An old fisherman:*
> *Unalterably intent*
> *In the evening rain.*

OK, so I have this self-image of being an old fisherman. Aged thirty-four, going on eighty-four! But that's me. It's a marvellous metaphor. But that phrase 'unalterably intent.' It speaks volumes. 'Unalterably intent.' Total concentration. On the mountain. Your fingers. The rope. Your companions. Or, in the workshop. Your tools. The grain of the wood. Everything. You need to trust. But you need to question what you're trusting. Even the familiar, frequently contains things which, although you do trust them, you still need to question as well. Trust and question must always go together. Otherwise you have only naïvety and childishness. And that has no place in maturity:

> *My native place!*
> *Even flies bite me.*
> *(by Issa)*

And in summer, in my workshop, they do! But that's the lesson. Familiar things do bite. They do need to be questioned ... and all these haikus and lessons can be traced back to experiences and conversations I had with people on my first time in the Japanese mountains. Because they made such an impression on me!

From conversations with other Buddhists, Pauline and Lizzie, two Biology students originally from Newcastle and Bristol in England, this combination of trust and questioning: acceptance and caution, was located within a broader discussion of the ways their faith was able to develop in Japan compared to the ways it develops whilst they live and work in England.

PAULINE:

In England, Buddhism is seen as strange. And I think you're always seen as an outsider. People don't fully know how to feel comfortable talking to you ... But in Japan, it's so natural to talk in terms of Zen for example, and to bring those ideas into your climbing.

LIZZIE:

Yeah, that was it for me. I'd never thought of Buddhism and climbing being linked before. And yet, now, when you think about it, well, why not? Climbing is all about concentrating on a single moment. Getting your fingers right. Keeping the rope OK. All that. And the recognition that there are these huge areas where you can use your Buddhism, and see it work, and know you can trust your faith in those situations really excited us, didn't it.

PAULINE:

Well, yes. Because it begged the question: 'well, if climbing is this whole new area where you can make your Buddhism work, then why not have the confidence to make it work elsewhere? ... And I think those (Japanese) climbs were a very practical way of sparking us off on that line of questioning. You know, where can you trust your faith next? ... It really was exciting to realize and think about.

In reflecting on their climbing experiences, and their conversations with other climbers and walkers, Pauline and Lizzie suggested the 'breakthrough' in this experience of trusting their faith more arose when they 'stopped treating Buddhism as an intellectual exercise, and started seeing how practical it can be':

PAULINE:

I found all the Japanese climbers were really fascinating because they bridge the pure logic of their economic success with the more ancient motifs and ideas. So you might be preparing for a climb, and you'll be very systematic and careful, but then ... one of them might just stand up and gaze at the sky, and quote a haiku. But, and this is important, everyone would take that poem, and the thoughts behind it, as seriously as the preparation for the climb itself. You know? The two were one.

The poem and the climb. So they became bigger experiences by being influenced from each other.

One morning in the Japanese Alps, Pauline, Lizzie and four Japanese women were preparing for a climb that would take them most of that day. Whilst they checked their ropes and supplies, one of the Japanese women suddenly stopped her work, looked up at the moon, which was low in the early morning sky, and quoted this haiku by Chora:

> The moon
> When I look at it — clouds:
> When I don't look — clear.

LIZZIE:

> *... and in those three lines, hearing them there, before the climb, I thought, 'that is so beautiful.' It summed everything up, about what I was able to take away from Japan in terms of developing my faith, and the ways I was able to trust my faith more than ever ... You start off in the poem with this beautiful moon. Like the one we saw that morning. Or any one, because it's such a beautiful and peaceful image. But why that haiku is so personal to us both, I think, is because we'd realized that although we'd been thinking about our Buddhism at home in England, we'd now seen that it was in the 'doing' of Buddhism: living it in every part of your life, where you're really able to grow into it, and to make it fully work for you. So, from the poem, when we'd been looking and looking at our faith, we'd only seen clouds, and partial views of its potential. But as soon as we'd taken our attention away from the purely intellectual approach to Buddhism, and started to 'live' it, like with our climb, suddenly it all became clear, and real.*

But whilst these Buddhist paths of insight toward spiritual trust were 'exhilarating' (Pauline), they were far more traumatic for some of the Christian travellers who contributed to these discussions. For many of these Christians, their discovery of spiritual trust, which they learned from their Japanese hosts, was contrasted with the ways in which Christian doctrine is sometimes presented as a 'catalogue of fears' (Michael). This 'Christianity of fears' had been learned and accepted only with considerable reservation by Michael, a systems analyst and devoted Christian believer, by the time he made his first visit to Japan. Toward the end of his first working-tour of Tokyo and Yokohama, he took a few days as a walking holiday near Mount Fuji. In the company of his hosts, he 'realized that so much of what (he) had learned in church had been based on fear.'

MICHAEL:

> *It was the most lonely time in my life. But don't get me wrong. No one was intentionally trying to make me question my faith. Because we were just talking very generally. You know, how we individually got value from the mountains ... But alongside my colleagues, who were all Buddhists, and who were able to accept, and relish, and cherish, and talk freely about the ways their faith could draw from the mountains, there was poor old me, thinking my own faith isn't based on accepting nature at all. No part of it had that facility. And yet towering above us, was this extraordinarily inspiring mountain. And I felt crushed smaller and smaller within myself by that realization. My Christianity had no place for this natural inspiration.*

In recalling his first night of the walking tour beside Fuji, Michael described how he lay awake, unable to sleep, with his mind 'frantically searching for some way to re-build (my) Christian faith from the rubble it had been reduced to.'

MICHAEL:

> *The more I thought about the problem, the more angry I was getting. With the Church. With Christian authors. With all those people. Why hadn't they highlighted these questions? Now, I know, there are a few authors, who deal with these questions, but they're very, very few and far between ... And as I was getting progressively angry, and frustrated and boiling, I realized I was getting absolutely nowhere fast in sorting myself out. So, I took out a blank sheet of paper from my brief case. And I wrote in the middle of it in small neat capitals 'Me and Mount Fuji.' It sounds terribly naïve to talk about it now. But that's what I felt reduced to. And then I stopped. What I wanted to do was to draw out a spider diagram from that centre with all sorts of references and ideas which could connect my Christian faith to the mountain and nature. And after a long time, I came up with a few rather weakly defined ideas.*

When Michael returned to England, he was determined to develop his spider diagram, and to 'drag' his Christian faith into a state of development where it could still accommodate 'the place for sin and redemption theology,' alongside 'the need to accept the inspiration of mountains,' and other natural landscapes.

Michael's research on these questions has now taken him four years of patient, private study:

MICHAEL:

I've done a lot of reading, and even now I feel woefully ignorant. But I've been able to sketch out some form of understanding on the Celts and Franciscans, with a lot of parallels to the Japanese mountains ... But I have to say that the mental pictures which I keep before me in thinking through this alignment between the Christian doctrine of sin, and the need to accommodate sacred nature, are the images of Fuji, with its vast, towering cone. That's the image, and the challenge. Understanding that!

In reviewing his search for satisfying links between this awe-inspired response to mountain landscapes and personal Christian faith, Michael suggested that it was only when he started keeping a notebook to record his thoughts, and those of others, that he really felt he was 'beginning to make sense of all the clues':

MICHAEL:

Everywhere I go, I take a notebook, because it's amazing the number of things you see which draw a parallel between this lost inheritance within Christianity and this strong feeling for nature. And every once in a while, I'll take out those notes to see how they fit into this expanding pantheon of references to Christianity and nature.

In keeping and reviewing this notebook, Michael remains aware of two persistent and conflicting themes. First, he relishes the sense of discovery and insight at finding out more and more elements within Christianity's 'lost inheritance' of teaching devoted to the inspiration of mountainous areas. However, the second persistent theme remains an intense frustration:

MICHAEL:

I've never yet found out why the Church doesn't weave these questions into its sermons. Among young people, you ask them what their main concerns and questions with life are. And they'll say it's the ecological crisis. And much the same often goes for adults. It's not just the young. I think if there's going to be one thing which brings people back to the Church, it's a fresh approach to worship. Worship which draws from a wider sphere of influences, and which is more interesting and relevant for people. I know it's there. I've been piecing it together for myself for the last four years!

Subsequent visits

Two themes dominated these people's conversations about further travels to Japanese mountains. First, there was a heightened awareness of the harmony which an individual can discover within the cosmos: a sense of the balance, order and proportion which can be encountered within all creation, through meditation and patient reflection. This particular facet of mountain spirituality is characterized by a receptiveness to fresh inspiration and a willingness to explore new avenues of sacred experience which may complement, or challenge, previously discovered themes. These conversations therefore confronted the opportunity of locating the microcosm of individual experiences, beliefs and attitudes within the macrocosm of all creation and all possible experience.

The second major theme, which became interwoven with the first, considered the unique inspiration of Mount Koya. Located within the forests of the Kii Peninsula, two hundred miles south west of Mount Fuji, Koya's intense significance draws from its close association with one of the most important of all esoteric Buddhist teachers: Kobo Daishi, sometimes referred to as Kukai. Born in 773 AD into an aristocratic family, Kobo Daishi subsequently abandoned his material wealth to become an itinerant monk. Through his travels, meditations and studies, he is credited with introducing the phonetic script into the Japanese language. For the people who contributed to this book however, Kobo Daishi is chiefly remembered as the founder of his own monastery on Koya's inspiring slopes. As a centre for learning and meditation, the monastery incorporates resonances of ancient Shinto belief through its reverence to Nibutsu Hime, the goddess of the mountain. However, the monastery also draws from the wisdom of Indian and Chinese Buddhist teachings which Kobo Daishi studied on his pilgrimages.

For Glenda, an artist and Buddhist from Colchester, England, each of her four visits to Koya have been inspired by this spiritual eclecticism within Kobo Daishi's monastery, as well as the obligation Glenda feels to explore and develop her own sense of harmony with 'those elements in the cosmos which can really speak to me':

GLENDA:

The moment I first saw that monastery, there was the biggest lump in my throat I could imagine. It had a totally quiet, gentle, unimaginable force about the place. And the one word which came immediately to mind was 'centre.' This monastery is a centre. A centre of harmony. A centre for the exploration of harmony. And a centre for reaching out to the whole cosmos ... And in each of the four visits I've made there, that sense of centredness always comes through to me. And I find I want to sit and meditate and reach out, and draw in from that incredible atmosphere there.

Even when she shared these experiences with her interview group during the research for this book, Glenda was wide-eyed with excitement as she recalled her first encounter with the monastery, with the mountain and its forests and this profound obligation to constantly reach out, and draw into her own Buddhist spirituality from 'as much of the cosmos as possible.'

GLENDA:

There's a continuing process which I found more clearly inspired on Mount Koya, and in the monastery, than anywhere else I've ever visited ... You find yourself discovering these amazing poems, or paintings, or even landscapes and places and other people's life-experiences and trying to fit them into your own vision of life. And it's that continuous reaching out to all there is, and drawing it in, and thinking about it, and feeling challenged or inspired by it, which really brings your whole experience of Koya, and the rest of your life, to the level of an amazing odyssey, because you're drawing from so much inspiration all the time.

This feeling of being inspired by Mount Koya: to reach out, and draw in, from the wealth of cosmic inspiration, was elaborated upon by two American Jews from Miami, Florida.

LIONEL:

... I remember very clearly, waking up on our first morning on Mount Koya and having this thought in my mind that there is no longer an inside or an outside to my feeling of being an American Jew. There is just this overpowering sense of dealing with the vastness of all creation and trying to claim as much of that richness for myself, and share it with others. So your religious experience becomes almost an unending regurgitation: drinking in as much as you can from everything you see, and then musing upon it to see how it fits with your own experiences of being an American Jew, and then trying to share it with others: either at Temple (the synagogue) or wherever.

SEB:

> *The quote I always think of when I hear you say that is from Mahatma Gandhi. You know? 'Earth and heaven are in us.' (Quoting from Iyer 1978, 176.) It's that simple. Earth and heaven, and the whole universe of inspiration, can be drawn into us if only we have the right attitude and draw those experiences into ourselves. And you really can feel that at Koya.*

Throughout these conversations with Glenda, Lionel, Seb, and others who have made repeated journeys to Koya, certain key words were used more than others. 'Wholeness,' 'centre,' 'unity,' 'interaction,' 'richness' and 'exploration' all marked out the distinctive ways in which Mount Koya is able to contribute to their lives. With its close association with Kobo Daishi's willingness to draw from as many references as possible to inspire his own Buddhist experience, Koya is today associated with an approach to personal spirituality which is marked out by its curiosity and vivacity. A sense of the microcosm of individual lives within the macrocosm of all that is imaginable and unimaginable. This mountain spirituality of the cosmos is therefore distinguished for these individuals by its potential to inspire visions and other forms of spiritual creativity.

On her second journey to Mount Koya for example, Glenda invited her friend Karen, an English artist who actively draws inspiration from her Christian faith to inform her painting and architectural drawings. Knowing that we would be talking about Mount Koya, Karen brought a copy of John Lobell's book *Between Silence and Light* from which she read an extract to illustrate the principal way in which Koya had inspired her:

> All in God's creation gives great delight to anyone looking
> upon it, for in some things there is beauty, as in flowers; in
> others healing, as in herbs; in others food, as in produce, in
> others meaning, as in snakes and birds ... A harmonious
> chord is sounded by spirit and body, angel and devil, heaven
> and hell, fire and water, air and earth, sweet and bitter, soft
> and hard, and so are all other things harmonized.
> (Lobell 1979, 18)

KAREN:

> *I've actually got those words printed and hung up in my studio at home, because I think they form the starting point to so much ... So in your spiritual experience, whether it's as a Christian like me, or a*

Buddhist like (Glenda), there's always more than enough to satisfy even the most curious person for the whole of their lives. No one's spiritual life need be dead after they've been to Koya. But, what makes me angry is the fact that, particularly the Christian churches, have always presented such a narrow set of doctrines and rituals. And so that's all people know. They don't get a chance to get in touch with these amazing themes of harmony with the cosmos, and meditation and prayer, because those themes are consciously excluded.

GLENDA:

Not always consciously excluded, because I expect you'd find that a lot of ministers and priests just don't know about a Christianity of the cosmos: a Christianity of harmony with that cosmos. So they're as ignorant as their congregations in that respect ... It's an inherited thing, isn't it. It's traditional, and probably unconscious. Handing down from one generation to the next a very, very limited Christianity.

As with so many conversations regarding the experience of Japanese mountains, Glenda and Karen had a haiku poem which captured the essence of these truths which they encountered together on Koya. Their favourite verse is by Hyakuchi:

> Silence. A cool evening.
> Thinking pleasant thoughts
> With a friend.

KAREN:

It's the relative weight of those words which is so important to us, I think. First, you start in silence. The silence of not realizing that your religious experience can draw from such a wide source of inspirations, and still keep its integrity. But also, silence in terms of prayer and meditation. And then 'a cool evening thinking pleasant thoughts.' That's important, because I came across my insights in the monastery, and subsequently, in a calm and pleasant way. These insights of cosmos, and harmonic oneness with that vastness all came upon me more like a gentle stream or waterfall.

GLENDA:

But you're fairly cut off on the Kii Peninsula there aren't you. And you can clear your mind and receive the imagery from the trees and streams and the rocks there. And, of course, the monastery gives off this amazing aura of disciplined exploration of spirituality. So it all helps. Every-

thing you see, and feel, and touch, all help to calm your mind and make these experiences very pleasant and more calm.

KAREN:

And then the last line of the Hyakuchi poem says so much too. With a friend. Because, if it hadn't been for (Glenda) I don't think I would have even taken myself off to Japan, and certainly not all the way down to Kii and then to Koya itself. So 'with a friend' is very special to us both, because it was about a shared experience as well as a personal one.

From their discussions about this inspired form of spirituality which draws from the vastness of all possible experience, everyone described different problems in weaving these new experiences into their pre-existing religious preferences. For Janice, an effervescent social worker, and practising Taoist from West London, this need to 'organize each new inspiration' is essential to the maturing experience of her faith:

JANICE:

I keep a notebook these days because I need to have some sort of order over all the things I want to write down ... I think what my own experience of (Mount) Koya taught me is, yes, you do need to be open to as much as possible. That's essential if your spirituality is going to grow and not stagnate. You can't get away from that. But then, at the everyday practical level, what do you do when you open yourself up to art and films and literature and ethnic cultures? And everything! You've got two choices. You're either going to end up with carrier bags full of scribbled notes, or you're going to try and put what you find into 'boxes.'

This apparent need to organize these new inspirations, and, as Janice suggests, to 'put what you find into 'boxes'' provoked a number of extended conversations over the perils of categorization. Ultimately, agreement centred around the compromise solution of 'categorize with care':

KAREN:

(Looking at Janice) You're right in what you say. Because you do need to keep a handle on what you're opening yourself up to. But at the same time, I think you've got to look at the whole of what you've collected, and do a sort of monthly revision on what you've collected. You

need to read through your notes and see how the whole of your spiri-
tual awareness is taking shape. That's why I like going back to Koya,
because it's the best place I've ever come across which encourages you
to make the effort, and look at the whole person. Or the whole experi-
ence. Or the whole of anything. Because it's only within the whole
where the true and full richness of life can be found.

The moment Karen finished that explanation, three members of her
interview-group reached for their own notebooks, all looking for a
haiku poem by Ransetsu which, they knew, expressed Karen's sentiments perfectly:

> Above the pilgrims
> Chanting on a misty road
> Wild geese are flying.

NANCY:
There was this amazing flurry of activity as we all started to look for
that poem! But it's interesting that after (Karen's) words, we all knew
which poem we thought summed everything up. And that one does it,
doesn't it. We're all pilgrims. We've all fallen in love with being on
Koya because that whole experience has taken us to new places in our
spirituality. You always need to get back to being in the whole. Like the
geese. Flying within the whole. And above the whole of everything.
Able to see and appreciate all the separate elements within the totality
of everything. I think that's a lovely image isn't it. Needing to be like
flying wild geese, flying in a state of grace, able to see all, and ap-
preciate all.

Other experiences of cosmic order, organization and wholeness
became introduced into people's recollections of Mount Koya through
conversations with work colleagues. For three members of a busy
Personnel Department from Colchester, England, all of whom walk,
climb and attend their Buddhist classes together, their four visits to
Mount Koya have helped them to deal with the range of business
problems which they encounter in their professional lives:

IRIS:
If you saw our office, you'd appreciate the sort of pressure we're under
at work. Paper is everywhere. Phones ringing all the time. And all sorts
of people expecting you to drop everything to help them with whatever
problem they have. So even getting away from all that, and going to

Koya the first time was amazing, because it was so cut off. But then on subsequent times when we've come back to work, we've all agreed, we do deal with people now with a much better sense of proportion.

JEFF:

That's right. I think we've come to sympathize more with other people who we work with. And that, I think, only comes from developing a sense of order, and disciplining yourself to organize priorities better.

JULIA:

But having said that of course, don't go away with the impression that we've all become saints from visiting Mount Koya. But at least I think we're walking on a better path these days, than in the past.

In anticipation of what Iris calls her 'impossible times,' when the pressures of work seem almost intolerable, she keeps a few lines from Yoshito Hakeda's book *Kukai: Major Works* taped on to the side of her personal computer. 'When the going gets tough,' Iris explains, she has the 'words of wisdom' from Kobo Daishi immediately before her:

> According to the meditation sutras, meditation should be practised preferably on a flat area deep in the mountains. When young, I, Kukai, often walked through mountainous areas and crossed many rivers. There is a quiet, open place called Koya located two days' walk from Yoshino ... (Quoted in Hakeda 1972, 47)

IRIS:

And then my memories and personal thoughts take over the rest. But those words really are special. And they've helped me more than once when I've been at work. They take me back, if only for a second, to Koya. And to all the lessons I learned there. And to the whole amazing, amazing experience of the place. But to have those words from Kukai, or Kobo Daishi as he's often called, it's special. It's as if you're sharing with his thoughts the first time he came across the place. And the way it probably bowled him over too.

On another occasion, Glenda read aloud from another section of Hakeda's book to emphasise the inspirational value of Kobo Daishi which, Glenda suggested, 'we're keeping alive in the modern world.' This extract is taken from Kobo Daishi's *Indications of the Goals of the Three Teachings*. Written in his early twenties, it is Kobo Daishi's semi-autobiographical description of a wandering monk, very similar to himself:

> The blue sky was the ceiling of his hut and the clouds hanging over the mountains were his curtains; he did not need to worry about where he lived or where he slept. In summer he opened his neckband in a relaxed mood and delighted in the gentle breezes as though he were a great king. (Quoted in Hakeda 1972, 22)

GLENDA:
Kobo Daishi knew that mountains hold a very, very special aura about them for meditation and learning. And that applied then, as much as it applies now. That truth doesn't change. But what I like about this extract is you get this picture of an immensely happy and content wanderer. And that image fascinates me. It's a wonderful, wonderful picture, which we can all appreciate. Certainly I can relate to it. And I'd like to become that happy wanderer, given time!

The final discussion theme on these individuals' maturing experiences of Japanese mountains, and specifically their growing appreciation of Koya, drew from a particular awareness of the 'erotic feeling of being on that mountain' (Glenda). In this context, 'erotic' refers to an intense love of living in a particular moment of time. A love of being in a particular place. A celebration of the sublime beauty of specific experiences, and a feeling of 'complete ecstasy and being alive to that one precious inspiration' (Nancy).

NANCY:
Now that I've been back to Koya a few times, I can feel the meaning of the place grow on me. And yes, I use this word erotic to describe my feelings toward that mountain, and the Kobo Daishi monastery, because that's the right word to use. Erotica, in its correct, unadulterated meaning does mean a sublime ecstasy of experience. And, through my meditations on the place, when I'm there, as well as when I'm home, that's the right word to use ... Also, I suppose if I'm going to be totally upfront about this, it's a great word to shock people with, and to make them think. I mean, if you're out shopping, and you're close to people there, and you start talking about 'erotic experiences,' and 'feeling the erotic meaning fill my mind,' you'd be amazed how the heads turn your way!

After Nancy had introduced this theme of sublime love for the inspirational meaning of Koya, and once she had identified it correctly as 'erotic,' others within her interview group conceded that they too had discovered the erotic aspects of their meditations on Koya. Indeed, for Martina, a pollution controller from Montana, her experience and studies on the erotic potential of Mount Koya have been doubly beneficial:

MARTINA:

I can remember on the third time I went to Japan, I was travelling alone that time, and I wanted to visit Koya. I mean, I knew I had to. And at that time in my life, things weren't exactly going well. So I was ready to receive something special within my Taoist spirituality. And after I was there (Mount Koya) for, about four days, I heard someone describe their meditations and insights and learning as being 'erotic.' So, naturally, I listened up! And she was right. It was a sublime, ec- static experience. That was it. It was erotic. Nothing pornographic. It was sublime love of place and experience. It was totally erotic. But I think erotic also carries with it a sense of fun. And that's a carry-over to the sexual side of things. You know, sex as something that's fun. And I'd say that discovering a lot of things about myself, and finding whole new avenues opening up to me has been fun, as well as ecstatic, and exciting, and breathtaking, and wonderful. So there are parallels between the correct way of seeing erotica, alongside the everyday use of the word.

In addition to finding these erotic discoveries to be spiritually in- spiring, Martina also found they can have a profound healing value too:

MARTINA:

On my very last day there (Mount Koya), I was at a teaching class on meditation, and I heard someone else share an experience like mine: finding the experience of being there had picked them up. And they described that process as 'cosmic healing.' And that was amazingly erotic for me because my mind really leapt forward in joy. I mean, I'd heard about cosmic healing before, and hadn't really understood it. But at that moment it all came together. Cosmic healing was this amazing, amazing empathy with the universe. And in reaching out, and drawing all that power and energy and richness into my own life, I felt my depression totally fall away. And I wish I could describe the feeling of knowing that I'd come to Koya for the right reason, for the right length

*of time, to receive exactly the right teachings for me. It was beautiful.
Really, really beautiful. And it will always be with me now, as something I can build on.*

When Martina had finished this explanation, she paused to hunt for
a notebook in her shoulder bag, whilst others confirmed that they too
had encountered this form of cosmic healing: an experience of being
enriched from the beauty and profound meaning of Japanese mountain experiences. Cosmic healing as a genuine form of therapy which
can help individuals and groups recover a sense of direction within
their chosen spirituality. When this further discussion had finished,
Martina read a haiku, by Matsuo Basho, which captured 'the moment
of my cosmic healing, and which sets it within a totally Japanese
setting: of mountains and sacred awe':

> Still alive
> At the journey's end:
> A late autumn eve.

MARTINA:
> *That one's very personal to me. I came away from Koya, happier and
> more fulfilled and far more purposeful than I think I'd ever felt. I felt
> incredible! So alive. Really alive! I felt I'd come to the end of a major
> part of my journey. I mean, it wasn't autumn when I was there, but I
> can see that it was a dying-off of my depression, and a complete end to
> all that. And like a New England fall, it was the most beautiful way to
> end those bad times for me.*

Turning points

Of all the interviewees who encountered profound spiritual insights in
Japanese mountains, the most dramatic were experienced by three
United States Air Force flight technicians, Andy, Bob and Maurice.
Their encounters with the Shugendo mountain religion during the first
time they visited the Ohmine mountains, between Yoshino and Kuma-
no, completely revised their previously held agnostic beliefs.[7]

The Shugendo belief developed in the eighth century AD through a
fusion of native mountain worship, Buddhism and Taoism.[8] Its princi-

pal emphasis has always been on self-discipline, self-denial, solitude and deep meditation. Practitioners of Shugendo, called *yamabushi,* are trained in remote mountain retreats where they receive instruction on the recitation of sutras, as well as mundane and humble tasks such as collecting fire-wood and water. Fasting is another hard-learned discipline. To conquer their sense of fear, the novice *yamabushi* are hung by their ankles over a precipice: sometimes for hours at a time. Even when bitter winds howl around them, making the rope creak and sway uncontrollably, the *yamabushi* will continue to hang. Concentrating. Meditating. Learning. Becoming at one with the rhythms of the mountain, and the wisdom and sense of understanding within the Shugendo tradition.

The supernatural powers on which the aspirant *yamabushi* set their sights were therefore attained through some of the most challenging physical and spiritual austerities known to humankind. But whilst most other religions pursue their rituals within temples or shrines, churches and cathedrals, the *yamabushi* require no such architecture. For them, the vastness of the mountains is their place of worship and meditation. Paths, rocks, caves, pools and waterfalls are all employed by the *yamabushi* to form natural elements of their ceremonial practice. Whilst a few small huts and temples have been constructed as well, they remain secondary to the mountains as the most important place for Shugendo spiritual development.

In 1872 however, Shugendo was prohibited by the Japanese government on the pretence that its attention to supernatural practices such as exorcism of evil spirits, making prophecies, and curing illnesses by magic were 'confusing' to the minds of ordinary people. The prohibition was not abandoned until the end of World War II.

When Andy, Bob and Maurice first heard of Shugendo, it immediately appealed to their admiration of mental and physical discipline. Only later did that respect grow into a sustained spiritual consciousness as well:

ANDY:

I was totally awe-struck by the idea of that discipline which demanded so much concentration that even the most bitter cold could be ignored.

MAURICE:

That's it. It's a concentration on overcoming pain, and suffering, and pressures. Totally. Because there are no half measures in Shugendo. You must be totally disciplined.

In other conversations, the three men spoke of Shugendo as de-
manding total command of oneself, total freedom from bodily limita-
tion, and a complete transcendence of everyday pain or anguish, stress
or dilemma. In the company of Japanese friends who were acquainted
with a group of mature yamabushi, the Americans were invited to
take part in a three-hour night-time meditation in the Ohmine mountains near Kyoto.

MAURICE:

*That, I know, was the turning point for all three of us. Because first off,
there was no way we were going to chicken out of this thing, no way at
all. So, we went along. And man, it was cold out there. But I think we
all wanted to really see what Shugendo meant in the raw ... Even to
survive out there, I've never had to dig so deep within myself in all my
life.*

BOB:

*I thought I was pretty tough. I'd climbed, and canoed white-water. I'd
done all that stuff. But there were some walls of pain I went through
that night that really took me places I'd never been before.*

ANDY:

*You know, we had to turn to places within ourselves, where none of us
had had to go before. I mean, other times when each of us have been
under pressure, like anyone else, I guess, you just grit your teeth and
go for it. But that first night of meditation, and all the other nights
we've been to out there, with the yamabushi, you realize that just going
for it isn't good enough any more. You have to transcend the pain. And
the only way to do that is to draw from new depths within you.*

During those three-hour meditations on the Ohmine mountains
Maurice, Bob and Andy encountered the most profound form of cold
they had ever been through. Cold which was only experienced as
pain. So cold, their bodily joints were no longer able to move freely.
Cold to the intensity where their eyes began to ache, and then sting,
and then feel 'as if they wanted to pierce right through the back of my
head' (Bob). Over a period of four weeks, the three men attended nine
different night-time meditations. They refused to miss a single invitation. And on each occasion, they felt themselves mining at progressively deeper levels of spiritual consciousness. Drawing upon
reservoirs of inner strength which they had never previously discovered. It was a process of spiritual enlightenment through inner excava-

tion. Mining for spiritual wealth. Digging deeper on each successive meditation for the strength to transcend the cold, and to focus more clearly on the sutras on which they were meant to be concentrating.

ANDY:

Thinking about those experiences when we'd gotten back to our hotel, really changed us. We were sitting around, totally silent. Thinking, and thawing out the best we could. But we were all realizing that there's now a dimension in our lives which we can really get something valuable from, if only we could keep practising these amazing disciplines.

MAURICE:

Yeah, that's the thing. You've got to keep at it.

Of their own admission, none of these three men have become Shugendo yamabushi. Rather, they simply and variously describe their spirituality as 'completely unorthodox,' 'free,' 'a disciplined mishmash,' but always 'the most important thing that's ever taken place in my life' (Maurice).

BOB:

We've talked a lot about this. And whereas before we discovered Shugendo, we were pretty critical about all things religious and spiritual, we're all a lot more accepting of those ideas. And although we usually keep to the meditations of the yamabushi which we picked up when we were out there in Japan, we'll take from all kinds of religious ideas. Anything which we feel will take us along this new path we've found out about ... It's totally awesome. And it's made the world of difference to my own sense of self-discipline, as well as the way I feel more in tune with everything around me.

It isn't easy to categorize this newly discovered, but immensely satisfying, spirituality which these men have found and nurtured for themselves. Whilst the first seeds in that nurturing were clearly drawn from an admiration of complete self-discipline and self-control, the further growth of their meditation has been drawn from Zen Buddhism, Taoism, and creation-centred Christianity.

ANDY:

It's liberating. That's the way I feel about it. And when we talk to other people, most of them respond positively, and they want to know more about how things have developed the way they have for us. And then,

*say, they'll tell me, or the other guys, about something they've found out
about, or read, or seen, or whatever. And you think, 'yeah, I like that.'
So you kind of move in on those ideas too. And it all takes you along
the way. It's great. But always rooted in the yamabushi traditions.*

Conclusions

The most distinctive theme within our conversations about the spiritual meaning of Japanese mountains was the continued presence of haiku poems. Almost everyone who had visited Japan and the mountains there, was able to quote at least one haiku which has a profoundly personal meaning which connects the person to a particular moment in a specific mountainous area.

GLENDA:
*Haikus are like the most exquisite photographs or miniature paintings.
They capture the truth of a moment forever. And in three lines: there
you have it, with nothing more to be said. And, for me, they mark out
the difference between things I learned from Japan, compared to elsewhere in my travels.*

But whilst the haikus were frequently employed as part of the way these people expressed their spiritual experiences within Japanese mountains, many of those experiences are also unique to Japan. In particular, Japanese mountains were always discussed by these contributors as being powerful inspirations for the development of a spiritual individuality which draws from the enormity and richness of the cosmos. Whilst this theme was hinted at and alluded to, regarding other mountains elsewhere in the world, it was never fully developed for these people in mountains outside Japan. It was a distinctive spiritual encounter with microcosm and macrocosm, unity and infinity, the atomic and the ultimate. A disarmingly simple truth, with infinite implications. Just like a haiku verse.

Much of this feeling of being at one with the cosmos came from concentrated meditations on single moments in time which are described by the haiku poems. But beyond the words of an individual verse, these people often formed their own personal moments of spiritual richness and grace. They found their own precious insights, from which they felt able to extend outwards, in their imaginations, to the farthest points of the horizon, or through the depths of the sky. And in doing so, feeling overwhelmed by the sheer enormity of treasures which that single moment had inspired. Sometimes, these inspirations were born from the way sunlight at dusk shaded the edges of clouds. Other times, a small bird resting beside a secluded rocky pool was enough. Ancient trees standing beside a waterfall. A path. A leaf. Tree bark. Or a panoramic view which held them motionless at the end of a walk up a hillside.

Other aspects of these Japanese mountain experiences support the conclusions drawn from elsewhere in the world. Among Jews and Christians in particular, many conversations were held which allowed people to voice their frustration with the absence of prayers, teachings, and scriptures which are devoted to single precious moments of spiritual wonder:

SEB:

Every rabbi I ever met was the same like that. They always want to say so much about so much. They never take time to slow down and just pause for thought, and look at one beautiful thing. Like a blade of grass, or one scene of God's creation, and talk about that. Maybe they should learn more about this traditional Japanese way of looking at things, then they'd see the value of what I'm talking about.

Christian contributors echoed Seb's concern:

DEREK:

There is, honestly, so much to learn, even from standing and thinking and listening in those Japanese mountains. And I would love to hear, if only once, a vicar standing up on his pulpit and asking his congregation to look at a picture of Fuji, or Koya, or any of those completely wonderful places. Because there'd be so many valuable lessons to learn: prayer, and faith, and growing in your faith. They could all be learned from looking at the mountains in this Japanese sort of way.

Another shared theme between these insights gained in Japan, and others encountered in mountains elsewhere, was a joyous celebration of individual faith.

NANCY:

So many times, I've been meditating in the mountains there. Fuji, say. And all of a sudden you're engulfed in a new vision of how things fit

*together. And it's incredible. You're totally, totally, full of it. And then
you drive back to Tokyo, say, and there's all this brash energy, and
pace, and people, and music and noise. And whereas you might have
previously thought, 'Oh God, what a din,' I've found myself on numerous occasions saying how brilliant and wonderful it all is. And in
doing so, shocking the people I'm with!*

Nancy's words glow with the erotic joy of living in a completely
fulfilling spiritual faith. There is fun, and laughter, and joy 'and the
most amazing, amazing sense of liberation I could possibly imagine'
(Nancy). This erotic love of being alive, and of learning about oneself,
and one's faith, was found by others, elsewhere. But for Nancy it was
first encountered in Japan. So, for her and others who contributed to
this book, it draws from her love of that country: its mountains, its
forests and streams, its poetry, along with its city life, and other forms
of human-made energy. The same is true for Pauline:

PAULINE:

*The more time I spend in Japan, the more I learn to love my spiritual-
ity, and to love life. And I think you can look at those mountains as
being unique, if only for the amazing simple poetry and wisdom they've
inspired. And you can draw from that wisdom and energy now, today.
In the cynical, aggressive, fragmented, late twentieth century, those
mountains have got something powerful and important to say. So their
voice needs to be heard. If I had to interpret that voice, I'd guess it was
saying 'adopt a clear, pure, simple, straightforward love affair with
being alive. Love your faith. Develop it. Take joy from watching it
grow. Like a child.' That's what the Japanese mountains have done for
me. And I know. Really. I really, really know deep down, that I will
always continue to grow, the more time I'm able to be there.*

CHAPTER 5

Himalayas

There is in the north a supreme king of mountains named Himalaya, possessed of a divine self. Bathing in the eastern and western oceans, he stretches like a measuring rod across the earth.
                                                    Kalidasa (1893)

Ancient wisdom

There are peaks within the Himalayan mountains which are sacred to almost one billion people.[1] For Hindus, Buddhists, Jains, Sikhs and followers of the Tibetan Bon faith, these summits form a divine land-scape of extraordinary inspiration and wisdom. A landscape which contains the birth place for all truth and understanding. A divine stage on which that wisdom can flourish and attain its highest possible expression. But within its darker sides, the Himalayan mountains are also capable of inspiring mortal terror and unprecedented agonies without a moment's warning. And any human life can be claimed with ease and indifference.[2]

To the east, the 1500 mile arc of the world's highest and youngest mountain range rises within the tropical jungles of Myanma, formerly called Burma. It then sweeps across northern India, engulfing Bhutan, Nepal, the southern edge of the Tibetan plateau and then further up to the glacial heights of the Karakoram in Pakistan. But this is an arc of mountains like no other. The light is unique. The air is thin. First-time travellers often describe the sensation of finding their minds and imaginations swimming and convulsing with exhaustion and inspira-tion, liberation, curiosity and an intensity of fear which they had never found anywhere before.

Within one of the most sublime sources of Hindu wisdom, the Kumarasambhava poem, written by Kalidasa in the fifth century AD, the Himalayas are held in the highest of all possible esteem. For this is the dwelling place of the Lord Shiva: destroyer of all life. Yet, here too remains the spirit of Vishnu, the preserver of life. Divine destroyer and divine preserver together, finding in the Himalayas the only place on earth worthy to serve as their home. Indeed, within Hindu mythology, Shiva took as his bride the beautiful Parvati, daughter of Himalaya, the god of these mountains. The young goddess had spent thousands of years in contemplation and austerity, developing her whole-self in preparation for her first meeting with the celibate Shiva. Then, at the end of a time spent in meditation, Shiva finally saw Parvati. A moment later, the love god Kama shot a flowered arrow at Shiva who retaliated by scorching Kama to ashes with a single glance from his flaming eye. But the deed was done. Love had been sown, and Shiva and Parvati were married within the magnificent surroundings of the Himalayan mountain kingdom. The union soon produced a first son, the supernatural Karttikeya: born with an extraordinary ability to defeat demons and liberate humanity from evil spirits.

As part of this dramatic and divine inheritance, the great epic of Indian literature, the Mahabharata, describes how Prince Arjuna climbed and performed austerities within the Himalayas in search of Shiva's power.[3] During a heightened period of consciousness, Arjuna addressed a summit which he had been contemplating:

> Mountain, thou art always the refuge of the good who
> practise the law of righteousness, the hermits of holy deeds,
> who seek out the road that leads to heaven. It is by thy grace,
> Mountain, that priests, warriors, and commoners attain to
> heaven and, devoid of pain, walk with the gods.
> (Mahabharata 2:308)

Arjuna's words are timeless. They remain fundamental to all pilgrims in the Himalayas who realize the sacred nature of these towering peaks. By the end of the Mahabharata however, only the most virtuous of all the main characters, Yudhishthira, is shown to have retained sufficient virtue to successfully enter the Kingdom of Heaven with his physical body. Previously, the various tests and trials of righteousness which are embodied within these sacred mountains had defeated the integrity and good intentions of all other aspirants. The lessons of the Mahabharata are therefore clear: it is possible to develop a divine wisdom from the Himalayas, and, in so doing, have one's life changed forever. But this is a wisdom which is always hard-won from these fortress walls of snow and ice. Secrets and insights can be understood, but they remain jealously guarded from all but the most persistent, wise and humble.

One such pilgrim was a prince who lived in the Nepalese Himalayas 2500 years ago. His name was Siddhartha Gautama. In later years, he became troubled by the consistent pain and suffering which people experience through their social and material attachments. Consequently, as the Buddha, he taught the virtues of wisdom and compassion: the path of abstaining from attachment to anyone or anything. A Middle-Way of detached concern. A Way which recognizes the value of sustained meditation on these simple truths, such as the contemplations which are still practised on the sacred slopes of Mount Kailas, north-west of Nepal, on the Tibetan Plateau:

> The prophecy of Buddha says most truly,
> That this snow mountain is the navel of the world,
> A place where the snow leopards dance.
> The mountain top, the crystal-like pagoda ...
>   (Chang 1977 1: 262)

After singing this lyric, the Tibetan spiritual master, Milarepa, described in awed reverence the snow-covered mountains surrounding Kailas in which five hundred Buddhist saints remain in a state of nirvana: the gracious experience of transcendence, free from attachment and suffering.[4] Indeed, every peak which surrounds Kailas corresponds to a deity on the mandala of Demchog, the principal Buddhist god of Mount Kailas.[5] On one side of the mountain for example, lies Ratnasambhava, the One Born of a Jewel. Directly opposite sits Amitabha, the Buddha of Boundless Light. Each of these two valleys carries with it a set of unique lessons on transcendent awareness which are cherished and studied by modern day masters and students alike.

But Kailas is also rich with Jain wisdom. Rishabhanatha, the first of the twenty-four saviours of this era, attained enlightenment on the golden slopes of Kailas. Close by, the founder of the Tibetan Bon faith, Shenrab, taught and meditated. But Kailas is not only the most sacred of all Himalayan mountains through its spiritual implications. It is also the luxurious home of Kubera, god of wealth, whose powers are described within the two great epics of Hindu literature: the Mahabharata and the Ramayana. In those texts, there are timeless lessons which teach the wise and discerning application of wealth: a form of wisdom which remains as valuable today as it did for the original authors and their disciples.

Whilst Hindu scriptures teach that Parvati spends much of her time with Shiva on Kailas, she is also blessed with other magnificent homes. Few can compare in their breathtaking beauty with Nanda Devi, the mountain called Goddess of Bliss, located in the Uttrarkhand region of northern India, close to the Nepalese border.[6] But around the summit of Nanda Devi there is a terrifying wall of rock and ice. Only one breach lies in that wall: the gorge of Rishi Ganga, another of the sources for the sacred Ganges river. For pilgrims, there is the opportunity to bathe within the purifying but icy waters at Gomukh, a glacial source of the Ganges.

Parvati's example can be a source of further meditation among pilgrims and climbers on Annapurna, the Sanskrit name meaning 'she who is filled with food.'[7] Here therefore, Parvati is in her most benevolent surroundings. Each year, after the autumn harvest, the faithful in the holy city of Benares dedicate the Annakuta festival to Parvati's name. The goddess' temple is filled with a symbolic mountain of food which is later distributed among those who travel in search of Annapurna's blessing and wisdom.

For most travellers and pilgrims who visit the Himalayas, the benevolence and favour of these mountains is only discovered after the most arduous experiences of physical struggle, pain, disillusionment, wonder and despair. Whilst this spiritual treasure is abundantly available to all those with sufficient patience and humility, the true splendour of Himalayan wisdom must always remain illusive and mysterious if it is to retain its full grace and infinite power.

First visits

For many of these visitors, their first encounters with the Himalayas were the most traumatic experiences of their lives.[8] Although they had arrived expecting to find soaring beauty, their abiding memories of these mountains are punctuated with recollections of searing pain, despair and the need for physical and spiritual re-appraisal. Louis, Rudi and Hannah for example, recalled their first trip to the Ladakh and Zaskar mountains of Kashmir State in northern India where they had arrived from London University in 1989 as environmental researchers. Their changes of mental attitude however, are typical of many others who described their first visits to the Himalayas:

LOUIS:

We'd all been excited for many reasons. It was a chance to see the back of beyond. But also to test ourselves in that type of incredibly challenging environment.

RUDI:

That's right. You do feel tested. First, because with all the rubbish from other travellers, you quickly realize this is not the pristine place you'd dreamed of. But second, you feel utterly dwarfed by those mountains.

HANNAH:

But therein lies its value! The Himalayas force you to explore aspects of your beliefs which you don't find in easier parts of the world.

Every element of this first expedition appears to have been a demoralizing struggle. Local guides had fallen into drunken fights. Equipment had been stolen. Other equipment failed to work correctly. And all the time, in the cold, thin air, every physical exertion felt unnecessarily burdensome. Even within the first week of being in those mountains, Rudi realized the experience would be as much of a spiritual exploration as a scientific expedition:

RUDI:

We were going to have twelve weeks of this kind of endurance. Twelve weeks of what looked like a lot of misery because nothing was going right in any way ... And I could feel my morale and whole spirit sink deeper and deeper into this profound physical tiredness you feel out there.

Rudi's Jewish background had taught him a great deal about the spirituality of pain and suffering. But this was the first time he had encountered those lessons directly as a personal experience.

RUDI:

Jewish history is the story of exile and loneliness and misery ... But it didn't occur to me that my own sense of inadequacy on that expedition could be compared to all that. What I was doing was to sink further and further into that black hole of misery, as more and more disasters kept falling in on us.

At the beginning of their third week, with very little progress being made on the expedition, Hannah found and shared the following passage from the Psalms with her companions:

I am worn out with groaning,
All night long I flood my bed with weeping
And drench my couch with tears.
My eyes grow weak with sorrow;
They fail because of all my enemies.
(Psalm 6:6–7)

HANNAH:

There was a wonderful silence after I'd read that to them (Rudi and Louis), because we'd all realized the wisdom we'd just heard. Each line spoke to us. We were tired, and even worn out with the effort of being tired because of all the things which had gone wrong for us. I don't know if any of us had gone so far as to drench their beds with tears, but it did sum up how desperate we felt.

These words from the sixth Psalm signalled the beginning of an entirely new form of spiritual exploration for these three scientists. They immediately felt a distant promise of hope return to their lives which they had not felt since their arrival:

LOUIS:

I think the Psalm reminded us that our faith could have a contribution to make there. And that was liberating. It added a new and really surprising dimension to being there in those mountains. I mean, we suddenly realized that there was an alternative to feeling crushed by all the disastrous events which had befallen us.

That sense of despair at the poor start to the expedition had previously drawn the three friends together as a team-within-a-team, whilst their other expedition colleagues had continued to seek recriminations and excuses. But in addition, on the basis of the sixth Psalm, Louis, Rudi and Hannah felt drawn together by a sense of spiritual insight regarding the integrity of their Jewish faith in this context. With that wisdom literature, they felt new questions develop in their imaginations. New insights became articulated. And fresh sources of Biblical literature came to mind which complimented the Psalm, as well as their developing curiosity at the ways in which their spirituality seemed to grow in its integrity. One complimentary passage which acted as a further major inspiration is the following extract from the Book of Job:

And now my life ebbs away
Days of suffering grip me
Night pierces my bones;
My gnawing pains never rest.
In his great power,
God becomes like clothing to me;
He binds me like the neck of my garment.
He throws me into the mud,
And I am reduced to dust and ashes.
(Job 30:16–19)

HANNAH:

Those words are amazing. And their true meaning is something which is often kept away from Jews, and I know, Christians too. It's about the endurance you need to withstand pain. To last the distance. And not to ignore the pain, but to see it as something which has been sent by God. And through the pain, you grow together. You learn together. And you become mutually compassionate ... And that was an incredible discovery to make with everything going wrong all around us, and the expedition morale getting progressively worse every day.

LOUIS:

But that spirituality of pain makes a lot of people uncomfortable if they haven't actually been through an experience where they need to call on it.

HANNAH:

Only because they've been taught to think about God as only having a rosy side, which is a nonsense. Anyone who's grieved for a close friend or partner will tell you that.

One section of the expedition which illustrates this transition in attitude among these three people arose when they were obliged to cross the thunderous Barai Nala river. The crossing was undertaken during a high, gusting wind while the first flurries of sleet and snow billowed around them and their two pack horses:

LOUIS:

From a previous way of thinking which was almost completely dejected and miserable, I know we faced that crossing with a willingness to accept the cold and winds. After all, they were as much a part of being in those mountains as their beauty.

HANNAH:

And at the very practical level, I think, for the first time during the expedition, we actually began to feel compassionate toward some of our less-friendly colleagues. So imagine their surprise when I answered their nasty grumblings and abuse with an offer of assistance. There was one guy who'd become little more than a bully, who was completely lost for words when I went to help him off with his pack!

In the face of extreme physical pain: the cold of the bitter mountain air, the stinging sleet on their faces, and the dejection of an expedition schedule which, until that moment, had been punctuated with failure and mishap, these travellers were able to draw constructive insights from their adversity. They used those problems to form the basis for renewed compassion within the group. They chose to look upon their pain as a resource which could serve the group, rather than destroy it. But Hannah, Louis and Rudi were not alone in choosing to look at the pain and emptiness of their Himalayan experiences in this renewed and inspired way. For three young German climbers, Roselle, Dee and Miriam, their experiences on the Annapurna and Machapuchare mountains in central Nepal led them to a very similar series of insights:

ROSELLE:

We'd been trying and failing in our climbing for over two weeks. But every route we'd been trying had been either blocked off with snow or ice, or the winds gusted too strongly. And so we were completely dead-beat.

DEE:

But you know how your mind swims around in air like that. When you're exhausted and feeling really down? Well, my mind swam back to a poster I had always liked as a child. And all it had, was a simple candle on a black background. I don't know what made me think of it, because I had plenty else on my mind. But as I sat there, freezing and miserable, I thought about it, and, gradually, I saw I could use it.

MIRIAM:

It was totally surreal. We'd pitched our tents, and made some drinks. And suddenly she told us to close our eyes and think of this candle picture! I mean, I thought she'd gone mad! But it was such a beautiful image, and it changed our attitudes almost instantly ... The candle is always there in your pain. You can turn your back on it, but it's always there.

The candle picture began to help these three women by healing their anxieties and shattered morale. It represented a sign of hope, just as the voice of God had helped Louis, Rudi and Hannah with the passage from the Book of Job. In common with God's voice therefore, the candle helped the three climbers to confront their pain. It showed that hope is as much a part of suffering as the despondency and misery it brings. Hope and despair, perseverance and pain are only two sides of the same experience of place — two ways of seeing a landscape of adversity. The important insight arises when both sides are seen at the same time. When loneliness, alienation and darkness are confronted alongside the knowledge that others have felt those experiences too — others who have found the right words of comfort and wisdom to heal their wounds and help pull them through the void of inner darkness.

ROSELLE:

The picture of the candle showed there are always two parts to any pain: the darkness and the light. And that light is always there so long as you have the right attitude to see it ...

MIRIAM:

Especially in a group, it helps to be more responsive to the misery of others in the team. And, in a way, you can become part of the candle in each others' lives. Encouraging each other onwards.

Both these groups of three travellers, the environmental scientists and the climbers, had used their experiences in the Himalayas to find new depths to their spirituality. A spirituality of pain and darkness alongside other aspects of their consciousness which had previously known only hope and optimism. In these mountains, those two sides of their religious experience had become moulded together. Hope had become identified as a consistent counterpart to pain. Optimism had been identified as always lying within the spiritual wreckage of suffering and loneliness. Two elements of the same process of inner discovery and realization.

Subsequent visits

Whilst first-time visitors frequently encountered this spirituality of pain, loneliness and despair, more experienced Himalayan travellers described the ways in which they were able to find deeper meanings within that 'sacred void.' In the following illustration for example, Amos, a teacher from Philadelphia, described how he developed his understanding of the darker aspects within Himalayan experience:

AMOS:

> I use the phrase 'sacred void' because it paints this picture of a feeling that's empty, lost, lonely and yet full of sacred meaning. Within that void, I find anyway, you can find new sides to God. They're deeper angles on understanding which I've never found anywhere else. And when I go to the Himalayas, first off, I know it's going to be a physical endurance. It always happens like that. But also, I always come away with a much deeper sense of knowing an unfamiliar side to God. And that's just amazing. It always is.

A deeper understanding about the spirituality of pain, darkness and desolation is therefore the treasure which Amos is consistently able to draw from travelling in the Himalayas. But whilst those experiences were frequently illustrated with reference to specific problems which were suffered in specific parts of these mountains, Amos suggested that all those lessons have universal application:

AMOS:

> We're used to being taught about the cosy and comfortable sides of God. God the loving Father etcetera. But often, I think, that's just 'nice' and 'pretty.' And I've never found God to be like that. There are deeper layers of meaning to Him which are only understood by going through some pretty uncomfortable barriers ... but what you find is that you come away from those mountains with a greater sense of curiosity about God, because He's brought you through such a lot ... And I've found myself able to use those lessons all over the world.

In a very similar discussion on the intensity of this darker spirituality, two English drama students, Patrick and Edward, described how they found this profoundly enriching inspiration from the Himalayas, within an extract of writing by the mystic writer John of the Cross. The section from which they quoted was the following:

> To reach satisfaction in all
> desire its possession in nothing.
> To come to possess all
> desire the possession of nothing.
> To arrive at being all
> desire to be nothing.
> To come to the knowledge of all
> desire the knowledge of nothing.
> (Quoted in Kavanaugh 1973, 103)

PATRICK:

I actually first read that in a tiny tent in a blizzard on Annapurna! And I was cold through to my bone-marrow. I was soaking wet, and only half awake. But those few lines taught me so much about the need to develop a well-rounded experience of God, which you just don't get from a comfortable church. You only reach anything near this form of profound understanding of yourself and God if you've been through those stages of pain and hardship. And for me, I always associate that with the Himalayas.

EDWARD:

Well, yes. But where else do you always find that completely soul-destroying and soul-enriching experience? I mean, I can't think of anywhere ... So John of the Cross captures so much of that roller-coaster way of learning about God. To find contentment in everything, be prepared to lose everything. And I can remember several expeditions I've been on in those mountains, when I've lost everything I brought with me. Including several times when I nearly lost my life ... But against that risk of losing everything, you also risk gaining so much insight and truth, and richness.

One of the most consistent themes for discussion among experienced climbers and walkers within the Himalayas is the way in which these encounters with spiritual upheaval and struggle concentrated their minds on specific details of individuals rocks, flowers, companions or even single moments within their Himalayan journeys. In the following illustration, Frances, a sculptor from north London, describes her experience of this intense appreciation for particular landscape details:

FRANCES:

Within that amazing intensity of struggle, and gasping for oxygen, you learn to appreciate the specifics of life. And all stereotypes just fly out the window. You learn to appreciate details. And you learn to see with eyes which have shared the same sort of pain as most other climbers and walkers there. So just as you see yourself as an individual composed of details and nuances, the physical and mental agony and ecstasy of climbing in the Himalayas teaches you to appreciate others in that fully developed and appreciative manner too ... The pains which you go through strip away all superficiality, and make you love the specifics.

As a believing Zen Buddhist, Frances often referred to her favourite haiku poems to illustrate the lessons she had learned from her travels within the Himalayas:

FRANCES:

There's an amazing mountain called Nanda Devi which is just near the Nepalese border in India. The feeling you get there is incredible. Anyway, I was climbing it in August 1990, and needless to say we were having to pitch our tents due to the terrifying winds you get there. And, from inside my sleeping bag, my note book fell open at this haiku by Shiki. And my mind just stopped dead:

> *As innocently as the clouds*
> *He tills the field;*
> *Under the Southern Mountains.*

It's an incredible picture, isn't it. An innocent guy, quietly, patiently tilling the field. Working for his harvest. A completely innocent man, working within sight of these amazing mountains ... But not only do I really like that picture of innocent toil, but having lived through the ravages of what mountains can do to you, I like to think the farmer is able to harvest this wonderful, fully rounded understanding of those Southern Mountains, and not just the pretty picturesque side of things.

Amos and his climbing companion Moisha described the same form of sympathy with the details of individuality inspired by a short extract from Shakespeare's Hamlet. As with Frances, these words were discovered whilst being unable to progress during a particularly violent and freezing wind-storm:

If thou didst ever hold me in thy heart
Absent me from felicity awhile,
And in this harsh world draw thy breath in pain,
To tell my story.
(Hamlet V:2:338)

MOISHA:

*There can only be one way of looking at people after you've read those
words. I mean, think about them. Only when you've been through pain
and anguish can you genuinely look at other people, and be ready to
hear their stories. For better and for worse. The 'whole' of people's lives.
And for me, I was only really able to do that, you know, listen to
people in that profound way of listening after I'd been through some
pretty harrowing times in those (Himalayan) mountains.*

AMOS:

*I think you can often think about Hamlet in the Himalayas because that
play is all the time dealing with your mortality. How do you deal with
that question? What does it mean to you within the intensity of those
storms? How does that question change when you're back home, some
place? Does it have to change? You know? Those are some powerful
questions. But not until you've been through the pain of being able to
empathize with them, can you begin to ask those sorts of things.*

In a separate conversation, Frank, a travel writer and photographer
from Detroit, Michigan, quoted from the sixteenth century French
essayist Michel de Montaigne to illustrate his point that an appreciation of these specifics of individuality can form a basis for understanding the harmony which exists within, and between, all created objects:

A man must keep a little back shop where he can be himself
without reserve. In solitude alone can he know true freedom.
(De Montaigne 1580, 39)

FRANK:

*'In solitude alone can he know true freedom.' Those are powerful words,
indeed. For me, they always conjure up images of Mount Kailas on the
Tibetan plateau, which is one of the best places I know if you want to
have a time of solitude. But, I think, in those times alone, you're able to
put together a lot of pieces and fragments of your journeys. And to
marvel at them. The ways people are able to live in such inhospitable
places. The ways the flora and fauna are able to survive. The whole*

marvel of that harmony of survival. And having the incredible opportu-
nity to see it, and think about it within the luxury of time. The luxury
of freedom. It's an incredible feeling, and one which I always carry with
me, but which I always identify with (Mount) Kailas.

Frances was also able to describe similar insights drawn from her
own experiences of solitude and harmony:

FRANCES:
> *For an artist, these are amazingly strong themes. And whenever I'm*
> *able to get away on my own, when I'm out there (in the Himalayas), I*
> *just sketch and sketch and sketch. I mean, they're such fertile themes*
> *aren't they: solitude and harmony. They're the source of so much poten-*
> *tial. But at the heart of that inspiration, you can never get away from*
> *the enduring meaning of those mountains. They're enormously tough*
> *places. You never get to know them unless you've been through the*
> *barriers of exhaustion and physical pain. But out of those agonizing*
> *periods, you do reach some amazing levels of insight.*

Others were able to provide recollections of insights into the harmony of Himalayan experience which they have been able to apply to
their everyday lives, as well as their travels elsewhere in the world.
The ability to find places in which to meditate, even within the most
inhospitable climates and circumstances was often described. Equally,
the achievement of finding the wisdom to appreciate the age of rocks
and landscapes, many of which are hundreds of thousands of years
old. Other landscapes may be millions of years in age.

THOMAS:
> *My experiences in the Himalayas have been some of the most traumatic*
> *periods in my life. And yet I'd never be without them. And I think, if*
> *there's one thing in common to all those experiences is the way I*
> *learned to meditate on the precious harmony which exists between*
> *everything you find. Even in surprising places and times.*

As part of one anecdote, Thomas described a period of three days
when he, and his climbing party, were trapped on the side of Machapuchare, in the Annapurna Range, by high, gusting winds:

THOMAS:
> *Those three days sum up my whole experience of the Himalayas. Bitter*
> *cold. Gasping for air. And then coming through those incredible strug-*

*gles to find an amazing empathy with the mountain, the wind, the ice.
And the necessity of that pain to an experience of that mountain as a
rich, provocative inspiration to my (Buddhist) faith.*

Thomas went on to describe an almost complete sense of oneness
he felt during that time with the howling wind, the ice, the age of the
mountain, the erosion which he imagined taking place to the rock face
all around him, the agonies, thirsts, hungers and fears going through
the minds of his companions, the destruction of hope within the
group, and the simultaneous creation of insight within his own consciousness.

THOMAS:

*In three days, I think I must have covered just about every philosophi-
cal question going! And I tell you, it was completely exhausting. But it
was totally wonderful too. To have that experience of finding empathy
with so much, all at the same time, and being able to relish those insights, and cherish them and treasure them as individual elements as
well as parts of a much greater whole was an experience I've never been
through again.*

Turning points

Whilst everyone who contributed to this book has described their
experiences of the Himalayas as being dominated by physical and
spiritual pain, and profound insight, only three of these travellers have
also suffered the agonies of personal tragedy following the death in
these mountains of their climbing colleagues. For these three men,
their loss occurred in the Zaskar Range of Kashmir, northern India.
The party of eight experienced climbers had been making their slow,
breathless way up to a pass in the mountains when a terrible dust
storm suddenly blew up without warning. From the most mild breeze,
the wind had suddenly hit them full in the face with a wild, punishing
strength which threw them into bewildered shock. Wet snow began to
swirl and whip around their petrified, frozen limbs making it impossible to see ahead, or to call out to each other. As the bitter wind
reached a screaming pitch, it knocked three of the party off the narrow
gravel path down the sheer rock face to their deaths. A moment later,

another climber lost his footing, but was able to grasp hold of the path. The closest man to him instinctively leant over to try and save him before both of them lost their grip and balance and fell helplessly to their fate. Of the eight men who had begun that journey, only three were able to inch their uncomprehending and exhausted way up the path, and then further up a succession of cols, before they found sufficient shelter and time to wait for the blinding wind to abate.

KEITH:

> *We all knew what had happened. And I can remember sitting against a boulder, gasping for my breath, holding my eyes tight shut, not knowing what to think, or what to do.*

LARRY:

> *It was about another two or three hours before the wind calmed down. So we all had time to privately figure out what we'd just been through ... But for me, I'd say those three hours were as much of a whirl of chaos as the wind. I mean, five deaths of good, good friends. Over in a second. And nothing you could do to help. It honestly threw me for a long time.*

LEON:

> *But in the years since that time, I've often said to folks that those hours we had to sit there sheltering from the winds, were probably the best way to help us deal with what had happened. Because, what you have to understand is just how quick it all happened. One minute we were together. The next, the winds blew up from nowhere. And then more than half the party was dead.*

In those exhausted hours, waiting for the winds to abate, the three remaining men privately reviewed their Buddhist faiths, searching for the wisdom with which to reconcile the disaster they had just suffered. At first, such a reconciliation was impossible. The screaming winds made it an effort to think. In the thin Kashmir air, their heads pounded with exhaustion and confusion, despair and grief.

LEON:

> *At times like that, you just sit there, reeling from the shock. You don't think, because you can't think. You just exist, in a form of coma. And I can remember the wind and snow blowing so fiercely that I kept my eyes closed, trying to shut everything out.*

All sense of time was lost to them. Time only became a numbing period of disbelief through which they waited for the wind to drop. It was as if all life had been suspended while they sat sheltering. Wondering how much of the nightmare had been real. Daring to speculate whether the sound of their colleagues falling away from them had been a hallucination, brought on by the lack of oxygen in their brains. But as their minds eventually calmed, each man knew the nightmare had been real. Nothing had been imagined. Nothing of the pain and devastation they felt had been an illusion. The nightmare was completely unfathomable, but it screamed for attention within their exhausted minds:

LARRY:

It's amazing to think of it now, but none of us could communicate during that storm. I mean, it was just impossible. But having spoken it over many, many times with the other guys, it's amazing that we were all thinking pretty much the same things.

KEITH:

We'd all started off in shock. But gradually, we'd started to search in our minds for some way to deal with this catastrophe. Some handle we could put on those events to help us deal with them.

LARRY:

I know I sat there with no sense of time, and suddenly a haiku poem came to me which summed everything up for me perfectly. It was so simple. I couldn't believe it, how clear it was. It's by Issa:

> *A dragonfly!*
> *The distant hills*
> *Reflected in his eyes.*

That's how I felt. More delicate and completely weak than I could remember. I mean, I was totally devastated by everything. But that picture, of a delicate, weak, fragile dragonfly, but with the capacity of achieving such vast insights, really appealed to me. And I wanted to be that dragonfly. And I wanted to find those answers.

In the months and years since that tragedy, Larry believes he has slowly moved toward a way of reconciling his Buddhism with the loss of his companions. The understanding does nothing to ease his sense of profound, earth-shaking loss, but it has helped him reconcile the events to his experience of the Himalayas both as a physical as well as a spiritual landscape.

LARRY:

Everyone who's been climbing or walking in the Himalayas knows about the pain barriers you go through there, because it's one of the toughest environments on this planet. And you can't get away from that fact. So in that kind of place, if you think about it, you've got to expect death. And you've got to expect to suffer grief when you lose friends. Because what are you doing if you don't face that truth? I'll tell you. You're making the Himalayas just pretty pictures. You're denying what they can do to you.

Larry's insights, using Issa's poem as a foundation, became shared by Keith and Leon.

KEITH:

The respect which you need to have when you go into the Himalayas connects you with some of the most ancient wisdom and beliefs known to mankind. It's simple, but it's also frightening. Really, really frightening ...

LEON:

It's that simple recognition that there are forces at work within the Himalayas, whether it's the winds, or the snows, which can kill you. And it's as simple and clinical as that.

From the oblivion of dark, numbing agony and loss, these three men have formed an enduring insight into the experience of spiritual upheaval which they encountered in the Zaskar Range. Having felt the void of confusion during which they neither knew what to think or believe, they have now reached an ability to conduct grief counselling meetings within their temple, in New Jersey, USA. Through that counselling, they believe, the deaths of their lost companions have been given a surprising but fulfilling meaning.

KEITH:

But that's another thing about the Himalayas. You'll never understand all the lessons it has to teach you. Because, I think, in the West, we always try to think in logical terms. Whereas, in an environment like the Himalayas, you need to expect surprise. And that's not a contradiction. You need to accept. You need to be ready to deal with that stuff. I mean, being prepared for the death of friends, never takes away the shock and pain of it when it happens, but it serves as a foundation to help you walk on, with greater strength in your heart. It's never easy, and no one can say it is. But learning to accept death as a part of life is the big step.

Conclusions

Alongside the inspiration which can be discovered within the Himalayas, these mountains also form a landscape which reduces its visitors to desolation and spiritual emptiness. At such high altitudes, and with the frequency of sudden storms and gales, the Himalayas can shred all romantic ideals of mountain landscapes in a matter of seconds.

However, out of those wrecked ideals and emptied expectations, new meaning can emerge. New insights can form. At first they may be as delicate as a dragonfly, but with careful reflection, they may also have the ability to take flight, and serve to create further wisdom within these unforgiving summits. In the case of Larry, Keith and Leon however, that new wisdom has not only served them whilst they recovered from the loss of their friends in those mountains, but it now helps to serve others, through their courses of grief counselling thousands of miles away in New Jersey.

Wisdom which is built upon sure foundations is always able to transcend boundaries — mountain boundaries, other physical boundaries, national and ethnic boundaries. None can prevent the voice of genuine wisdom being shared to all those who are wise enough to listen. As the haiku poet Buson suggests:

> Voices of two bells
> That speak from twilight temples:
> Ah! cool dialogue.

A wisdom shared carefully can be one of the most powerful forces known to humankind. It can bring light and understanding into lives which did not believe such insights were available. For the travellers who have contributed to this chapter, their wisdom has been won in the face of bitter agonies. But from such a genesis, real strength is found. The Himalayas have therefore become one of the most provocative learning environments known to these people. Many of them return simply to breathe the chilled and rarefied air, and to gaze in silent wonder at such enormous, jagged peaks. Others return to learn more of the ancient wisdom of Hindu, Buddhist, Sikh and Bon scriptures, poetry and legend.

> This is the great place of accomplished yogis;
> Here one attains transcendent accomplishments.
> There is no place more wonderful than this,
> There is no place more marvellous than here.
>   (Quoted in Chang 1977, I, 262)

The Himalayas are truly a wonderful and marvellous landscape. But here, the wonder and the marvel never develop without a profound awareness of its accompanying horror and emptiness.

AMOS:
When you really learn to see the Himalayas, wherever you might be out there, you really feel the full majesty of the place in terms of its lighter sides as well as its darker, more disturbing aspects. You only really get to see the light, when you've also seen the darkness. You know? The problems, and the dangers. But at the same time, you have to understand that I find that those darker, gloomier and sinister times can really form the basis for some pretty major insights into a lot of questions which we try and avoid in the West. You know, death, and loss. And personal direction, and a sense of true priorities. It's true. The more you spend time there (in the Himalayas) the more you get to understand how much you can learn, and how much those lessons can change your life for ever.

CHAPTER 6

China

High rises the Eastern Peak
Soaring up to the blue sky.
Among the rocks — an empty hollow,
Secret, still, mysterious!
Uncarved, and unhewn,
Screened by nature with a roof of clouds.

Tao-yün (in Waley 1919, 120)

Ancient wisdom

The writhing, arching dragon is a vital key to every intriguing element of Chinese mountain spirituality. For five thousand years, these ancient mountains have inspired stories of giant and mysterious dragon spirits with an ability to terrify invading armies, and destroy them with cascading rocks, falling trees or gusting, frozen winds. Over the millennia therefore, dragons and mountains have been woven into the Chinese legends and wisdom of national permanence, protection and peace, timeless social order, eternal security, the preservation of human life, and the consignment of that life to death. Even in their physical appearance, the mountains have held a close resemblance to a dragon's lithe and powerful body. Whilst rock formations outline the animal's bones and physical features, rivers and streams are often considered to be equally sacred as the dragon's life blood. Trees, plants and grasses have been interpreted as areas of hair and bristle on the dragon's face and flanks. Even the rain clouds, from which life-giving rains fall, are nothing more than vapour which rises from a dragon's nostrils according to its grace and inclination.

It is also five thousand years since the reign of Shun, a legendary ruler who drew personal inspiration from the ways mountains and dragons could bring wisdom, strength and insight to his sovereign duties. According to the classic Confucian history of China, *Shu Ching*, written in the fifth century BC, Shun's reputation identified all the fundamental requirements of subsequent Chinese leaders.[1] Like the mountain and the dragon, Shun ensured national order and stability. His reign was long and wise, benevolent and reasoned. Also like the dragon and mountain spirits, Shun guarded China from invasion. Chinese life was kept apart from barbarians. It was protected. It received strength from its ancient mountains and their ferocious dragon spirits. China was given divine rights, a deity, and the confidence and fertility to cultivate one of the greatest civilizations ever witnessed by humankind.

To the north of China, it has always been possible to see the peaks and troughs of a dragon's back as it lies across the undulating dry hills and mountains of those landscapes. Where the gentle plains are broken by cliffs and escarpments, clearer views are afforded of the spirit's sides, tail and legs. Toward the east of China, even more mysterious dragon spirits can be discerned and contemplated. Among them, the magnificent T'ai Shan mountain has remained one of the most inspiring peaks in China for over two thousand years.[2] As the highest summit in eastern China, T'ai Shan is first to receive the earliest morning light. As such, it has been associated with new life and resurrection, renewal and the spring season.[3] Even among Chinese rulers, T'ai Shan has been of enduring inspirational value. For the powerful Han dynasty emperor Wu-ti, T'ai Shan was a place of seclusion and profound reverence. In 110 BC, he chose only one attendant to join him on a solemn pilgrimage to the mountain's peak. A few days later, the attendant died, refusing to describe what he had witnessed on that journey with his emperor. But four years later, Wu-ti returned to the mountains. And again in 102 BC. And again four years after that. Then, for a final time, five years later in 93 BC. An explanation for this curious obsession is provided on an inscribed ceremonial mirror dating from the first century AD which suggests that Wu-ti's fascination with T'ai-Shan was part of his quest for immortality:

> If you climb Mount T'ai, you may see the immortal beings.
> They feed on the purest jade, they drink from the springs of
> manna. They yoke the scaly dragons to their carriage, they
> mount the floating clouds. (Quoted in Loewe 1979, 200)

Further south, the dragons change shape again into the form of delicate limestone pinnacles. And in the west, the mountains and dragon shapes transform again, and rise from the valleys of green river basins in massive blocks. Across all these ranges, and over two millennia, groups of hermits developed a unique form of mysticism which sought to discover the most harmonious way of navigating through life's treacherous and tortuous paths.[4] For these early hermits, who lived up to 2600 years ago, this harmonious and mystical Way, or Tao, might simply have meant a particular way of life. Alternatively it may have referred to the ways, habits, laws and operations of the cosmos. Finally, the Way may have been similar to the Buddhist Void: an emptiness never to be filled, but a source from which all life and creativity flows in abundance. All these ideas of life and nature, spirituality and inspiration were collected in the poems of the Tao Te Ching, a book ascribed to Lao-Tsu, when it reached a general audience during the life of Confucius in the fifth century BC.[5]

Throughout the subsequent development of Taoist contemplation, mountains were regarded as natural temples of profound mystery, sublime instruction and compelling intrigue. In the year 320 AD for example, the Taoist sage Ko Hung wrote of the overwhelming physical and spiritual risks of travelling in mountains.[6] In a spiritual quest for so much, it was equally possible to lose everything. On the brightest day, a single moment of lost concentration can destroy any pilgrim. Protective spells and amulets may provide some sense of peace, but all peace is only transient. In the mountains, no guarantee can ever be given that a man, woman or child is completely safe. For Ko Hung, and other Taoists, mountains were therefore landscapes of the most sacred horror. They were landscapes of ultimate dread and regret, humility and longing. They were landscapes of fear.

In a very real sense, the wisdom of Ko Hung, and other Taoist mountain thinkers can be closely compared with the elements of Buddhism which had been accepted into China two hundred years before Ko Hung's birth. Nevertheless, equally clear differences show the unique Taoist contribution to Chinese ancient wisdom. Whilst Buddhism included an aspiration for transcending the painful round of birth and death, Taoism sought to discover the most virtuous route through the everyday problems of human life. Whilst Buddhism sought to spiritually transcend the mountains, Taoism sought to navigate them. Buddhism contemplated the vast, sublime emptiness of precipitous rock walls and cliffs, whilst Taoists tried to find a path along those walls in sympathy with the physical constraints and barriers they discovered on their journeys. But despite these differences, Buddhism developed a significant and sustained contribution to Chinese mountain wisdom. Between the sixth and ninth centuries AD for example, the mysterious Buddhist poet Han-shan provided a valuable and contemplative re-interpretation of the same dangers in mountain exploration which had occupied Ko Hung's attention more than three hundred years earlier.[7] Han-shan's particular area of interest lay in the south-eastern Chinese mountains in the T'ien-t'ai range of modern day Zhejiang Province. From those bare, precipitous walls of rock, he found words of inspiration and spiritual contemplation, words which challenged Han-shan's followers during his life-time, as well as other travellers today.

During that same era, the Buddhist monk Chih-i began to devote his life toward a re-unification of all the various strands of Buddhism. Inspired by the T'ien-t'ai mountains, Chih-i saw that all humankind responds to its environment in very similar ways. Fear is caused by similar types of threat. Laughter is caused by similar forms of surprise and delight. Peace always flows from individual security. Personal inspiration is found in the unique, the vast and the indescribable. And the need for spiritual enlightenment, persuasive wisdom and sustained benevolence is common to all people. Upon these fundamental observations, the T'ien-t'ai school of Buddhism spread throughout that range of mountains. Then throughout the whole of Zhejiang Province, and then beyond. Through China, as well as Japan where it became the equally influential Tendai school of Buddhist wisdom.

But from landscapes of fear and horror, the last two millennia have witnessed an important evolution in the spiritual evaluation of mountains within Chinese wisdom. Increasingly, mountains have been seen as places of retreat, sanctuary and calm in a world of blatantly prevalent corruption, chaos and bureaucracy. The Tang dynasty poet and painter, Wang Wei, for example, described his complete relief and personal joy at being able to leave behind his official post, and retreat to a life of contemplation and creativity in the northern mountains close to modern day Xian. There, he could pursue his art and studies, uninterrupted by the distractions of city life, spiteful competition and personal greed.

Within the early twentieth century too, the poetry of Communist Party leader Mao Tse Tung was written along exactly the same themes of finding sanctuary and inspiration in mountain landscapes. In order to avoid defeat at the hands of the Nationalist Army, Mao led his people on the Long March, the route of which took them within sight of the eastern Tibetan mountains.

> Mountains!
> You pierce the blue sky,
> Without blunting your peaks.

> But for your support,
> Heaven would fall.
>> (Mao Tse Tung 1976, 18)

More recently, travellers have found the mountains in China to be an extremely welcome landscape of retreat from the rapid industrialization which began to flourish in the 1980s. The mountains are therefore an opportunity to consider, from a distance, the social processes of modernization which borrow so much from the western world, but which also dispense with practically all the ancient wisdom accumulated by Chinese spiritual masters over the last five thousand years. From the mountains, modern travellers have a vantage point on this stampede toward industrial improvement. They are able to reflect upon what is being built for the future, and what is being destroyed and lost from the past.

First visits

Among the contributions to this book, one Chinese mountain attracted more first-time visits than any other: Wu-t'ai Shan in China's northern Shanxi province. Known as Five Terrace Mountain, Wu-t'ai Shan is a hand-shaped collection of peaks where a series of five flattened summits radiate from a palm-like grassy plateau over 160 miles wide.[8] Across the entire area, more than three hundred Buddhist temples have been built. Wu-t'ai Shan was therefore a compelling magnet for these contributors. It inspired their Buddhist faith as well as their independent study of the region's spiritual meaning. Each of these people had also read John Blofeld's autobiography, *The Wheel of Life*, in which he described his journey as a western Buddhist to Wu-t'ai Shan immediately before World War II. But whilst each visitor had these themes of study and inspiration in common, they were all able to offer distinctive reflections on the mountain's inspirational meaning. For Kathy and Don, a married couple from Felixstowe, England, their Buddhist inspiration was drawn toward Wu-t'ai Shan after a friend had sent them Blofeld's autobiography as an anniversary present:

KATHY:

> *I think our trip arose from two very happy coincidences. First of all,*
> *we'd been vaguely planning a trip to China for some years ... But when*
> *we'd both read John Blofeld's book, we both knew we had to visit the*
> *area around Wu-t'ai Shan because something told us it would bring*
> *our (Buddhist) faith along, and strengthen it.*

DON:

> *... John Blofeld isn't a widely known Buddhist writer these days,*
> *but some of his descriptions really grabbed our attention in a big*
> *way.*

One passage from Blofeld's work remains particularly ingrained within both these travellers' imaginations:

> We found ourselves looking down on a sight which might
> have inspired the original conception of Shangri-La. The wide,
> grassy plateau lay only a few hundred feet below the pass.
> Wild flowers grew in such extraordinary profusion that the
> old cliché 'carpeted with flowers' seemed the most apt
> description possible. Here and there, nestling against the
> surrounding slopes or clinging to overhanging rocks were
> monasteries, some large enough to house hundreds of monks,
> others small temples with only three or four living rooms ...
> (Blofeld 1972, 121)

Before they arrived at Wu-t'ai Shan, Kathy and Don had spent four days in Hong Kong, Shanghai and Xian before driving out to the mountains. The visual impact of those rapidly expanding cities therefore stood in marked contrast to the simple, inspiring strength of their first encounter with Wu-t'ai Shan.

DON:

> *For me, I've got this memory of standing on the southern terrace of*
> *Wu-t'ai Shan, with the two of us being together, and gazing out over*
> *that amazing succession of valleys and peaks ... And when your mind*
> *relaxes, that whole panorama draws you into it.*

Both travellers saw immediately the power and grace of this landscape which had originally attracted the attention of Chinese Buddhists almost 1700 years ago. The land was more than beautiful. It was more than tranquil. And it was more than peaceful. Wu-t'ai

Shan had about it an aura of calm wisdom, an ancient wisdom which spoke to these visitors in a clear and thoroughly contemporary voice. Originally, the mountain was seen by Buddhist writers as the home of Manjushri, the Bodhisattva spirit of Wisdom.[9] Like all Bodhisattvas, Manjushri is both a spiritual guardian, as well as a guide who can help believers overcome their pain and anxieties. Pilgrims to Wu-t'ai Shan can therefore develop an intimately personal relationship with Manjushri as they become increasingly confident in praying to the spirit, and in receiving the Bodhisattva's inspiration and instruction. Consequently, within only two days of Kathy's arrival at Wu-t'ai Shan, she felt 'overwhelmed' by Manjushri's protective and inspirational presence:

KATHY:

I definitely felt a presence of wisdom there (Wu-t'ai Shan). And I'd definitely say that feeling matched everything I'd previously read about Manjushri.

Having established that presence of wisdom, Manjushri used the memories which Kathy and Don had formed earlier in their brief tour of Chinese cities to contrast those urban landscapes with the landscape of wisdom before them.

KATHY:

I'd never felt anything like that before in my life. And to begin with I was frightened. But, patiently, I felt these questions being put into my head. And only when I fully understood the first question was another one put into my mind.

DON:

But the eerie thing was that although all that was going on in silence as we stood there on the terrace, those same questions were being gently put into my head too ...

The first of these questions concerned the dignity of individuals living in modern Chinese cities. Within their imaginations, Kathy and Don were shown the crowded apartments of Hong Kong, Shanghai and Xian. They were reminded of what they had read and seen of increasing traffic pollution, domestic violence, drug addiction and adolescent alcoholism. Then they were drawn back to Wu-t'ai Shan. How much more dignified could those lives be if they were able to live and work in landscapes like this? How much potential would those city people have to expand their lives if they lived here, instead of their tiny apartments, crowded streets and factories? From Wu-t'ai Shan, the human spirit can soar. But as the Chinese government faces rapidly increasing urban unemployment, it has finally begun to recognize this need to move people away from the cities. Consequently, in 1995, the government announced new plans to return 150 million unemployed workers and their families to the rural districts. However, those noble intentions have not yet been supported with the necessary new homes, new roads or new schools. And with Chinese inflation approaching 30% in 1995, the costs for such projects are already being questioned by government advisors.

The wisdom and clarity of Manjushri's words therefore continue to be extremely relevant to Chinese social and economic trends. And as they continued to listen to Manjushri, Kathy and Don were filled with complete astonishment. But the extraordinary value of Manjushri's words are further emphasised in the following contribution by another traveller, a photographer from Dayton, Ohio. Ian visited Wu-t'ai Shan the previous year to Kathy and Don, and yet his own experiences of the mountain are equally insightful and socially astute:

IAN:
> ... I felt new questions being put into my mind which I'd never thought of before ... And what's more, they were given to me in words which, although I understood them OK, they weren't exactly the sort of phrases I'd have used for myself ... But there was this recurring phrase of 'natural justice.' The natural justice which obliges us to conserve areas like Wu-t'ai Shan. Yes, we can live there. And yes, we can build there. All that's OK. But you have to do it sensitively. That's the key. It's OK for China to expand and try and improve the lives of its people. Of course it is. But what Manjushri was trying to tell me was there's a right and a wrong way of doing that development. And at the moment, China's making the same mistakes as the West. All for the sake of short-term gain ... Whereas Manjushri is a spirit of very, very long-term wisdom. That's the key difference.

To add further emphasis to the clarity and persistence of these questions and observations offered by Manjushri, two more travel experiences may be identified. Julian and Joe are history students, originally from Felixstowe, England. They too are practising Buddhists, and they also visited Wu-t'ai Shan without realizing they would receive the wisdom of the ancient Bodhisattva spirit:

JULIAN:

At first, I thought I was daydreaming because I was so tired from all the travelling we'd done getting there (Wu-t'ai Shan). But this one phrase just dreamt its way into my head. 'These mountains are entrusted to the leaders' ... And it took me a few minutes to work it all out. But China has almost no history of conservation within the twentieth century. Mao wore the land out within a few years. And even now, they're (the Chinese government) pushing ahead with some potentially dangerous projects without any acknowledgement of the conservation ... So Manjushri was right ...

JOE:

But thinking about all that later, I just wondered why Manjushri had chosen us to speak to, and not someone else. I mean, we're not journalists, or television people, who could make a big deal from those experiences ... but I think we both try and tell people about that issue now, whereas we might not have bothered before ... and maybe taking part in this (book) is all a part of that bigger connection with Manjushri.

All these Buddhists have found at least two major benefits from their encounters with Manjushri's voice on Wu-t'ai Shan. First, their own spiritual practices of study and meditation have been given a strengthening confidence and individual purpose. Whilst each of these people conceded that their meditations had 'lacked a real focus' (Ian) before the visit to Wu-t'ai Shan, or they had been 'less than regular' (Don), Manjushri seemed to gently remind them of the personal value of those meditations. It was worth making the effort to find time for contemplation. It is worth working at. It will repay patient attention.

The second theme which Manjushri left with these travellers was the need to reflect not only on the particular costs which China is suffering within its current programme of development, but also the broader parallels in other countries. Other cities in which people are crowded beyond the point where their individual dignity can cope with the social pressures. Other towns where the long-term wisdom of Manjushri has been ignored in favour of short-term advantage, short-term competition and long-term cost. None of the people who contributed to this section had any professional or previous commitment to these questions of industrial expansion and the implications which ensue at every level of society. And yet, these people were chosen by a voice of wisdom who transcends all immediate concerns, but who can nevertheless gently weave those concerns into a message of timeless grace. Immediate problems can illustrate broader, universal pictures. Specific case studies can enlighten a listener to the full power and weight of eternal words. In the case of Manjushri, those wise words clearly bear repetition. An ancient voice is sufficiently concerned about the social problems of modern China that visitors are given these words to take with them on their further journeys. The words of these travellers are therefore of incalculable power and wisdom. They must be learned. They must be listened to. They must be acted upon.

Subsequent visits

Among experienced Buddhist climbers, the spiritual voices of other Bodhisattvas have been heard on other Chinese peaks. To the west of China for example, in Sichuan Province, the terrifying precipices of O-mei Shan have been known to resonate with the words of Samanta-bhadra: the benevolent spirit, who rides a white elephant across O-mei Shan's highest slopes.[10] For the pilgrims who are sufficiently coura-geous to climb to those heights, Samantabhadra will willingly perform acts of benevolence. He may heal wounds which climbers have suf-fered on their ascent. He may also offer food, or water, or directions to travellers who have lost their way. As in the following illustration, encounters with this sacred benevolence can leave the individual sublimely grateful, enlightened and at peace:

FREDDY:
A group of us were camping there (O-mei Shan, in 1993) and some-thing had gone desperately wrong with our supply logistics. Nothing had got through for days. So there we were. Completely stuck. Frozen cold, and starving ... Twelve hours of this utter misery passed during which we formulated new plans to get food out to us, all of which were totally impractical ... Until I thought one of the others told me, 'Don't be so foolish.' Those were the words. And, of course I looked to see who it was. But it was only then, when I realized the voice was inside my head. And the very next moment, I spotted a tiny procession of traders making their way through the valley, and we were saved.

When Freddy heard that voice, he had never heard of Samantabha-dra. Indeed, following a recent personal crisis, his newly found spiritual path within Buddhism was only in its infancy. However, a year later, when he was told of the Bodhisattvic spirit of O-mei Shan, Freddy immediately connected the two experiences:

FREDDY:

> *Of course you can't prove scientifically that the voice I heard was Samantabhadra. But all the same, in my own mind I'm satisfied to make that connection ... What I heard was something wholly otherworldly. A voice which spoke clearly and gently even in a crisis and drew my attention to the answer ... The voice was gentle, but the more I think about it now, the more I'm filled with complete humility and astonishment ... And I think I learned more about the sheer power of Chinese Buddhism in that moment, than I've ever learned since.*

As with Manjushri on Wu-t'ai Shan, the spirit of Samantabhadra on O-mei Shan is an eternal voice of responsibility. Manjushri spoke of a responsibility which rests with all humankind, at all levels of society, for Chinese industrial development and its social consequences. On O-mei Shan, Samantabhadra clearly felt responsible for Freddy and his companions to the extent where he was led to a source of food supplies to save his camping expedition. Similarly, other travellers, on the southern mountain of Chiu-hua Shan spoke of finding a distinctive voice of responsibility which they later recognized as belonging to the Bodhisattva Kshitigarbha whose task it is to journey into hell and rescue as many sinners as she can find from their eternal punishment. By prayerfully ascending through Chiu-hua Shan's maze of gorges and rock-walls, pilgrims may be able to attract Kshitigarbha's attention so she can save them if ever they descent into the underworld. Alternatively, Kshitigarbha may be requested to rescue the soul of a pilgrim's ancestor. As with all Bodhisattva spirits, Kshitigarbha's words can also bring wisdom and insight to a climber regarding a particular anxiety within their lives. For Hillary, a policewoman from Ohio, USA, Kshitigarbha's voice was one of intimacy, responsibility and breathtaking strength:

HILLARY:

> *I'd reached a point in my life when I needed space to get right away from things going on with me ... And through various opportunities and coincidences I had the chance to go climbing in southern China ... And we all got out to Chiu-hua, which isn't that big at just over 4400 feet, but it left a real hold on me because of the way I felt myself sat down and taught to see the beauty of that wilderness in incredible*

*detail. I mean, I was taught to look and see ... But the invisible hand
which led me was just as incredible. Only later on, I realized that it
must have been Kshitigarbha because all the pieces fitted together so
well.*

Hillary visited Chiu-hua in a state of mind which she described as
'depressed and disenchanted' with almost every part of her life. With
the benefit of hindsight however, she suggested that was the 'perfect
state of consciousness' from which to receive the wisdom of Kshitigarbha.

HILLARY:
*I know myself pretty well. And if I'd been feeling feisty or over-
confident, I just wouldn't have listened to Kshitigarbha ... But the way
I felt, I was ready to be picked up. And out there, in that raw, powerful, amazing mountain wilderness, away from crowds, and problems at
home, that was the perfect spot for it to happen. Perfect place and perfect timing! ... But also, it was what I was told, and how I felt after-
wards that I associated with Kshitigarbha's spirit because not only did
they match what I needed to hear, but they've also struck a real big deal
with people who I'd never have thought would have been interested in
that kind of message.*

Hillary is therefore convinced that she has become a messenger for
Kshitigarbha. A messenger brought from the West to receive a distinctive message from an eternal voice of the East. Subsequently, Hillary
believes, she has been granted the safety and personal confidence to
share that wisdom with friends, family and work colleagues in Ohio,
as well as on her travels:

HILLARY:
*I guess the main thing I was told, was about the way China's destroy-
ing its land at this amazing, frightening rate. I mean, they're pulling
down mountains which have been around for millions of years ... But
the words I always pass on to people, and which made such an impression on me was the expression, 'Future generations will judge you.'*

When she was given these words, Hillary only understood them as
a voice of environmental conservation. A voice of concern from Kshitigarbha for the destruction caused to Chinese mountain landscapes.
However, more recently, she has found further use for those same
words within a much wider set of social circumstances. A year after

her return from China, Hillary was asked to take part in a review meeting on crime prevention techniques among adolescents. When asked to comment for that review, Hillary began her reply with the words she had received from Kshitigarbha on Chiu-hua. A message from a Chinese mountain Bodhisattva finding contemporary relevance within late twentieth century Ohio. A transcendent wisdom with very particular implications:

HILLARY:

It stopped the meeting! Because I used those words 'future generations will judge you,' at the start of what I had to stay. And then I used it again at the end. And there was this awful silence which people later told me was the turning point of that review. Before then, the academics and criminologists were getting too much of their way. But after my little speech, it seemed as though the cops working the street were given far more credibility ... and eventually I was pretty pleased with the outcome.

Experienced Taoist climbers and walkers found an equally powerful set of encounters with the Chinese mountains which had been dedicated to their spiritual path. Of those mountains, T'ai Shan's inspiration attracted more return visits among these contributors than any other.[11] Located in the northeastern Shandong Province, T'ai Shan is relatively accessible to western travellers since it is located between the principal cities of Beijing and Shanghai. But beyond that accessibility, T'ai Shan has inspired some of the most sublime verse within Chinese literature.

For Perry and Joan for example, two linguistic translators originally from Toronto, Ontario, their abiding appreciation of T'ai Shan has always been shaped through the words of Tu Fu: a Tang Dynasty poet regarded by many as one of China's finest writers:

PERRY:

T'ai Shan isn't the highest mountain in the world, that's for sure. I think it's a little over 5000 feet. But that doesn't matter half as much as the power which that place has assumed within the Taoist consciousness ...

JOAN:

If you're there at dawn or at sunset, its subtlety can blow you away ... in one sense you can see it all before you, but if you really look hard, you realize the inspiration which comes from that place can only be

glimpsed at, even if you could stay there a life time ... But the best
we've found are the words of Tu Fu, because he's caught a lot of that
gracious aura so beautifully.

To illustrate that point, Joan read aloud from the following extract
of Tu Fu's verse, 'Gazing from Afar at the Sacred Peak.' Although this
version was read from Joan's private note book, another translation
has been published in Kroll (1983, 228-230):

> With what can I compare the Great Peak?
> Over the surrounding provinces, its blue-green hue never
>   disappears from sight.
> Infused by the Shaper of Forms with the soaring power of
>   divinity,
> Shaded and sunlit, its slopes divide night from day.

JOAN:

I could read on and on, but that shows what I'm talking about. T'ai
Shan's a mountain experience you carry with you for ever. And we just
love to go back there whenever we need to re-charge our batteries and
we need to get in touch with the classical spirit of Taoism again.

For Perry and Joan, as well as other travellers to T'ai Shan, there
are two ways to see the mountain. One is to join other tourists and
pilgrims who climb the snaking stairway of over one thousand steps
leading to the South Gate of Heaven: a terracotta red coloured arch
with a dazzling gold roof.

PERRY:

Seeing T'ai Shan is always an awesome experience if only for all the
stairs!

JOAN:

But they're there for a purpose. You don't just climb those stairs like
an athlete. You climb a few. Think for a while. Gaze around you. Talk
to other travellers. And then carry on some more ... If it takes you all
day, then you're probably doing it right.

The second way to see T'ai Shan is to find an area of woodland or
rocks away from the tourists. In that temporary seclusion, it is possible
to gaze in wonder to the far distant horizon, across a panorama which

Above: Sunset on Uluru (Ayers Rock),
Australia. (Image Colour Library)

Right: Detail of Uluru
(Image Colour Library)

Above: Mount Fuji and Lake Motosuko, Japan. (Image Colour Library)

Top Right: Mount Fuji with trees, Japan. (Image Colour Library)

Below right: Tateyama and Murodo Plateau, Japan.
(Toyofumi Mori/Image Bank)

Top left: Annapurna and Gangapurna, Nepal. (David Patterson/Tony Stone)

Below Left: Bridge with prayer-flags, Lhasa, Tibet. (Harold Sund/Image Bank)

Right: Lijiang River, Guilin Hills, China. (Ke Lin Jin/Image Bank)

Below: Guilin Hills with giant banyan tree, China. (Zhen Ge Peng/Image Bank)

Opposite top: Guilin Hills with paddy fields, China. (Paul Slaughter/Image Bank)

Opposite below left: The Thousand Steps to Heaven, Taishan, Shandong Prov., China. (Peng Zheng/CTP/Image Bank)

Opposite below right: Mount Tienzhi, Zhangjiajie, Hunan Prov., China. (CTP/Image Bank)

Above: Huangshan (Yellow Mountains), Anhui Prov., China (Bob Elsdale/Image Bank)

Right: Huangshan, China. (Jun Ling/Image Bank)

has inspired and eluded the finest Chinese painters and writers, teachers and disciples. First-time visitors almost invariably try and draw conclusions and lessons from such scenery. But with more experience of T'ai Shan, subsequent visits to the mountain teach travellers simply to accept. Accept the subtle colours and lines of the landscape — the changing hues caught by natural light and cloud shapes — the voices of thousands of pilgrims who are satisfied to arrive with wordless questions, and who remain completely satisfied to depart with wordless answers.

For Waylon, a teacher and practising Taoist from near Tulsa, Oklahoma, his five journeys to T'ai Shan have all helped him to build from these simple, eternal truths toward a Taoist faith which draws daily inspiration from the mountain, but which also provides a daily wisdom for his everyday life:

WAYLON:

For anyone who's not thought too much about Taoism, I know it can seem real naïve. But when you do give it some thought, and when you spend time in places like T'ai Shan which are dedicated to Taoist teaching, it falls into place ... For me, T'ai Shan can be thought about at many different levels. It can be seen as just a big rock. It's also a sanctuary. It can be a barrier to struggle over. It can be a public place, or a private one too ... Many, many aspects of the mountain which mirror real life.

Waylon continued by recalling many occasions, as a teacher, when his Taoist beliefs have helped him resolve confrontations with his pupils and their parents or relations. But instead of trying to match their aggression with his own assertiveness, Waylon has tried to defuse the incident by listening attentively. Trying to discern ways in which he can satisfy the individuals. Sometimes, he concedes, it is simply not possible. However, the more Waylon pursues his Taoist meditations, and the more he reflects upon the personal meaning which T'ai Shan has for him, the more often he finds ways of amicably resolving such confrontations:

WAYLON:

It might sound strange to talk about using a mountain in everyday life, but that's pretty much how it is. There are so many lessons to be learnt from T'ai Shan. And they're all very practical as well as mystical ... Take for example, the mountain as a barrier. Something to climb. Well, just like any other barrier, or confrontation, you take it slowly and

Opposite top: Mount Bromo, view from Borobudur, Indonesia. (Denis Waugh/ Tony Stone)

Below left: Borobudur Buddhist temple, Indonesia. (Image Colour Library)

Below right: Krakatoa, Java, Indonesia. (Guido Alberto Rossi/Image Bank) *patiently. Every once in a while, you stop and take stock of where you've got to. You wonder how you feel about heading up the next stage. And then you do it ...*

In a very similar way, two Taoist climbers from Felixstowe, England, Gavin and Dale, also find an alignment between the mystical qualities of a Chinese mountain, and its practical implications. In the following illustration, both men are recalling their three visits to Heng Shan in Shanxi Province. A towering block of heavily weathered gorges, ridges and cliffs, Heng Shan has been one of the most valued of all Chinese mountains among Taoist believers for over two thousand years:

GAVIN:

The first time we went there, we'd only just got into Taoism as a religious faith, so it was a bit difficult to take everything in.

DALE:

But there definitely was something very strange about the place. As if it was on another planet ... But after three visits, and with a fourth being planned, I'd say Heng Shan is now the most important thing about our faith ... in terms of having a real, solid memory to think about when you're trying to understand Taoist meditations ...

GAVIN:

But also at work, whereas you might be surrounded by people losing their temper, say in the shipping offices where we work, you can think back to Heng Shan and always feel really, really humbled by that complete massiveness. And that memory actually helps you to keep your head ... You feel humbled by the place, and I think that helps you deal with problems at work more carefully and in their proper context.

One of the distinctive themes within all these conversations has been a sustained preference by Taoists to visit the Chinese mountains which have been most closely associated with their literary heritage. In the same way, Buddhists have visited mountains which have been aligned with their own faith. The only exception to this preference was demonstrated by Jade, a Zen Buddhist believer and railway information officer from London:

JADE:

> *For me, I always say I'm a Zen Buddhist. But that doesn't mean I'm not willing to learn from other faiths too ... And I've actually had four trips to various mountain areas in China now, and on each time, they've taught me something really valuable about my own faith ... On the last visit I made to T'ai Shan, I met so many Zen believers, as well as Taoists, and they taught me so much, that it really became an amazingly educational time for me.*

To illustrate this educational value, Jade was able to quote and explain a series of Zen haiku poems which she had learned at T'ai Shan, and which captured the essence of her repeated visits to that mountain:

> As bell tones fade,
> Blossom scents take up the ringing:
> Evening shade!
> (Basho)

JADE:

> *I remember walking around at the foot of the steps at T'ai Shan's South Gate of Heaven, just trying to reconcile it all in my mind, when all of a sudden, I was aware of this amazing silence. Just for a moment, there was a perfect, delicious silence ... and later when I was telling someone about it, they showed me that poem. In other words, in that beautiful silence as the bell tone had faded, the aroma of the trees and plants brought their own subtle beauty to the moment in a really wonderful way.*

> *The skylark*
> *Sings in the field:*
> *Free of all things.*
> *(Basho)*

> *Into the cold night*
> *I spoke aloud ... But the voice was*
> *No voice I knew*
> *(Otsuji)*

JADE:

> *Zen is all about finding enlightenment and wisdom in single moments. Living in the now, and focusing on the moment. And these two poems*

sum up the need to respond to precious moments which you find in really powerful places like T'ai Shan. Places where you just need to look all around and take it all in. You never do. And you miss most of it. But still, to hear a bird's singing, and to treasure the moment. Or to find thoughts going through your head which you'd never come across before ... Those are amazing learning experiences. And you need to keep hold of them in your memory and really think them through and explain them to others ... There's an amazing power to those Chinese mountains which a lot of people haven't found elsewhere in the world. So if you're able to pass that power on, in whatever way, then you've got to take that opportunity while it's there for you.

Turning points

T'ai Shan's South Gate of Heaven is familiar as a place of pilgrimage and reflection to many of the people who contributed to this chapter. It has inspired and encouraged, informed and sharpened the conviction and joyous experience of their individual faiths. But one man found the South Gate to be a profound spiritual turning point as well. A sacred place on a sacred mountain where his fundamentalist Christian beliefs were examined, challenged and completely transformed 'with the compassionate grace of a true spiritual master' (George).

GEORGE:
I was making my steady way up the stairs there on T'ai Shan, and I'd stopped for a bit of a breather. And as I looked around me, I saw this tiny, stooping, old man. Less than five feet tall, with two younger men who I assumed to be his sons ... We'd never met before, but the old man smiled at me so warmly that I felt drawn across to say hello, and to pass the time.

Each of the three Chinese visitors was able to speak in faltering English, and George fell into amicable conversation with the two younger men about their ascent toward the South Gate. To begin with, it felt like any other occasional discussion between travellers who enjoy sharing a mutual interest. But whilst the two younger men spoke openly about their feelings toward T'ai Shan, and about their annual pilgrimage to the mountain with their father, the elderly man simply remained in silence. Only when George turned to glance at him, was he able to appreciate fully the power and clarity of the old man's dazzling brown eyes. From deep within a wrinkled and darkly tanned face, those were the eyes of an astonishing but gentle charisma. A compelling grace and a smiling curiosity.

GEORGE:

I'd never met anyone who looked so wise and completely content in all my life ... As an evangelical Christian, I'd always believed what I'd been told that there's always something missing from other religions, and that fundamentalist Christianity was the only true path to salvation ... But in one glance from his eyes, I saw that he had something which I was still searching for. In just that moment. It was incredible. In one look, something told me, I still had a lot to learn about what makes a religious faith work for people.

George was invited to join the small family group as they made their way up the stairway. He accepted immediately. The two younger men stepped purposefully ahead, leaving George beside their father. After a moment in silence, the old man spoke to George for the first time.

GEORGE:

He asked religious questions which I'd never come across before, but which I saw were immediately worth thinking about. Did I think T'ai Shan could heal people of their worries? Did T'ai Shan inspire me to tell others about the place: about its beauty and its gentleness? ... They were great questions, but I just had to say I couldn't answer them.

The elderly man then stopped again, and told his sons, in Chinese, to carry on walking, and invited George to join him while he rested against the wall beside the stone stairway. George wanted to listen, so he was pleased to stay there. In that moment, his ambition to climb the full stairway was no longer important. It was far more important to listen and to learn.

The father began by explaining to George why he asked his sons to bring him back to T'ai Shan each summer. The mountain, he explained, was a place of retreat. A place of meditation. Did George have such places at home, where he could go to draw on nature's spiritual strength? George had to confess he didn't. The man's wise old eyes smiled in quiet understanding.

GEORGE:

And that's how we carried on. The man with his thought-provoking questions, never telling me too much, never making any rash statements. Just asking these amazing questions which challenged me, and which really grabbed my attention ...

Questions about the ways in which George's faith led him to reflect on social trends. Questions about George's interpretations of the passing pilgrims: their aspirations; their questions; their dilemmas; their doubts and their inspirations. Each new question patiently and quietly followed George's hesitant, uncertain answers. Each new question taking George a little further along a completely new and wider spiritual path beyond the confinements of literal Biblical interpretation. It was an educational journey of the imagination which built on that Biblical wisdom, but which also identified strong, ancient links with complementary eternal truths. George was therefore continually aware that the conversation was being led with the piercing clarity of a high, noonday sun.

GEORGE:

Slowly but surely, I was gently being made aware of the limitations in my narrow Christian faith, but also the potential of that faith to grow and lead me into a whole new set of questions ... I saw that fundamentalist Christianity was no more a panacea for all ills than any other faith which based itself on wisdom and love, and the worship of God.

Had George ever felt there is an increasing urgency to try and help others discover more in their faith? Yes. George had. But finding the time, and the opportunity, was always a problem. As a busy building inspector, time was always his enemy. The old man smiled again. 'Is time your enemy, or is it the confidence you need to share your faith?,' he asked. Like many religious believers in the West, George was always hesitant about discussing his beliefs outside his church or home.

GEORGE:

The old man said nothing when I'd told him that. He just looked away for a moment. Still smiling. And he gazed back down the stairway to look at all the other pilgrims puffing and panting their way up toward us. And, of course, the answer was so simple. You don't always need to use words to help someone along. An outstretched arm can often be more helpful than a mini-sermon.

Had George thought about the sacred qualities of time? Another fascinating question. No, George hadn't. So his elderly companion explained. Time is sacred because it is so scarce but so immensely valuable. The time to dwell on spiritual wisdom is indeed a rare treasure. But time is also sacred because in just a single moment, a piece of wisdom can change a person's life for ever. They may suddenly find a great urgency to tell others of their experience and insight. They may also find that time has become transformed into this rare and wondrous and sacred resource. Time to learn is always scarce. Time to share with others is equally limited. Time is therefore sacred because it must be sought out and treasured. It must be allocated for essential priorities. Time must be devoted to oneself and to others, to study and meditation, to laughter and the joyous appreciation of life itself.

The conversation continued for a further two or three hours. At each stage, George was patiently led toward an expanded awareness of human need. A wider context in which he could understand the diversity of contrasting spiritual paths. A heightened awareness of the need for tolerance and compassion, sensitivity and openmindedness. An understanding that now, as never before, there is a time of increasingly profound need where people all over the world desperately search for a set of values with which they can make sense of the world. Values which can be sufficiently flexible to deal with life's increasing transience. Values which can help an individual to understand why personal crises will always take place. A form of contemporary wisdom which draws people away from the attrition of petty spite and unproductive competitiveness, toward a more inspiring appreciation of the cosmos as a sacred creation. An inspired belief which draws daily from that divine beauty — from the subtle shades of dawn to the more vibrant sunset colours of dusk. All these things were a complete new discovery to George. But through the gentle and patient way in which he felt invited to reflect upon them, George agreed it was the single most powerful and moving spiritual experience he has ever encountered. Whilst the high emotion of charismatic Christian celebration meetings were loud and joyous, George's meeting with the elderly Chinese father had been far more personal, mind-expanding, profound, and ultimately, more valuable.

From the way in which George described this single encounter on T'ai Shan, it was clear that the meeting has left an extraordinary impression on his spiritual life. Now, George has a much clearer understanding that no single faith has a monopoly on truth. At best, it will be a contribution to humankind's quest for spiritual inspiration and understanding. Now, George also has a much clearer vision of himself as a pilgrim. An apprentice. A student who will never learn all the answers, but whose imagination and curiosity have been ignited sufficiently to yearn for a greater appreciation of sacred meaning. Finally, George has a far greater understanding of the sacred meaning of time. He knows that now is the time to try and sensitively help others to learn what he learnt at T'ai Shan. Not necessarily through formal seminars, sermons or lectures, but through occasional acts of assistance. Through sensitivity and compassion. And through an attempt to emulate the personality and easy-going grace of the elderly father he met on the steps leading to the South Gate.

Conclusions

The experiences and insights which have been recorded in this chapter contain a rich diversity of inspiration and ancient Chinese wisdom. It is a wisdom which retains an undeniable relevance today. And it contains a range of eternal lessons which can still be continually learned, contemplated and shared.

IAN:

> *For most people, China only means communism, or, more recently, capital investment and construction. But if you spend any time there, and if you visit the mountains, the wisdom and gentleness of it all just pours over you. You just need to give it time. Look, listen and wonder at it all.*

Hillary's conclusions were closely comparable:

HILLARY:

> *There are so many threads to Chinese wisdom that you can only pick up on a very few of them. But I'll always tell anyone that I'm a changed woman every time I go out to those mountains there. To Chiu-hua, or around there ... At one level you can take it in just privately. Like a meditation. But then you can also use it. And, for me, if you can find a wisdom which works in twentieth century United States, then you've got to use it! ... For me, the voice and inspiration of the Kshiti-garbha Bodhisattva blows my mind every time. It takes you to another*

dimension. But I feel so privileged to have been spoken to, or touched, or call it what you will. But what ever you want to say, it works. And that's always the test. It's a discipline to me, so it's helped me. It's really inspired a lot of my friends, and other people. And everyone has found it's brought meaning to their lives.

For all these people, their experience of wisdom which they have found within Chinese mountains has been more of a dialogue than a single lesson of received instruction. During their time at the mountains, all these travellers felt able to examine the mystical voices they heard, or the inspiration they received. Even at the initial stage in their education into Chinese wisdom, a dialogue was taking place — an exchange between sources of wisdom and insight, and novice visitors eager to learn. Subsequently, these dialogues have continued. At home, in Europe or North America, each traveller has reflected upon their experiences. They have read more on these subjects. They have thought more deeply. They have even sought to apply this fresh wisdom to their lives at work and leisure. At each moment of this more recent experience, their knowledge of Chinese wisdom has been further examined. Its integrity has been probed and scrutinized. It has been discussed and questioned among colleagues, friends, family and neighbours. A fresh, modern audience has therefore developed for this most ancient of wisdom. New ways of interpretation. Fresh questions to bring before this historical understanding which maintains a sparkling contemporary relevance. Simple truths which remain breathtakingly valuable in a bewildering, shifting and incalculably complex modern world.

If there is a single common theme to all these lessons, it is the dignity of the individual. A reminder of individual integrity. The need for individuals to have a voice which is listened to with sensitivity and compassion. A need for governments and other authority groups to build and develop their countries in collaboration with the fundamental requirements of their people, rather than in direct confrontation with those needs.

JADE:

I definitely believe these Bodhisattva spirits should be listened to because they seem to strike a very interesting balance between transcendent themes of compassion and love, and a more specific need which you see all over China today ... There are cities which are growing up there which are no better, and sometimes a lot worse, than in the West. And whole families are being crammed into tiny, tiny apartments and

*told to get on with it ... So what those Bodhisattvas are saying is 'hold
on a minute and think of the costs and the damage you're doing.'*

*Maybe there are ways of gaining the same degree of economic devel-
opment but without squashing human beings so blatantly ... It's a
message worth saying.*

There is a definite urgency to these eternal voices. From the apparent tranquillity of Chinese mountains, cries of warning are being
raised which need practical attention now. Guardian spirits living in
some of China's most sublime landscapes are identifying problems
which could completely change their country's spiritual and physical
maps within a matter of a few short years. Examples of such problems
are numerous. In April 1995, Wen Wei Po, a Communist newspaper in
Hong Kong, described the need for a comprehensive eradication of
corruption across the whole nation.[12] Almost every economic report
being issued in the mid-1990s confirms that China's government has
insufficient control over its economic growth. The current-account
deficit is destined to continue rising. Consumer panic-buying is an
increasing social phenomenon. In Hong Kong, there are rising pressures on the authorities to develop social-welfare schemes.[13] Each of
these problems is serious. But together, they represent a major cause
for concern over China's future. Given the magnitude of these concerns, it is no surprise that so many of the travellers who contributed
to this chapter have described the words of warning and despair they
have received from the Bodhisattva spirits.

GEORGE:

*It's amazing that everyone I've spoken to who's visited these moun-
tains, and has gone there with an open mind, ready to listen to this
inspiration, has always come home with something which has changed
their lives ... Whether it was me, unexpectedly meeting that amazingly
wise sage, or others who've heard the spirits talking about these things
... there's definitely something incredible going on in those mountains,
and I just hope upon hope that these questions and messages are listened to, and something's done about them ... before it's too late.*

CHAPTER 7

South and Southeast Asia

Now man possesses insight and, on departing from this
world, he will attain the world beyond in accordance with
his degree of insight.

Satapatha Brahmana X.6.3.1

Ancient wisdom

The sacred mountains of south and southeast Asia are a composite of many worlds. They have inspired an incalculable variety of sacred visions, all of which have been interpreted and re-interpreted, refined and reflected-upon over the last three thousand years. Not surprisingly, the physical landscapes which contributed to these diverse spiritual insights are as varied and numerous as their corresponding geographies of visionary wisdom and enlightenment. South of the Himalayas, the Indian mountains bordering the Deccan plateau are a combination of open, gently undulating foothills, moist pastureland and high, rain-swept peaks. Further south, on the island of Sri Lanka, steep escarpments of ancient gneiss and schist rocks are covered with tropical jungles. Along the southeast Asian peninsula, the valleys of the Irawaddy, Salween and Mekong rivers separate the mountain ranges which curve away from the Tibetan plateau in the north as they smooth out under more rainforests. But among the islands of Sumatra, Java, Borneo and the Philippines, mountains soar once again in their volcanic magnificence and sacred vitality.

For Buddhists, Vulture Peak in northern India has maintained a profound spiritual importance since the days when the Buddha gave a series of sermons there. On the slopes of that rocky hill, pilgrims still contemplate those original insights described by the Master — insights which have subsequently travelled the world, consistently maintaining their integrity. A wisdom of enduring strength and disarming simplicity. A wisdom which is learned more through silent reflection than by intellectual study. A universal wisdom, yet one which developed in its early years among small groups of devotees, and curious on-lookers, in places which, then, were only of local importance, such as Vulture Peak.

Just as Buddhist disciples founded further sites of sacred meaning on other mountains within their own localities which looked similar to Vulture Peak, the third century BC saw Hindus also starting to borrow from mountain symbolism, inspired by the summit of Mount Kailas on the Tibetan Plateau. Quite simply, Kailas is the breathtaking abode of Lord Shiva, one of the principal deities within the Hindu pantheon of gods (see Chapter 6). At his side, Shiva is accompanied by his wife, Parvati, and their two sons, Karttikeya and the elephant headed Ganesha. For those Hindu believers who were unable to complete the pilgrimage to Kailas however, local mountains were invested with the same towering spirituality and traditional wisdom with its reverence for all life and its appreciation of natural cycles. The virtue of compassion and the wisdom of adhering to lessons described within ancient texts such as the Mahabharata and the Ramayana. One of the most frequently visited of these local hills in which the inspiration of Mount Kailas has been invested is Arunachala, the Mountain of Light, in southern India. Within the Skanda Purana text for example, there are no less than five hymns devoted to Arunachala, each line of which emphasises the fact that Shiva's eternal spirit has become manifest. Within the heart of this humble looking rock, the mighty Shiva lives and observes, ready to punish and destroy:

> This is the holy place! Of all, Arunachala is the most sacred.
> This is the heart of the world. Know it to be the secret and
> sacred heart of Shiva. In this place, He always abides as the
> majestic Arunachala. (Adapted from Sri Ramana Maharshi,
> 1946, 8)

The mythical glory of Arunachala is re-emphasized each year in November, after the rains have abated, when pilgrims converge to worship Shiva while he is represented as a phallus of fire: the source of divine power, and the pillar of spiritual strength for the coming year.

Jains too are able to trace an inspirational history during which mountains and sacred hills have served to focus their meditations on abstaining from any form of violence. That inspirational history of contemplation within mountain landscapes also accommodates the

Jains' discipline of adhering to a controlled and sensitive diet which is composed in harmony with their beliefs extolling the most profound reverence and celebration of nature. In the north of India for example, Mount Abu is the site of Jain temples carved with extraordinary intricacy. Circular ceilings present the visitor with a mandala: a perfectly round collection of symbols and pictures on which they can contemplate the interwoven harmonies within the cosmos which were identified and taught by the Jain Tirthankaras, or saviour teachers. These are characterized by a human reliance on divine inspiration and natural chains of predator and prey, flora and fauna, birth, death and re-birth. Similarly, to the south, Shravana Belagola is another major centre for Jain pilgrimage, drawing its visitors with the prospect of contemplating the magnificently hewn statue of Bahubali, son of the first saviour teacher.

Along the southeast Asian peninsula, mountains were regarded as sacred territories as early as three thousand years ago. As sources of water, and therefore of agricultural fertility, mountains were the subject of reverence and ritual celebration. But as burial sites, these same mountains inspired more profound questions of death, impermanence and the fragile balance between humankind and the forces which could destroy fields, crops, families, and, on occasions, entire generations living in villages which were swept away by floods and landslides falling from neighbouring slopes. Given this reverence in which mountains were perceived, ancient peninsula civilizations such as the Cambodian Funan people of the second century AD, enthroned their sovereigns and emperors on these mountain summits. Indeed, the word Funan can be translated as either Sacred Mountain, or King of the Mountains. Similarly, the Pyu kings of seventh century AD Burma constructed their royal palaces as replicas of the goddess Indra's residence on the mythical Mount Meru.[1] Consequently, the Pyu royalty were obliged to act with the wisdom of the gods. A wisdom of balance and harmony. Thus for example, the number of ministers and court wives could never exceed those believed to have served within Indra's palace. With such attention to the details of universal harmony, Burma was believed by its people to act as a cosmic centre, a land of divine right, a kingdom of destiny, a people in empathy with the requirements of the deities and a civilization of unquestionable authority.

Following the downfall of the Cambodian Funan kingdom, the Khmer dynasty began to spread its civilization from Cambodia in the ninth century to govern most of southeast Asia over the next six hundred years. But not only did the Khmer people continue to draw inspiration from local mountains, they also built their cities and temples on these sacred and strategic vantage points. Through that combination of spiritual and pragmatic wisdom, the Khmer remained as one of the most dominant forces in the historical development of this region.

The evolution of this reverential concern with mountains has not always been a story of uninterrupted harmony. Sixteenth century Java for example, was a land invaded by intolerant Muslims for whom the indigenous Javanese beliefs, and the imported resonances of Buddhist and Hindu mountain spirituality, were nothing more than pagan heresies. The strict discipline of the Koran allowed no accommodation for cultures, civilizations and forms of wisdom which had served their people for thousands of years. During that period of rejection and intolerance however, nearby Bali remained as a sanctuary in which Hindu beliefs remained strong. Indeed, within Balinese legend, the Hindu gods were described as moving from Java to the land of Bali where they clearly felt their wisdom and divinity would be more appreciated and maintained within the culture of everyday life.[2]

Today's visitors to south and southeast Asia are presented with a bewildering collection of local variations to the universal themes in mountain spirituality. Rich and vibrant colours in the diverse physical landscapes of volcanoes, tropical jungles, and rain swept hillsides, as well as the equally rich and provocative spiritual insights of Hindu, Buddhist and Jain wisdom, all serve as a continuing source of inspiration and enlightenment to the modern pilgrim.

First visits

Three themes dominated all the conversations with first time travellers to these Asian landscapes. First, the vast diversity of local interpretations in mountain spirituality inspired these visitors to compare that variety with the relatively restricted patterns of ritual, celebration and worship which they encountered in their churches and temples at home. But as with so many of these discussions, the following extract of conversation between four English business partners, suggests that these restrictions in their Christian worship at home are less necessary than they previously believed. In describing their observations, the four partners recalled their first visit to the volcanic peak of Gunung Agung in northeast Bali:[3]

ALEX:

> *Of all my mountain travels, that's the clearest example I can think of where you have just the one massive, terrifying volcano, likely to go off at any time, but the most amazingly diverse range of ways to worship. I mean, some people would just sit and meditate. Others would chant quietly. Others would bring flowers and offerings ...*

BILL:

> *And what was so wonderful, there was no requirement to use only one form of service, like you do in a church, where the service follows a set format.*

STAN:

> *But that just reminds us all of the ways the Church has tried to control people's lives so much. And you only need to look in John's gospel to see that God never intended worship to be so restricted:*

> > *I am the vine;*
> > *you are the branches.*
> > *If a man remains in me*
> > *and I in him,*
> > *he will bear much fruit.*
> > *(John 15:5)*

STAN:

> *In other words, God remains the centre of Christians' lives, but He allows for, and anticipates, a full variety of different ways of worship ... And what I saw, say at the Besakih temple, was a complete variety of worship, with those rituals helping to bear fruit in the people's lives ...*

TRACY:

> *Variety is definitely the word, because those worshippers had so much religious variety within them that they didn't need to rely on an institution to tell them what to sing next, or pray next. They already knew. It was part of their pattern of worship to have that spontaneity and variety within their knowledge.*

Stan's identification of Biblical passages which encourage Jews and Christians to explore richer and more varied patterns of worship was echoed by other first time visitors to Gunung Agung, as well as other mountains within the south and southeast Asian region. For Amy, a public relations consultant from New York, the following passage from the New Testament letter to the Hebrews recognizes the spiritual value of exploring more broadly based forms of ritual, prayer and contemplation:

> The Son is the radiance of God's glory and the exact
> representation of his being, sustaining all things by his
> powerful word. (Hebrews 1:3)

AMY:

> *I was totally blown away by the worshippers I saw on Gunung Agung, because everyday I was there, there were different groups doing their thing. Praying. Meditating. Making offerings. All in different ways. And I compared it to worship I've been to in Europe or the States where you have a priest at the front of the group of worshippers telling them all what to think next, and do next. And yet you've got passages like that one from Hebrews which describe Jesus as sustaining all things by his powerful word. And yet Christians and Jews don't seem to have the confidence in their faith to accept that sustenance. And it's all very sad, and an amazing contrast with the Balinese.*

Other first time visitors to these Asian mountains felt more strongly about this contrast in freedom to worship. For Toni, a photography student from London, the ways in which western worshippers have been 'trapped' into such a narrow way of worshipping is both 'morally and spiritually wrong':

TONI:

> *My first visit to the Jain temples on Mount Abu (northern India) is the best example I can think of to show how wrong it is for Jews, and Christians as well, to be so impaired in their rituals ... Jains have managed to combine a set of doctrines about dress and diet and morality, but they also allow their minds to float free through meditation. So they don't seem to be imprisoned and trapped so much as western worshippers ...*

In pursuing this line of thought, Toni suggested that one of the reasons why attendance in synagogues and churches in the west is declining, is because the worshippers are 'trapped' into a pattern of worship which is imposed on them from 'out-of-date' prayers and rituals.

TONI:

> *If you look at what happens on (Mount) Abu, and elsewhere in India, you find people making their own rituals within the broadly defined limits of their faith. I mean, it's never anarchy, because each person is really into what works for them. But they also respect different things which work for other people too.*

The second major theme of conversation with first-time visitors to these mountains identified ways in which this freedom of worship can be incorporated into their own spiritual experiences. In describing this receptiveness, many of the Christians suggested that they found these new resonances of freedom to be a further experience of salvation. The house-church style of Christian worship described in the following illustration from Paula, a housewife from Felixstowe, England, is an informal gathering of believers where services take place in the privacy of a member's home. The worship is therefore contrasted to a formal church service by its intimacy, relatively small number of worshippers, and flexibility of ritual:

PAULA:

> *... I have to say that after I'd travelled all through southern India, and seen their worship, I wanted to introduce some of their ideas to our group. And in particular, I wanted more quiet times, when we could just sit and think. Taking time for ourselves. And now we do it every week, because for many of us, with children in particular, it's the only time we get to close our eyes and reflect ... and then we have another time — which I also saw those people do (in India) — where we share our thoughts, if we want to ... but it's all really, really liberating ... and I owe that to those people I saw (in India).*

In a similar manner, Lesley and Lindsey, who describe themselves as eternal students (of Modern History) and professional hitch-hikers from London, found that a small group of Hindus meditating on the Nilgiri Hills in southern India were able to offer them one of the 'most liberating pieces of wisdom I think we'd ever come across' (Lesley):

LESLEY:

> *We got talking to those people in their broken English, and, of course, we wanted to ask them about their faith, and how it contrasted with our own (Buddhist) feelings.*

LINDSEY:

*But when our question had been translated to the others in the group
who didn't understand English, they all smiled and looked at us both
with the eyes of really patient wisdom. And for a minute I wondered if
they'd understood what I'd asked! ...*

LESLEY:

*But the guy who'd been doing the translating, when he'd eventually
stopped grinning, looked me straight in the eyes, and said 'There is
only one illusion. Only one.' And I think my heart stopped, and I felt
all colour drain from me. I mean, think about it. No boundaries. No
contrasts, you know, between Hinduism and Buddhism, or anything
else. Just one focus ...*

LINDSEY:

*Which in itself is only an illusion. I mean, explosive stuff, or what ... It
just opens you up to everything you can learn ... But it all amounts to
just one form of wisdom if it really works for you.*

Over the years since meeting those Hindus in the Nilgiri Hills,
Lesley and Lindsey have grown to appreciate the simultaneous unity
of their advice along with its universal implications.

LESLEY:

*Every once in a while I'll be reading something which immediately
reminds me about those people we met, and that amazing opening up of
our minds. And one really good example, is a Japanese poem, by Matsuo Basho, which captures that 'one illusion' idea, but in a slightly
different way:*

> *No oil to read by*
> *And so I'm off to bed ... Ah!*
> *My moonlit pillow.*

LESLEY:

*As soon as I read those lines, I was back with those people on the Nil-
giri ... Look at what the poem says, as well as what it doesn't say. The
silences within the poem. 'No oil to read by.' So he has to reflect on his
studies. But then, on his 'moonlit pillow' inspiration falls upon him.
And in my mind's eye, I saw him become inspired, like we were in
India, by simple truths and understanding. And it's so beautiful. Imag-
ining his head resting on a moonlit pillow, suddenly understanding so
much, in a calm, half-sleepy way.*

The third theme within these conversations emphasised the price which some of these travellers have had to pay for trying to practice this much more open, accommodating and rich form of worship and meditation. Sometimes, the price has been almost complete incredulity and rejection, as in the case of Margaret, an administration clerk from Colchester, England:

MARGARET:

I'd been travelling through the south of India, and I'd seen more different styles of worship, you know, among the Hindus there, than I'd ever thought were possible. And so, when I got back to my own church, I suggested to our youth group that we should try new forms of worship, and other new ideas. And it was as if I'd said the Bible was a load of rubbish, or something like that. No one wanted to listen, and all they wanted to do was to tell me how wrong and misguided I was.

Although Margaret soon chose to keep quiet about her suggestion, she suffered almost two years of rejection and loneliness at her church before she decided to leave and join a house-church in which her suggestions have been only cautiously accepted:

MARGARET:

It's a lot better than at my first church, because at least people listen here (at the house-church), and we have a lot of quiet times when we can pray or think, so I'm able to think about those Indian Hindus, and the freedom they had in their worship ... Your mind floats away from the words of a hymn, or a part of the Bible, and seems to float in a cloud, and I find that incredibly beautiful.

Through the pain of recent experience however, Margaret has learned to be careful how she describes the inspiration she draws from her meditations. Any reference to Hindu spirituality among Christian groups almost invariably brings with it a reaction of shock and rejection from those with whom Margaret is conversing. Consequently, these days, she simply describes the genesis to those meditations as having arisen generally from her 'travels.'

For Dianne, an unemployed mother and committed Christian from south London, her experience of this type of rejection led to an even more radical consequence:

DIANNE:

> *About a year before my divorce, I travelled through India with a*
> *group of friends, ending up in Madras. And we were all really*
> *humbled by seeing these Hindus spontaneously making offerings,*
> *and praying, and not restricting their religious habits to any one set*
> *day ... But after I'd suggested some of those ideas to my church in*
> *London, I had a very terse phone call one evening from the vicar*
> *saying that if I wanted to spread this 'rubbish' among his congregation*
> *then perhaps I'd better leave. And I couldn't believe it! After all, all*
> *I'd done was to suggest we loosen up a bit, and do new things on*
> *different days. You know, community nights on a Friday, or visiting*
> *the old folks homes, and any other expression of Christian love people*
> *could think of.*

After she received her vicar's telephone call, Dianne became tearful
and rapidly disillusioned. With her impending divorce, she concedes
that these events occurred at a difficult time for her: one during which
she had expected some measure of sympathy from the Church. However, alongside the way she felt rejected, her private Bible studies
identified a verse from the Old Testament Book of Hosea which not
only gave her profound comfort, but also formed a sense of empathy
with the Hindu women she had seen making their occasional offerings
to Indian holy men:

> I will say to those called 'Not my people,' 'You are my people' and
> they will say, 'You are my God.' (Hosea 2:23)

DIANNE:

> *It says 'We're all one' in God's eyes, aren't we. We're all one. Those*
> *(Hindu) women, me, their worship, my worship, their experiences of*
> *their gods, my experiences of my God. All the same. All one. And the*
> *more I was able to see that, the happier I became.*

But whilst Dianne gained contentment from this passage, and with
the impression of empathy it formed for her, she continued to feel
increasingly unwelcome at her London church. Eventually, after a final
confrontation with the vicar, which Dianne preferred not to describe,
she decided to leave that church altogether. At the time of writing, she
visits other churches, on an occasional basis, without having formed
any deep roots within those communities of worshippers. However,
although she feels almost completely rejected by institutional Christianity, Dianne suggests that she has a much clearer understanding of

her faith alongside the insights she continues to draw from the memory of those Hindu women who so profoundly inspired her:

DIANNE:

As I look back on travelling through those (Indian) mountains, and seeing that group of people making offerings: women helping the holy men, children learning their religious books, I feel those mental pictures, along with those sentences from Hosea really brought me through some very difficult times. And in a way, I think I've learned to have enough faith now, in Christ the saviour, the creator of salvation, to give me time to breathe, and take stock of where I'm going. And then, who knows!

As with all the other first time visitors to this diverse collection of Asian mountains, Dianne's discussion fell within a consistent set of three themes. First, there was the inspiration drawn from a richness, vivacity, variety and frequent spontaneity of worship and spiritual expression encountered within those mountains. Second, there was a further inspiration which that richness sowed within these people's imaginations to try and incorporate this spirit of openness and spiritual exploration within their own worship. Finally however, whilst this inspiration of Indian and southeast Asian worship remains strong and clear, Dianne and Margaret continue to feel frustrated at the varying levels of rejection their suggestions received from their religious leaders. Ultimately therefore, those women's inspiration and memory of Asian mountains is retained and developed only as an element within their private contemplations. Personal experience has shown painfully that such powerful and important themes observed in these mountains can only be shared among others with the greatest caution.

Subsequent visits

Among the more experienced travellers in these mountains, there was clear evidence of the ways in which their spiritual maturity has helped them resolve these frustrations of not always being able to encourage others to fully appreciate the inspiration and value of the diverse and creative forms of spiritual expression found within these varied Asian landscapes. In the following illustration for example, Philippa, a journalist from Washington DC, suggests that it is simply naïve to expect western believers to readily accept the forms of worship and devotion found in these mountains:

PHILIPPA:
> *It's like a fear of the dark. Without the right encouragement, you can't expect people to snap out of it ... And over the centuries Christian and Jewish leaders have wanted to control their people. And to keep them under control, they've used two devices. One is guilt for sins, and the second is the fear of stepping outside the dictates of the institutional authority ... So sometimes, you just have to learn to let them carry on in their blinkered way.*

To further illustrate her observations, Philippa drew from her memories of a working visit to the volcanic island of Krakatoa, located in the Sunda Strait of Indonesia between Java and Sumatra. In 1883, Krakatoa exploded with its most infamous eruption sending ash and dust high into the world's atmospheric air-streams. A merciless tidal wave was also sent rolling across the narrow Sunda Strait drowning 36000 people.

PHILIPPA:
> *... ever since, Krakatoa has maintained this aura of danger about it. Even its name still conjures up images of vast Hollywood-style destruction. But for the local people who worship on those foothills, or even higher up, you can see they've made up their own rituals. Each family does its own thing. And the first time I saw that, I was reminded of some very wise words written by T.S. Eliot in his 'East Coker':*

> > *I said to my soul, be still,*
> > *and let the dark come upon you*
> > *which shall be the darkness of God.*
> > *(Eliot 1952, 126)*

The wisdom which Philippa found within T.S. Eliot's words was that of a recommendation to accept the darkness and mysteries of an inspired spiritual life, and to trust in God to guide the believer through. In recalling the families and individuals worshipping, praying and meditating on the slopes of Krakatoa, Philippa believes she found a clear example of people who have overcome their fears of the dark mysteries surrounding that infamous volcano. Not only had they felt able to travel toward Krakatoa, but their spirituality and imagination had created individual responses to this mountain of incalculable destructive power.

PHILIPPA:

> *After I'd interviewed some of those people, I learned that every fresh visit they made there, seemed to be a religious exploration of the new. They felt as if their faith had allowed them to come to the edge of life and danger and human understanding, and to literally gaze over the rim in wonder ... Fear was never completely conquered, but it was overcome enough to make the place (Krakatoa) into a powerful symbol for their own beliefs on their own terms.*

These descriptions of individual faith which is able to overcome fear, and become creative and growing, were developed further by Quentin, a freelance lecturer and writer from Atlanta, Georgia. In drawing from travel experiences and insights gained throughout the south and southeast Asian mountain regions, Quentin suggested that the only way in which people can overcome their fears of exploring new forms of spiritual experience is to step outside the language and doctrines which they have inherited from religious authorities. In the following illustration, Quentin recalls the impression made on him by the vast edifice of Borobudur in central Java.[4] Constructed by the Sailendra kingdom between the eighth and ninth centuries AD, it remains the largest Buddhist monument in the world.

QUENTIN:

> *I'm not a Buddhist. I'm a Taoist, but the feeling you get from being at Borobudur immediately crosses all the boundaries between any type of faith. And the reason why so many people get so much from being there is because they go to receive. Most people will just sit down, make themselves comfortable, relax and accept. They'll stare at the carvings and let their minds start to work. And in those mental wanderings, their religious awareness will expand. They'll find themselves led on to new insights: building on what they know already, but going a little bit further each time.*

Against those memories of Borobudur, Quentin contrasted his observations of fundamentalist Christians in the southern states of the USA where, he suggested, meditation and free thinking are virtually prohibited.

QUENTIN:

And that's why they'll keep hold of their fears and suspicions of new forms of spiritual awareness, as long as they live. They refuse to go outside what they know, so of course they'll be suspicious of different ideas. They bring it upon themselves!

Quentin's contrast between the visitors to Borobudur and these fundamentalist Christians was most frequently punctuated with his prescription of the need to 'let go' of the familiar ways of worship, and to explore beyond them, trusting one's own instincts to maintain the integrity of a chosen belief. In further explaining this need to 'let go,' Quentin identified the following verse which, he suggested, 'always comes back to me again and again whenever I'm trying to explain what Taoism is, and how creative it can be':

> Tao is beyond words
> And beyond things.
> It is not expressed
> Either in word or in silence.
> Where there is no longer word or silence
> Tao is apprehended.
>   (Quoted in Merton 1965, 152)

QUENTIN:

That's a very familiar extract, and a lot of people know it already. But, for all that, it sums up the need to relax, and to allow your mind to drift into new insights. And, for me, there's a little bit of that Taoist creative mentality within all religious ritual and worship which tries to adapt to the moment. You know, to problems which are on someone's mind. Family problems, or whatever. You always have to trust in the strength of your faith, whatever it is, and to go from that foundation into fresh encounters ... And that's the beauty of what you see throughout the whole of Asia. People explore what they believe in. They ask questions of their faith. They allow it to take them to new places, and they take their faith to new places too.

A very similar set of observations were offered by Andrea, a colour therapist and Zen believer from Liverpool, England. However, in distinction to Quentin's memories and discussions, Andrea's were presented from a consistently feminist perspective. In the following illustration of her conversation, Andrea was able to recall her three visits to the volcanic Mount Semeru, the highest summit on Java at

12600 feet. Its significance for local peoples is that of a cosmic centre within Indian Buddhist legend. Semeru is therefore a mountain which bears the imprint of the mythical Mount Meru: a symbol of divine grace with the approval and protection of the gods:

ANDREA:

Semeru is a great place to think about the possibility of building on your faith. Because, it's like returning to the womb, isn't it? And out of the womb, new insights are born. And as with any small child, those insights need attention, and nourishment, and protection from those who may reject or misunderstand what's been born. It's a perfect analogy, between reaching out to discover more of your spiritual journey which you see people doing there (Mount Semeru).

Andrea continued with her birthing analogy to suggest that further and subsequent insights and discoveries about one's beliefs can be conceived of as forms of rebirth — the birth of new wisdom, the abandonment of past despairs, and the growing love for fresh energy and renewed life.

ANDREA:

I travel all over Asia, not only for my work, but also to keep my own (Zen) beliefs alive and responsive ... and this is the lesson which I'm always reminded about, which I find over there, but which is almost always neglected in England, and, I suppose, in Europe as well.

The final point which Quentin and Andrea emphasised is the need for westerners to avoid their frequent preoccupation with 'naming' and 'labelling' their spiritual insights:

ANDREA:

When I come home, and I might be telling people about what I've seen, I'm almost always asked, 'well, is that from Hindu belief, or is it Buddhist?' Or, 'I thought you were a Zen believer, shouldn't you spend more time in Japan than in these other (south and southeast Asian) places? Honestly, it's true! I get all those questions. And I always have to tell them, it doesn't matter what label you put on these revelations. Call them whatever you like. Whatever makes you feel comfortable, that's the name for you!

To further illustrate this need to avoid undue concern over names and labels to identify religious insights, and thereby discriminate from other, contrasting, experiences, Andrea read the following haiku by the poet Sampu:

> Their names I know not,
> But every weed has
> Its tender flower.

ANDREA:

> *I've never found anyone in those (Asian) mountains who felt in any-*
> *way restricted by wanting to avoid thinking about particular subjects*
> *because they're too close to someone else's faith. And that's the simple*
> *beauty of Sampu's poem. Names don't matter. And boundaries between*
> *faiths don't matter either. It's the thought which counts. The inspira-*
> *tion which is the precious thing. And it's that which should be show-*
> *ered with love and attention, and not the superficial details of asking*
> *yourself, 'is this a Christian thought, or a Buddhist thought, or maybe*
> *even a Hindu thought.' It doesn't matter. Just think, and explore and*
> *create, and you won't need to worry about those labels!*

Turning points

Among a group of four Cambridge University students, their discovery of these insights about openness to fresh inspiration and personal creativity instigated a profound dilemma and spiritual transformation during their first visit to Adam's Peak on Sri Lanka.[5] Their curiosity to visit the Peak arose from its sacred status to more religious believers than any other mountain in the world. Hindus, Buddhists, Muslims and Christians have all woven this jungle-covered mountain into their own mythology. For Hindus, the Shaivite priests of the sixteenth century described the Peak as being an imprint of the Lord Shiva's footstep. Previously, the mountain had been the abode of wise Hindu sages and mystical teachers. Among Buddhists, the mountain, which they formerly knew as Sumanakuta, also bears the footprint of the Buddha which he is said to have left on Sri Lanka during his third visit to the island. Muslim belief also holds that the mountain bears a footprint of sacred inspiration to them: that of Adam, the man created by the breath of God, the first Islamic prophet and patriarch of all the world's people.

Inspired by the wish to see this legendary footprint of Adam, the four students, Giles, Wesley, Lincoln and James, had made the Peak the first place they wanted to visit on Sri Lanka in early 1995. Whilst they had all begun their journey as evangelical Christians, their curiosity drew as much from their undergraduate studies in archaeology, as it did from spiritual desire. They knew, for example, that Christian legend tells of the famous footprint also belonging to St Thomas the apostle who, it is thought, travelled to India and Sri Lanka to teach the Gospel after the crucifixion of Jesus.

LINCOLN:

> *We were there for many reasons. The isolation, the legends, and also the simple wish to see this foot-shape which appears to crop up in so many forms.*

The first disturbing experience which began to trouble these first-time travellers to Sri Lanka was their encounter with small groups of worshippers at the foot of the Peak. Even the most cursory glance at the faces of those devotees showed the students that they were witnessing ordinary people in profound spiritual grace:

GILES:

> *As evangelical Christians, you're always told that it's good to try and convert other people to Christianity, or to be an instrument for God to make that conversion. And you're told that somehow, other religions are less worthy and less correct than Christianity ... But when we saw those families praying by the roadside, on the very lowest hills, it was blatantly obvious that there was nothing second-class about what they were experiencing. And I suddenly found myself staring at them, absolutely dumbfounded ... and I realized how arrogant it is to suggest that our faith is any better than theirs. I mean, it's imperialism in just another guise.*

The seeds of doubt and dilemma had been sown. Although the new light of their Christian experience was yet to emerge from these young mens' spiritual horizons, the beginning of their re-education by this mountain's aura had begun.

JAMES:

> *If you can imagine a seven thousand foot, jungle-covered cone, you've got Adam's Peak in your mind. And although we were there early in the year, the humidity was up in the eighties and nineties. I say that to*

explain why we had to pace ourselves. Our progress was slow, tiring,
hot and very damp! And in those sort of conditions, I think our minds
returned to those worshipping families, and their faces of complete
contentment ...

WESLEY:

To be perfectly honest, I think we'd all realized by seeing those people
sitting around in a really calm way, that we were missing something.
None of us felt drawn toward Hinduism, but within our own Chris-
tianity, we knew we needed a lot more than the evangelical doctrines if
we were going to develop a sort of Christian equivalent to those fami-
lies' experience of their beliefs.

As the humidity continued to dilute their strength, rest-stops became more frequent. But in the breathless silence of those times, the
mind of each man continued to wonder and speculate about these
questions. The need for a more fulfilling Christianity. But how? The
need for new elements within their worship and prayer. But which
ones? The need to have sufficient confidence in the integrity of their
faith to explore the works of Christian authors and teachers whose
words lay outside the restrictions of fundamentalist belief. But where
to begin?

GILES:

During our rest-breaks, we didn't actually say too much at all. But in
our ways, we were all mulling over those questions ... And then sud-
denly, I had this amazing, amazing experience. Because, the answer was
so obvious, we'd all missed it.

LINCOLN:

We'd all been too intellectual about it. That was the problem.

GILES:

That's right. I mean, where were we? Adam's Peak. What is Adam
most closely associated with? God's creation. Eden. Paradise.

Giles' insight identified immediately the genesis of his new-found
breadth of Christian consciousness — creation spirituality. Mythical
reminders of that wisdom were all around him. The story of Adam.
The Biblical record of earthly Paradise. The lessons within the Book of
Genesis warning about the implications of breaking God's laws within
that perfect place. And yet, the men were all tramping beneath that

extraordinary tropical canopy of trees, heads down, exhausted, worried, and looking at their watches 'every ten minutes.'

Ironically though, after having encountered this precious insight, Giles felt unable to share it with his friends. Quite simply, within Giles' experience of evangelical groups, new suggestions of fresh ways in approaching Biblical appreciation were viewed with the 'greatest suspicion.' He therefore spent the rest of the day trying to compose the most diplomatic 'and vague' way in which to introduce his inspiration.

GILES:

At last, all I could think of was to try and make a weak joke of it. 'We walk through God's earthly Paradise,' I announced with pseudo-Shakespearean bravado. Then there was the most awful silence between us ...

LINCOLN:

Until I was forced to agree. I mean to say, it was just that simple. That was what the Hindu families were venerating and praying about. It was the missing piece to our own Christian jigsaw. And, subsequently, we've all found it's opened up the most amazing opportunity to discover more about our own faith, its history, its links to other religions ...

WESLEY:

And the really beautiful thing is that it's operated at different levels. For us as Christians, it's taken us into a much broader basis for learning about our faith. But also, on the academic front, these same questions obviously have an archaeological dimension, in terms of the ways in which past Christian groups and individuals described their relations with the land and natural resources.

With the seeds of this new discovery fresh within their minds, each of the students was seized with a dilemma. Whilst they had come to Adam's Peak with a simple curiosity to see the legendary footprint, each man realized he had encountered a wisdom of much greater and more profound importance. In wanting to dwell on that wisdom, to pray about it, to discuss it, and to develop it among themselves, none of the students wanted to continue their ascent to the summit:

LINCOLN:

We'd all gone through the most profound, exhilarating Christian enlightenment we'd ever felt. And yet, if you think about it, if we'd continued to climb, we would have carried on slogging our hearts out in getting there. And what do you do when you get to the top? You come all the way back down again. And whilst sometimes that's great, we just weren't in the mood. Because we had more important things to occupy our minds ...

JAMES:

But also, if we'd left the mountain, where would we have gone? Carried on with the (travel) programme? Well, no. Because that wasn't important any more either ...

GILES:

So we literally set up camp, I suppose half way up the mountain, and spent the rest of the time, until our supplies ran out, talk, talk, talking. And even though we'd never actually considered these creation-sided aspects to Christianity before, I think we all felt inspired and heightened by the feeling of being there (Adam's Peak) ... Amid a real earthly paradise we felt our minds expand, and our awareness of the breadth of Christianity.

In a very real sense, each of these four men encountered the tropical slopes of Adam's Peak as a womb, just as Andrea had described earlier in this chapter. From that spiritual birth place, new insights were discovered which have profoundly changed each of these men's Christian and academic interests. For these four travellers, Adam's Peak saw the birth of these inspirations. Subsequently, when they camped beneath the tropical canopies, that place nurtured the embryonic development of these insights. It provided illustrations of created beauty, change, stability, erosion, old age, youth, variety, silence, and bird and wind song. A womb of multisensual inspiration, and a classroom where each man felt instructed in the richness of south Asian spiritual opportunities, and in an early empathy with those who are blessed with lives which can be spent in prayer, worship and meditation within such landscapes.

Conclusions

The principal source of inspiration which these travellers discovered in south and southeast Asia was the rich variety of individual and family ways of worship, prayer and meditation practised by local people. For some of those people, it was enough to sit and contemplate their ancestors, or to gaze in wonder at the aura of eternal magnificence which clothes these sacred mountains. Other local families had developed their own rituals: their own prayers, their own chants, their own manner of lighting incense sticks, and their own ways of making offerings to the gods or other divine spirits. In contrast to many other journeys described in this book, the inspiration of these mountains drew as much from the local people, and their spiritual creativity, as it did from the experiences and imaginations of these travellers.

ANDREA:

But that's the thing which stands out about that part of Asia. The people there have been free to make their own forms of celebration and meditation. No one's sat on their shoulder, telling them what to do and think, so they've had no alternative but to be creative with their faiths. And the results always knock westerners backwards because it's so beautiful and inspiring to watch.

But alongside the beauty and inspiration which Andrea and many others have taken away with them, Quentin also has experience of having listened to people who sometimes travel home from this region of Asia in a state of profound disquiet.

QUENTIN:

What often happens is that I hear people talk about their desire to let go of their formal patterns of worship, and to develop new ones. I mean, that's a great idea. But then you almost always get Church or Synagogue leaders stopping that form of creativity. So the dilemma remains. You have people inspired and wanting to change, and become more free. But you also have religious leaders who won't let them. So what happens? A very, very few will leave and do their own thing. But the majority will just carry on going to their church, or temple, feeling frustrated and confined and as if they're missing out on some amazing new experiences. Which, of course, they are!

The most responsive set of believers to this opportunity of encouraging the discovery of new patterns in devotion were the small groups of Buddhists who gather in numbers of less than a dozen. As a member of one such group in Washington DC, and another in London, Philippa was able to speak with direct experience of this contrast with more institutional responses to the desire for innovation and experimentation:

PHILIPPA:

... it's really healthy to the overall life of the groups. So, what happens, someone will come back from their travels some place, or even someone will have met another Buddhist and they'll have shared their thoughts. So, suggestions are made to the group. And they're talked about, and tried out. And if the whole group likes it, then it's used. And if only a few people like it, then you often find they'll do it round one of their homes on another occasion. So then, you get this whole tapestry of inspirations and suggestions coming in, and being thought about ... And you find that some of them can really work, and take you to new places in your meditation.

Among these smaller groups of Buddhist practitioners, there appears to be a willingness to let go of their egos and desire to control each other's contemplations and spiritual development. Instead, there is a creative receptiveness to new ideas, new inspirations, fresh insights, innovations which contribute to the momentum and life of the groups. Within Quentin's Taoist meditation group, the same flexibility is practised:

QUENTIN:

Flexibility lies at the heart of the Tao. You need to respond to the moment. So it's always great to listen to new experiences which people have discovered on their vacation some place. And it's good to try them out. A new meditation. A poem. A chant. A new story. They all add so much to the rich experience of bringing the lessons of areas like the south Asian mountains home to the west so we can learn from that wisdom.

CHAPTER 8

Central Asia

Having enjoyed paradise's vast realm,
they return to the human world,
merit exhausted;
Those who follow the three Vedas,
desirous of enjoyments,
win only the changeable.

Bhagavad Gita, IX.21

Ancient wisdom

The forbidding landscapes of central Asia form one of the most barren, hostile and punishing regions on earth. It is a land of ferocious extremes: in winter, temperatures can fall to −30° Celsius. In summer, highs have been recorded at +50° Celsius. Away from the few sheltered areas, winds in excess of 110 mph have whipped up dust storms to lash and tear at the face of anyone or anything in their path. But in addition to its climatic extremes, this is also a land of monumental height and plummeting depth. It is a region of summits which can compete with the Himalayas. North of the Tibetan Plateau for example, there is Ulugh Muztagh, soaring to 23923 feet. Far to the west, rising from the wide valleys of the Pamir mountains on the Chinese border with Afghanistan, Muztagh Ata towers to a height of 24757 feet. And only a few miles to the northeast of Muztagh Ata, Kongur stands 25325 feet tall. At the other extreme, this is also a land which descends along the Turfan Depression to a depth of over 500 feet below sea level: the world's second lowest basin.

For many of the teachers and spiritual masters of Taoism, Hinduism and Buddhism, these remote, untamed mountain landscapes have always been a source of inspiration and wisdom. Among early Taoist thinkers for example, the labyrinthine K'un-lun range held a mysterious route to paradise.[1] A heaven of eternal freedom and complete understanding for the immortal beings who were worthy of a place there. In their quest to become one of those immortals, Taoist masters contemplated the astonishing and beguiling mystery in these mountains. A mystery and a fascination which keeps this apparently barren wilderness full to abundance with fresh, provocative and fertile inspiration and spiritual encouragement.

In contrast, Hindu and Buddhist mystics have focused their search right across the Chinese mountains of Pamir. From that focal point, a series of further ranges radiate like the spokes of an enormous wheel: a divine circle on which a lifetime of meditation can be concentrated. Within that wheel, the ranges of T'ien Shan, the Hindu Kush, Karakoram and K'un-lun support the central axis of Pamir. And at the heart of that divine axis, within a region believed to be the centre of all human life, understanding and experience, the mystical Mount Meru is thought to lay hidden among the jagged spires of rock and ice.[2] But the search for Meru is not an easy task. None of the ancient texts show any precise geographical coordinates. Nor do they describe the route to Meru. Instead, those poems and scriptures, such as the great epic poem, the *Mahabharata*, were written with an emphasis placed on the sublime power of Meru and its ability to inspire and challenge teachers and their disciples across the centuries, an emphasis on what the mountain might represent for different individuals, rather than the brief and ultimately destructive facts of Mount Meru's physical location — a wisdom which keeps that mountain alive and inspirational within the inquisitive minds and imaginations of those Hindus and Buddhists who concentrate on a creation-centred belief.

For most of the first millennium AD, Tibetan scholars, artists and storytellers developed myths and legends about the mystical paradise of Shambhala which, they believed, would be found far to the north of their plateau.[3] One school of thought suggested that Shambhala would be finally discovered beyond a vast ring of snow-capped mountains. And once found, Shambhala would not only be of immense inspirational value, but it would also have a sound practical and educational application as well. From the teachings of Tibetan prophets, it is said that, during the time when Shambhala is discovered, the world will be at war — a war more brutal and destructive than any other within the history of humankind. A war which will reduce entire cities to rubble and burnt ash in a single heart-beat, and destroy national populations. A war which will crucify the world's spiritual awareness, burn its scriptures and banish its teachings, including those of Buddhism. Only the Buddhists living within the sanctuary of Shambhala will be saved from this apocalypse. That faithful community will then form a new foundation for humankind. And within their number, a divine king will be born. From the womb of this barren mountain wilderness, he will inspire and lead an army of followers who will crush all the forces of evil which previously conspired against humanity. He will be a king like no other king. He will guide his people like no other ruler. His wisdom will herald a new, golden age of justice and celebration, wisdom and understanding, eternal truths and profound insight.

But whilst the search for Shambhala continues, the landscapes immediately to the north and south of western China's Tarim Basin have already been witness to riches of a more earthly nature. Along the dry and dusty tracks in those areas, ancient routes were developed by traders, scholars, pilgrims and adventurers from China and India in the east, and from Europe and the Middle East in the west. In both directions, along this Silk Road, a rich diversity of products and ideas were transported in an exchange of philosophies and wisdom, arts and inventions, learning and inspiration. And beside the Silk Road, at oases such as Tun-huang, Turfan, Khotan and Kashgar, small towns began to grow. Over the years, they attracted their own pilgrims. They gained new reputations for literature and teaching. Consequently, during the first thousand years AD, the paintings, scholarship and sculpture of these oasis towns became influenced with traces of east and west. Chinese patterns and colours were mixed with Iranian and Iraqi ideas. Indian art influenced Greek art. And vice versa. As never before, travellers were learning from a vast treasury of human imagination and exchanged achievements. And the insights gained from that meeting of minds and mentalities often led to the most sublime inspirations within these forbidding landscapes. As a response to this surprising discovery of sublime grace, many of the Chinese travellers named the mountains on the northern edge of the Tarim Basin as T'ien Shan, the Mountains of Heaven.

As the Chinese fascination with the Silk Road increased during the seventh century AD, a monk named Hsuan-tsang journeyed west for sixteen years in search of Indian Buddhist scriptures.[4] From the pages of his extraordinary account of that pilgrimage, it is possible to appreciate the combination of fear and exhilaration which Hsuan-tsang felt as he struggled on through this bizarre and threatening route. At one point, he confesses his impression that much of the way was haunted with ghosts, demons and evil spirits. Indeed, on many occasions during his sixteen year journey, Hsuan-tsang found groups of men who were completely lost among the mountains. Unable to understand their language, Hsuan-tsang could only observe and record those terrifying encounters, as the lost wanderers became completely inconsolable with fright and confusion.

But whilst the Silk Road allowed European and Asian cultures to share the richness of their distinctive wisdom and cultures, there was also a consistently darker side to these routes. From the eighth to the twelfth centuries AD for example, Muslim armies sought to destroy as many of the Buddhist temples and shrines as they could find, trying wherever they could to convert local peoples to Islam. Also during the eighth century, Tibetan forces took control of large sections along the Silk Road. To consolidate that military initiative, they subsequently annexed many of the oasis towns which had formerly been under Chinese authority. A century later, Kirghiz armies forced the Uighur peoples to move from their fertile valleys to the more barren and desiccated Tarim Basin. Bloodshed continued through, and beyond, the thirteenth century when the Mongol armies of Temujin, later to be re-named Genghis Khan, swept across the Tarim Basin in the early years of their extraordinary empire.

Among modern travellers, these mountains still combine an impression of extreme contrast. They have been landscapes of traumatic nightmares and rich spiritual enlightenment. Despair and encouragement. Frustration and inspiration. As such, these peaks continue to provoke fresh, vital and contemporary wisdom. Beyond their superficial appearance of dry, empty wastelands, it is therefore possible to discover in these mountains some of the most profound spiritual lessons on earth.

First visits

All the travellers who contributed to this chapter are experienced mountaineers. Indeed, when they first began to discuss their travel and spiritual experiences with me, they all had at least five years of climbing to their name. That experience had given them the confidence and ability to venture into these remote landscapes. But it also gave them a breadth of travel experience to truly appreciate, and respond to, the unique inspirational qualities of these mountains. In the case of Alfred for example, a retired archaeologist from Phoenix, Arizona, his first climb on Muztagh Ata had been provoked partly by his academic interest in the western Chinese Pamir range, and partly by his Buddhist and creation centred beliefs:

ALFRED:

> *I'd spent a lot of years studying the writings of Hsuan-tsang, so one of my main intentions in making that first trip was to visit the Pamir ... But of course, when I saw it for myself, it was far beyond how I'd pictured it ... and I think the first thing I realized when I first got there, was the need to make time for myself to be especially receptive to those moments of being in that environment ...*

The first time Alfred saw the 24757 feet high dome of Muztagh Ata was when his travelling companions sailed him toward the mountain across the Little Karakul Lake. It was dawn. And the early morning light shone low over the gently rippled water, and against the dome's snow covered sides. In the face of such rare and extraordinary beauty, Alfred knew he had to concentrate on every precious moment of the experience. But in order to truly receive the inspirational value of Muztagh Ata, Alfred also knew he had to let go of his anxieties about the archaeological expedition he was leading in this remote Asian wilderness. He had to learn to relax. He had to learn to quieten his mind. To find peace. And to find the solitude to meditate on Muztagh Ata's instructive value.

ALFRED:

> *Some places you visit, you immediately know it's going to be incredibly special ... And so, at my first opportunity, I went off on my own. Partly to see what I could see. And partly to meditate in order to reconcile this giant mountain dome with my hang-ups about being so far from the kind of support I was used to ...*

But throughout the expedition's first month, Alfred's leadership responsibilities continued to prevent him from relaxing sufficiently in order to concentrate on the sublime grace and monumental presence of Muztagh Ata. During Alfred's fifth week therefore, he reached the conclusion that this imbalance between academic and leadership responsibilities and his desire to receive spiritual inspiration from the mountain had to change. A more fulfilling balance was essential.

ALFRED:

> *To put it simply, I was so pre-occupied with the logistics of our (archaeological) expedition that I was missing the main value of the mountain, the main reason why Hsuan-tsang felt the way he did, and the reason why the tribes people feel the way they do. You've got to accept the mystery of the place and you've got to put aside your anxi-*

eties, and accept all the sounds and sights and smells and feelings of being there. That's all you need. No fear. Just accept. It's that simple. But often the simplest things are the hardest to achieve!

However, with the benefit of hindsight, Alfred suggested that, for his spiritual sensibilities, those five weeks of managerial and academic preoccupation were not wasted. With the benefit of that hindsight, those five weeks are still instructive.

ALFRED:

I wasn't listening to myself. You know, my whole self. As an academic, yes I was fine. As the expedition leader, I had everything under control. But, with those pressures on me to make sure everything went right, I wasn't looking deeper into myself to really see the anguish those pressures were causing me ... That's hard, of course, because it's like being your own analyst. But I think you sometimes have to try and be that analyst for yourself, and really try and think 'am I able to get the most from being here?' Because if you're not, then it's time to do some major soul searching.

Among the profound lessons which Alfred discovered on that expedition was the need for sufficient strength to delegate more responsibilities to those he could trust. He therefore had to learn to trust. He also had to admit his anxieties and vulnerabilities to himself and to others. Alfred learned that he had to stop 'wearing the mask of invulnerability.' He learned that some of the most profound spiritual insights and inspirations are discovered during, and after, times of intense stress and anxiety. Sometimes an individual's spiritual path cannot lead them away from the pain of confrontation, dilemma, depression or worry. Rather, it is often unavoidable for that spiritual path to lead an individual directly through a time of pain, worry and stress in order to confront the need to abandon that 'mask of invulnerability.'

ALFRED:

I could never emphasise too much the importance of these lessons for me. The need to banish for ever the need to appear invulnerable ... Admit your fears. Bring them to the front of your mind. Talk about them. Let them out. Let go of them all ... Because only then, can you turn round and look again at something like Muztagh Ata and really understand what it's all about ... to be inspired by it. To carry that inspiration back home, and to keep it alive for yourself and others too.

Although Alfred approached these fundamental lessons from his Buddhist perspective, they were also encountered, from a Christian view, by Jeremy, an art student from Cardiff, Wales. Jeremy's initial climbing experience in central Asia arose from his first climb in the Amnye Machen range, near the source of China's Yellow River.[5] Although he had gained considerable experience from climbing in Europe before that first visit, Jeremy's recollections of mountaineering on the southern Chenrezig peak showed that his strength, stamina and climbing techniques were challenged to their limits by the unexpected winds which gusted around the mountain:

JEREMY:

I'd never climbed in anything like it! The winds were completely contrary to all the weather forecasts we'd received. But their strength! They almost pulled me off on more than one occasion.

With successive days of similar weather, the expedition's morale became increasingly deflated. But whilst Jeremy sheltered one evening on Chenrezig during a particularly ferocious storm, he read the following passage from the Letter from St Paul to the Romans:

The Spirit himself testifies with our spirit that we are God's children. Now if we are children, then we are heirs — Heirs of God and co-heirs with Christ, if indeed we share in his sufferings in order that we may also share in his glory. (Romans 8:16 and 17)

JEREMY:

To understand how that passage affected me, you have to try and understand just how dejected the whole (climbing) group of us were. We really were down, with all the problems from the weather ... So in the middle of all that soul-searching, I found that those words really spoke to me about the way I was feeling, and the way God shepherds his children through a disastrous time, and doesn't chose to take those children around the problems. You know, away from it. You sometimes have to go through problems ... and confront them. But you know that he comes with you, and that's the major difference.

The principal lesson which Jeremy drew from reading that passage, at that point in his life, was an appreciation of the continuous relationship which an individual can develop with God. It is a continuous process of being offered the wisdom of Biblical scripture alongside the individual's prayerful listening to God's additional words of guidance. But those lessons also form a continual process of being strengthened in the face of adversity, as in the case of Jeremy's troubled climb on Chenrezig. For children of God, a time of painful adversity does not have to be a time of lonely disillusionment. It can be a time of instruction. Sometimes, painful instruction. Frequently, the lessons will be longer than an individual believes is right and fair. Often the lessons will also be more intense than the individual may believe they can tolerate. But during all such times, those children of God are being taught to rely on God's strength, not their own. They are being taught to rely on his wisdom, not their own. And they are being taught to follow his guidance, and not their own.

Subsequent visits

Beyond the point of simply accepting these spiritual truths, the more experienced mountaineers and walkers were able to describe how they have developed an increasingly active and creative response to their faiths. It is an individual response to the opportunities and priorities of a spiritual commitment which is more personal, more intimate and more deep-rooted in who they are, and where their lives are going. But for all these experienced travellers, this creative spirituality is a union between two contrasting elements: the inspiring elements of their faith, and the troubling distractions from that commitment. It is a creative and fertile union between the profound value of ancient insights, and the need for individuals to abandon their destructive obsessions which prevent them from being fully receptive to their sacred inspirations. Theirs is a spirituality which actively responds to divine guidance as well as to the darkness which threatens the unfulfilled spirit.

In one series of conversations which highlighted this type of spiritual creativity, anecdotes were drawn from the K'un-lun mountain range, which stretches between the Taklamakan Desert to the north and the Tibetan Plateau to the south. From their repeated, independent, travels throughout the K'un-lun, Shaughn and Basil, business managers from Dublin, Ireland, and Chicago, Illinois respectively, discussed their experienced Christian responses to these challenges:

SHAUGHN:

When you're spending time in an environment like the K'un-lun, you're really down to facing the absolute basics of life. There's you. There are the mountains. And there is God. And that's it. That's all you've got out there. And so, in order to survive, you have to get a creative relationship going with those three participants in that experience: God, you and the mountain environment. It's got to be creative. It's got to be simple. And yet, above all, it's got to work.

BASIL:

It's life in the raw, isn't it. And, I guess, for people who haven't been to places like that, it's kind of hard to understand. But when you're there, you know it's a fact of life.

Among the many literary references to which these men referred, was the autobiography of the twentieth century prophet, Dorothy Day. The following passage from that autobiography exemplifies the essential simplicity of this active creative relationship between God, individual people and the spiritual power of mountains:

God is our creator. God made us in his image and likeness. Therefore we are creators. He gave us a garden to till and cultivate. We became co-creators by our responsible acts, whether in bringing forth children, or producing food, furniture or clothing. The joy of creativeness should be ours. (Dorothy Day 1952, 255)

BASIL:

Those experiences in the K'un-lun mountains are the building blocks which God used in my life to heal some pretty major wounds I'd suffered over the years. You know, spiritual and emotional wounds. Through broken family relationships and such ... And, for me, I think it was the fact that in being so far away from any other source of help in those mountains forced me, finally, to turn to God, and to receive from him ... But then, in learning to go beyond simple and passive receiving, to pray with questions on my mind, and waiting for him to show me the answers ... and being led like that right through each of those climbs ...

From the conversations with Basil and Shaughn, as well as other experienced travellers to these remote, central Asian mountains, it was clear that, within their perception, contemporary society increasingly serves to erode spiritual creativity and, indeed, all forms of individual creativity. In discussing this opinion, these travellers suggested that instead of being encouraged to be creative, people are manipulated to be passive. There is blatant as well as subtle pressure to watch television, videos and movies from the producers and managers of those media. There is also media pressure simply to listen to music, instead of composing and performing it as well. Among adolescents, there is also peer pressure to dance, but negligible opportunity to choreograph new dances. In churches and cathedrals, worshippers are expected to passively follow a prescribed order of service, instead of being able to influence that order, and respond to it in new ways which emphasise their individuality.

An opinion which all these travellers shared is that, at school, contemporary pupils are not taught how to face the profound difficulties of everyday life: they are given neither the vocabulary nor the experience to develop a creative and inventive response to those problems from within the resources of their spiritual beliefs.

BASIL:
> ... I know I learned the hard way. Because at school, I'd just been taught to learn and memorize basic passages of scripture. I was given the so-called right answers ... And basically I was indoctrinated. Literally. That doctrine was force-fed to me. But years later, when I'd finally got around to accepting those scriptures in a more adult and mature way, I still didn't have the intellectual and emotional equipment to run after God ... To ask him questions. I mean, I didn't know if I was allowed to do that, until, in the K'un-lun, my third climb there, I was forced to ... And many, many times out there (in the K'un-lun) I've been faced with problems following accidents, or weather problems, when I just had no choice other than to ask (God) for help. But only in that really gritty and tough environment did I eventually learn to develop this more active and intelligent and questioning relationship with God ... And all that came from me being in the K'un-lun ...

For Shaughn, this negative force within contemporary education stands in marked contrast to the 'astonishing potential for spiritual growth' within humankind's relationship with its environment. And yet, the trend persists. Children are rarely taught to listen to the wind after they leave junior school. Adolescent pupils are rarely encouraged to trace their finger tips over differing textures of rock, tree bark, leaves, grasses, mud, clay or silt. Pupils, of any age, are almost never taught to see beyond the obvious, superficial level of visual meaning.

Their sense of culinary taste receives virtually no attention whatsoever. And there is virtually no school curriculum in the world which is focused directly and consistently on stimulating young imaginations as individuals as well as in small groups or teams. Shaughn particularly emphasised his opinion that, within the world's universities, creativity is still denied its full potential. This denial is particularly evident within the theological colleges at which future religious ministers and other spiritual teachers study before moving into communities to teach, lead worship and, ideally, stimulate other imaginations in their search for a greater understanding of the divine resonances of life:

SHAUGHN:

The more I visit those incredibly wild places, such as the K'un-lun range, the more I understand about this amazingly blatant black-and-white issue that's going on these days. On the one hand, even in the most remote places, you've got an absolute tide of things to inspire you. Things which you see, you hear, you smell, you touch, and which you taste. And they're coming at you all the time ... But then, you've got a technological society which crushes every ability to appreciate that sensuality ... I mean, it really does make me angry when I watch kids who, through absolutely no fault of their own, do not know how to find any beauty from a mountain, or even a picture of a mountain ... They're not taught how to develop that creative relationship in school, and they're certainly not taught about it in any church I've ever been a part of ...

For the Zen teacher and writer, Buster, from Dublin, Ireland, this simultaneous and persistent denial of spiritual creativity, alongside the increasing need for it within contemporary, technological societies has always been exemplified by his five climbing expeditions to the K'un-lun range. In particular, Buster mourns the way in which school children and students are 'taught to sleep walk, instead of being fully alive to the moment':

BUSTER:

For me, the K'un-lun is one of the ultimate multi-sensual experiences. You have to fully see, fully hear, fully taste, fully touch and fully smell the scent of that area ... So from that foundation, that multi-sensual foundation, it inspires the spiritual soul. And each moment in that range can become another piece in the jig-saw of piecing together our individual enlightenment. It happens slowly, but it does need our constant, vigilant and active participation ... and above all our creative awareness.

As he continued to discuss the need for an education in the multi-sensual appreciation of these mountains, as well as a personal and creative willingness to create opportunities to develop a chosen spiritual path, Buster identified a series of Japanese haiku poems, often used in Zen meditation, to illustrate the 'latent potential' within each moment which is spent alive to the prospect of creative spiritual development:

> The long night:
> The sound of the water
> Says my thought.
> (Gochiku)

BUSTER:

I've actually had a night like that in the K'un-lun. I just wanted to lie awake and listen. And since I was camped right close to a stream, those gentle sounds brought out a whole procession of thoughts, and ideas, and wonders, and questions. All night ... So that single sense, the sense of hearing, provoked all that astonishing richness.

> *Loneliness!*
> *It, too, is joy:*
> *An autumn eve.*
> *(Buson)*

If there's one season which is open to the senses more than any other, it's autumn. You've got the sound of crunching dead leaves. The sound of the howling wind. The sight of death and decay and hibernation all around you. You've got the taste of the cold on your tongue. The sharp tang of life composting down for the winter. It's all there in autumn ... So even in the gloom of loneliness, life offers the opportunity, if we're willing to actively respond to it, of breaking free of that inner solitude and becoming more in contact with all those sights and smells and sensual appetizers!

Each of these haikus was illustrated, at length, with numerous anecdotes drawn from Buster's solitary and shared mountain travels in the K'un-lun range. But as with all the experienced travellers who contributed to this chapter, Buster's principal theme of conversation was that, upon the foundation of an educated and inspired imagination, there are absolutely no limits to the constructive creativity which people can bring to their chosen spiritual faith, even within an apparently forbidding mountain wilderness, such as the K'un-lun. With imagination they can respond to adversity in prayer. With inspiration, they may respond to sorrow through painting, crafts, music, writing, or many other avenues of creative expression. And when faced with the combined threats and inspirations of the K'un-lun, all these experienced travellers described personal encounters with the uplifting joy of finding inspiration within that most isolated of mountain landscapes. Private moments as well as shared times can be immeasurably enriched through an ability to respond creatively to the spiritual power of those places. Consequently, such wondrous moments can remain precious, treasured and shared with awe and thanksgiving.

In emphasising this need for individuals to respond creatively to their life-experiences, many of these travellers also expressed the need to develop and share this inspired spiritual creativity in a thoroughly responsible way. For Kent, a Buddhist and teacher from New York, this is a fundamentally important lesson which he drew from his last journey through the Amnye Machen massif near the source of the Yellow River.

KENT:

I think one of the key themes, for me, in my meditations in the Amnye Machen has been to consider the checks and balances needed within a spirituality. I mean, you just can't go off in a whirl of enthusiasm from the first thing which inspires you ... There's got to be time for those ideas to develop. You have to be patient ... And in those really harsh and challenging environments, like the Amnye Machen, you come to be powerfully aware of the constraints which govern what you can, and can't do out there ...

Kent's meditations, which were originally inspired by the summits of Amnye Machen, have universal implications. For a spiritual lifestyle to develop fruitfully, it must be guided with care and awareness past the temptations of impetuosity and foolishness. There are more than enough opportunities to develop an individual's insights and inspiration based on the sure foundation of responsibility, patience and sensitivity. Consequently, within Kent's more recent meditations, he has developed a belief that individuals need to be 'co-creators' with the sacred elements of their life-experience.

KENT:

On my last visit out there, I was sitting by this melt-water stream, taking a breather, and daydreaming as the water swirled by ... And in my imagination, I began to swim within that stream, and to turn and dive, and be totally at one with the water. Where its currents went, I'd go too ... And that was such a beautiful time for me that I kept thinking about it ... how I could develop this spiritual empathy with a stream, and that area, by becoming at one with it. Learning its power as well as its limitations ... but not taking my own spiritual inspiration beyond what that environment will allow me to do.

Using the language of the nature conservation movement, Kent also calls this creative side to his environmental inspirations 'sustainable spirituality': an intuitive response to the mountains, or other inspirations, which affirms both the full creative potential of those moments, as well as their natural and justifiable limitations. And in order to achieve that responsible and sustainable balance between spiritual potential and natural constraint, Kent finds that his meditations and insights require a patient and careful approach. They must be reflected upon. They must be nurtured, like a delicate plant or small animal. They may be discussed with other people who are sympathetic to those particular spiritual insights. Upon that sure foundation therefore, a creative spirituality can be allowed to flourish. It can be celebrated. It can be enjoyed to the full. It can be shared among friends and offered to others as gifts from one life to another.

KENT:

The more I think about these ideas of co-creativity and sustainable spirituality, the more I feel confident in the directions which my experiences are taking me. And on the basis of that confidence I can take my own spiritual inclinations into places as wild as the Amnye Machen, as well as places back home, and know they've been nurtured, and developed carefully, in a way which works ... and which continues to inspire me, and the people who I share with in my meditation class.

Turning points

When Casey first began to discuss his mountain travels for this book, he did not mention his experiences in central Asia. He discussed his mountaineering and hill-walking in North and Latin America, but no mention was made of any other travels. During the fourth week of his participation in this research however, he asked me if we could discuss some of his experiences on a one-to-one basis. Only then did Casey describe his first journey through part of the K'un-lun range, and why he had kept it a complete secret until he felt sufficiently confident in the integrity of the interviews.

In 1987, Casey was a respected business manager, living in Tennessee, USA. However, since the age of seventeen, he had also been a member in a group of satanic worshippers. At first, Casey suggested he joined the group partly out of curiosity, partly for 'fun,' and partly out of secret rebellion against his devoutly Christian parents. But by 1987, Casey had wanted to leave the group for over five years. He was appalled by the violent rituals, and by the way other teenagers were enticed into the cult, only to be transformed 'into the same kind of sadistic monsters as the people who ran the group.' However, Casey knew that no matter how strongly he wanted to leave, such resignations were never tolerated. No one ever left that group alive. Consequently, in desperation, and following his second nervous breakdown during his divorce, Casey took the decision to leave his job, sell his house, and spend time travelling alone through Asia:

CASEY:

At that time, I was a complete bundle of nerves. I'd break down in tears three or four times a day, and I was totally messed up ... Every dream I had was a nightmare from those (satanic) rituals. And there wasn't a single vestige of innocence or happiness in any part of my life.

In his state of profound mental trauma, Casey knew he was unable to consider any form of strenuous mountaineering. However, he did want to travel through part of the K'un-lun on foot. Casey therefore set off with a pack of supplies sufficient to last him for four days.

CASEY:

To show you what sort of a mess I was in, I even packed with me a couple of books of occult scripture. I didn't want them with me, but those things don't leave you so easily.

The course of his chosen path had no particular significance other than its virtual guarantee of complete solitude within the mountains. The main object of the walk was simply to try and establish a new plan for his life, a new direction, and a new set of goals.

Within the biting winds and clear mountain air of the K'un-lun, Casey felt he was beginning to make the break from his past which he

needed. The morning of his third day in the mountains began brightly
with the sun shining low in the perfect blue sky. By mid-morning, he
was making good progress along the narrow gravel path. The next
second, he tripped and fell head first over the side of the trail, and
continued to fall in a helpless whirl of uncontrollable terror. Jagged
fragments of stone tore at his clothes, face and hands, piercing and
slicing his skin. Without knowing how far he was going to tumble,
Casey's mind locked into a wordless panic. Three hundred yards later,
he slumped to a bruising halt against a rounded boulder half his own
height. In breathless exhaustion, he lay completely still, gathering his
splintered emotions. Then without warning, Casey's legs were covered
in a cascade of sharply angled stones and pebbles which had followed
his terrifying slide.

CASEY:
> *By any rule of logic or reason, that fall should have killed me. I was out
> of control, and if I hadn't fallen against that boulder, I'd have carried
> on falling to the bottom of the valley ... But I was alive! And for the
> first time since I was seventeen, that was a real good feeling. I was
> aching all over. I was half-covered in rock. And I was winded. But I
> can still remember getting my wits together and realizing I had a smile
> on my face!*

Having slowly and painfully hauled himself to a standing position,
and having wrapped his bleeding hands and arms with bandages,
Casey stood gazing across the valley at the snow covered peaks stretching away into the next succession of valleys and summits:

CASEY:
> *... and while I was taking it all in, I realized something was missing
> from my life. I didn't feel any threat from Satan ... It was as if, in
> cheating death up in that valley, I'd cheated the whole occult thing once
> and for all. And I was dumbfounded. You know, it's hard to describe
> that feeling to someone who hasn't been through it, but it was like
> leaving prison for the first time in twenty years.*

Casey's next instinct was to start a fire and celebrate his freedom
by cooking a bowl of hot soup. But in making the fire, he realized
there was another task which had to be completed first. From the
bottom of his back pack, Casey pulled out both the books on occult
scripture which he had felt compelled to bring with him. Holding
the first book open by its hard back cover, Casey allowed the flames

to ignite the pages. When it was alight, the second book was also set on fire.

CASEY:

> *It felt like a complete liberation, watching those books burn like that. I stared deep into those flames and there was the most enormous feeling of being free and being alive, and appreciating every sound I heard and every sight I saw ... it was as if my senses had had some sort of muffler taken off them ... and it was amazing.*

As part of his new life in Europe, Casey currently pursues a private course of study and meditation which broadly corresponds to a Buddhist creation-centred spirituality. Many of the books Casey reads are written by Buddhist authors. His meditations are comparable to a Zen style of contemplation, and he shares the personal goal of heightened awareness and understanding which other Buddhists recognize. However, within the spirit of Casey's sense of spiritual liberation, he belongs to no formal study class or meditation group.

CASEY:

> *Although my spiritual understanding has leapt forward a thousandfold since K'un-lun, I'm really aware that I'm spending a lot of my time picking up the pieces of my life again. So I make it a rule to keep everything (spiritually) in a very low-key and relaxed. That works for me well. And I mean to keep it that way.*

In one sense, Casey's pilgrimage to K'un-lun is no different from the accounts of other experienced mountain travellers who contributed to this chapter and who find a distinctive, raw, isolated, and elemental inspiration from the mountains of central Asia. However, in another sense, Casey's experiences have been among the most traumatic and harrowing of any contributor to this book. Even at the time of writing, Casey freely admits that he has still not fully recovered from his past associations with the satanic group. Their mark is still with him, although it remains in a 'massively reduced and diluted form.'

Conclusions

Two related themes have identified the mountains of central Asia as being spiritually unique for the people who contributed to this research. First, there have been the ways in which these travellers learned to understand how their spiritual paths can often lead them through emotionally painful experiences, instead of leading them around, and away from, those problematic encounters. Second, these mountains have inspired a deeper appreciation of the creativity which can develop within an individual's spiritual path. Whilst part of that creativity will arise from the sublime inspiration of beauty and wondrous power in these peaks, a further source to that spiritual creativity also arises from the darker experiences of life: the distractions which prevent the individual from flourishing to their full potential.

KENT:
> *If you talk to anyone who's spent time in different mountain areas, they'll all tell you that there's a different feel to each range you're in. And I think the thing about central Asia is that you're so far from any of the cultural comforts we all take for granted that, in a major way, you feel reduced to the absolute basics of life. And so you can really examine your spirituality in landscapes like that. And you soon find out where your spiritual weaknesses are ... and what your hang-ups are.*

For many of these travellers, the mountains of central Asia are the most challenging in the world. Whilst they are certainly not the highest mountains, they still serve to present arduous physical challenges, as well as further profound challenges to individuals' emotions and spiritual integrity.

CASEY:
> *I'd recommend to anyone who wants to find out more about themselves that they should take time to visit the K'un-lun, or any of those mountains (in central Asia). Out of all the world's mountains, that's the place where you're going to come face to face with who you are and what you're made of ... And for a lot of folks, that's not going to be a nice experience. But although that's true, I'd still say get out there, because what you come back with, in terms of new ideas and new goals, could radically change your life for ever. So it's worth the effort and the pain you go through to get to that understanding.*

CHAPTER 9

Middle East

The Lord is my shepherd, I shall lack nothing.
He makes me lie down in green pastures, he leads me
beside quiet waters.
He restores my soul. He guides me in paths of
righteousness for his names's sake.
Even though I walk through the valley of the shadow of
death, I will fear no evil, for you are with me; your
rod and your staff, they comfort me.

Psalm 23:1–4

Ancient wisdom

From the towering volcanoes of Iran and Turkey to the desert peaks of
Sinai and Saudi Arabia, and from the abundant heights of Israel and
Lebanon to the barren ranges of Jordan and Syria, the mountains of
the Middle East have been an influence in the imaginations and
philosophies of almost all western peoples. Ancient civilizations —
Sumer, Babylon and Canaan — all bore the unmistakable imprint of
these mountains. And clay tablets dating from over five thousand
years ago show us today that those people found something profoundly mysterious and intensely sacred in these scorching, and
frequently desolate peaks.

But unlike many other parts of the world, it is not the size of these
mountains which first inspired their importance. Mount Sinai for
example, rises to a height of less than 9000 feet. But despite that
relatively small physical stature, Mount Sinai has been of fundamental
importance to the Jewish and Christian faith:

> ... arrival at the foot of Mount Sinai marks the beginning of
> Israel's history. We reach what was the kernel and core of the
> nation's life, the Covenant by which all the tribes were united

in allegiance to One God, the Covenant by which a priest-people was created, and a kingdom of God on Earth inaugurated among the children of God. (Hertz 1961, 290)

A single mountain as part of the kernel and core of an entire nation. As God's ambassador among the Israelites, Moses was chosen as both law-giver and judge. It was Moses who led the people of Israel from slavery to the foot of Mount Sinai where they heard the voice of God speak to them as his children — His chosen ones, His ambassadors to the rest of humankind:

On the morning of the third day there was thunder and lightning, with a thick cloud over the mountain, and a very loud trumpet blast. Everyone in the camp trembled. Then Moses led the people out of the camp to meet with God, and they stood at the foot of the mountain. Mount Sinai was covered with smoke, because the Lord descended on it in fire. The smoke billowed up from it like smoke from a furnace, the whole mountain trembled violently, and the sound of the trumpet grew louder and louder. Then Moses spoke and the voice of God answered him. The Lord descended to the top of Mount Sinai and called Moses to the top of the mountain. (Exodus 19:16–20)

Mount Sinai was the setting for two movements of colossal significance which have shaped the minds of all Jews and Christians ever since. But two movements in opposite directions: God coming down to the bare face of Mount Sinai, whilst Moses, the people's leader, walked up that mountain to meet and talk with God. It is therefore as a meeting place between a man and his God that Sinai claims its central role in the spiritual development of Jewish and Christian peoples. But what a meeting! Man and God: the profane and the sacred, the mortal and the eternal, the dependent Moses and the benevolent, divine Father figure. A human answer to the call of God. And what a call! What a message! Nothing less than the Ten Commandments: the ten sacred themes which have remained within the laws and moralities shared by every generation living since that moment in the West, as well as other peoples living in lands colonized and otherwise influenced by the West. Indeed, Moses urged his people to remember Mount Sinai all their lives, and to tell their children and their children's children, of Sinai's inspiration and the wisdom embodied within that inspiration.

Only be careful, and watch yourselves closely so that you do
not forget the things your eyes have seen or let them slip
from your heart as long as you live. Teach them to your
children and to their children after them. Remember the day
you stood before the Lord your God at Horeb, and when he
said to me, 'Assemble the people before me to hear my words
so that they may learn to revere me as long as they live in the
land and may teach them to their children.' You came near
and stood at the foot of the mountain while it blazed with fire
to the very heavens, with black clouds and deep darkness.
Then the Lord spoke to you out of the fire. You heard the
sound of words but saw no form; there was only a voice.
(Deuteronomy 4:9–12)

Powerful words. But in their attempt to remember the inspiration
of Mount Sinai, modern day Jews and Christians have one overwhelming problem. The mountain's exact location is no longer known for
certain. No existing scriptures or carved tablets are able to provide any
definitive answers. Even the Bible offers no clear direction. In the Book
of Deuteronomy for example, readers are told that Mount Sinai is
eleven day's journey from Horeb by way of Mount Seir to Kadesh-
barnea. At first, this instruction appears to be clear and concise. However, the location of Mount Seir has also been lost with that of Mount
Sinai. Still though, theories abound. Some scholars suggest Mount
Sinai is on Jebel Helal in the north of the Sinai desert. Others maintain
it is actually located further to the south around the higher and shar-
per peaks of Jebel Musa and Jebel Serbal, rising up to 7500 feet. Ultimately therefore, it is only the inspiration and the aura of Mount Sinai
which can be allowed to live on through the generations. The mountain's moral and legal implications. Its spirit. Its eternal truths and
ancient wisdom. And it was this appreciation of Mount Sinai which
was expressed perfectly by the first century AD historian Flavius
Josephus: a man who knew that God's spirit, and that of Mount Sinai
can live for ever, through his people. Whether that spirit would be
kept alive through the tent which God commanded his people to build
for him, or through other means, the spirit of Sinai will remain eternal:

God also desired that a tent should be built for him, in
which he would condescend to meet them, and which could
also be carried with them on their journey, so that in the
future it would no longer be necessary to ascend Mount Sinai,
since God himself would descend into the tent and in that

very place would hear their prayers. (Quoted in Skrobucha
1966, 12)

But whilst God's people marched on toward the land which is
modern day Israel, the spirit of that meeting between humankind and
its God remained back in the desert. And in particular, it stayed
around Jebel Musa in the south of the Sinai desert. It was a spirit
which created possibilities for other followers of God: the early Christian monks and hermits of the third century. Those men came to Jebel
Musa and found a real, moving and profound inspiration in the
landscape there. That arid, scorching wilderness where God had
walked, and in which some men could still hear the whispers of that
divine presence. In recording his own discovery of this profound and
divine spirit on Jebel Musa, one of those early monks, Nilus Sinaita
wrote the following account:

> A powerful longing towards Sinai seized me, and neither with
> my bodily eyes nor with those of the spirit could I find joy in
> anything so strongly was I attracted to that place of solitude.
> (Quoted in Skrobucha 1966, 31)

On Jebel Musa, men with a similar sensibility to Nilus Sinaita
found a solitude for contemplation and prayer. Above all though, it
was a solitude for cleansing the soul. And within the ferocious heat of
the day, and the bitter cold of the night, they found a solitude for
banishing all dependence upon material comfort. Finally, upon that
contemplative foundation, these monks discovered complete dependence on God alone. Indeed, with that goal in mind, an early abbot of
the Jebel Musa monastery described what he called 'The Ladder to
Paradise': a spiritual guide for monks and novices which showed how,
within the aura of Mount Sinai, they could completely renounce the
world and all its temptations. Through that renunciation, they could
also find a perfect peace and a perfect love of God himself. As an
illustration of that Ladder to Paradise, there is a solid stone staircase,
carved in rock, leading up from the monastery, consisting of three
thousand steps. According to tradition, it was that bare rock staircase
which served as part of the monks daily contemplations on the
strength and integrity of their prayerful vocation. A vocation which
would inspire some of their number to take that intense feeling of
communion with the Word of God right across Europe. Six hundred
years ago for example, Gregory of Sinai had helped spread this austere
and devotional life as far as eastern Europe. And there have been

other monasteries, all of which have been strongly influenced by the Sinai spirituality, which have been built in India, Greece, Romania and Russia.

Even today, this strong sense of preserved ancient wisdom and an abiding wonder at the eternal presence of God still haunts the soaring peak of Jebel Musa. For the Englishwoman, Lesley Hazleton, her first encounter with this wisdom, and this mountain, were among the most moving experiences of her life:

> I was standing at the top of a giant mountain altar. It rose gradually, majestically, over many miles, flowing upward in straight lines from the multiple crests of distant low ridges to the framed triple peak, up and higher to the double peak, and then up to the apex of the altar — to the single peak of Jebel Musa and myself, standing upright, atop this single peak. Suffused with the sheer physical logic of this being the holy mountain, the metaphysical logic of mysticism, I felt that never had I stood higher than this, that there could be no higher place in the world. (Hazleton 1981, 37–8)

But whilst the true location of Mount Sinai remains shrouded behind veils of mystery, and generations of pilgrimage and wonder, the location of Mount Zion in the Kidron valley, near Jerusalem, is far more certain. Consequently, it remains one of the most important magnets for Jewish pilgrimage in the world. But to the Old Testament writers, Zion was another holy mountain of God. It was the high place, chosen by God, just as he had chosen Mount Sinai where he could remain among his children. Within the Psalms for example, Mount Zion is described in words of absolute reverence:

> Great is the Lord, and worthy of praise, in the city of our God, his holy mountain. It is beautiful in its loftiness, the joy of the whole earth. Like the utmost heights of Zaphon is Mount Zion, the city of the Great King. God is in her citadels; he has shown himself to be her fortress ... Walk about Zion, go round her, count her towers, consider well her ramparts, view her citadels, that you may tell of them to the next generation. (Psalm 48:1–3 and 12–13)

Two psalms later, there are more wise words about the inspirational value of Zion:

From Zion, perfect in beauty, God shines forth. Our God comes and will not be silent; a fire devours before him, and around him a tempest rages. He summons the heavens above, and the earth, that he may judge his people. (Psalm 50:2–4)

The similarities with the lessons of Mount Sinai are clear. Both mountains are intensely sacred places enveloped with fires and storms which themselves envelop the presence of God on earth. But equally, Zion does differ in important ways from Mount Sinai. Whilst Sinai was purely tempestuous, violent and terrorizing, Psalms 48 and 50 represent Zion as a mountain of fragrance and beauty, gentleness and contemplation. Whilst Mount Sinai is located within the imaginations and spiritual sensibilities of its believers, Zion is the location for a modern city, Jerusalem, which reverberates with the sounds and busy activities of God's people living their lives. Ultimately therefore, whilst Sinai has become a mountain exclusive to the contemplative faithful and spiritually sensitive, Zion is available to all. But in contrast to the pessimism and depression found in most contemporary cities, Jerusalem's place on Zion has always maintained a strong association with the ancient Biblical wisdom which portrayed Zion as a symbol of optimism. An optimism which has persisted within the city's ancient and modern history. For the Old Testament prophet Isaiah, this optimism was part of the eternal value of Mount Zion:

In the last days the mountain of the Lord's temple will be established as chief among the mountains; it will be raised above the hills, and all nations will stream to it. Many peoples will come and say, 'Come, let us go up to the mountain of the Lord, to the house of the God of Jacob. He will teach us his ways, so that we may walk in his paths.' The law will go out from Zion, the word of the Lord from Jerusalem. He will judge between nations and will settle disputes for many peoples. They will beat their swords into ploughshares and their spears into pruning hooks. Nation will not take up sword against nation, nor will they train for war any more. (Isaiah 2:2–4)

It is through words and expectations like these from Isaiah, that it is possible to appreciate the enduring link which Zion has formed between the hopes of Jews and the faith of Christianity. It is a link between a sacred mountain and a place of power and change. A place where God will bring to life a promise of new hope, of radically changed relationships between his people, and further changed ways of understanding God himself. For Christians, Isaiah's promises and prophecies have already been fulfilled through the life, the teaching and the resurrection of the Messiah, Jesus Christ:

> Those who trust in the Lord are like Mount Zion, which
>   cannot be shaken but endures for ever.
> As the mountains surround Jerusalem, so the Lord surrounds
>   his people both now and for evermore.
>   (Psalm 125 1–2)

But whilst Mount Zion remains as a fundamental element within the ancient wisdom of both the Judaic and Christian faiths, it is equally fundamental to Islam. Indeed, Zion ranks as the third most visited place of Muslim pilgrimage in the world after Mecca and Medina. It was at a point immediately beneath the mosque built at the summit of Mount Zion where Mohammed ascended to heaven. To mark that ascension, the Islamic architects built one of the most perfectly proportioned mosques in the world. On top of this beautiful and poignant place of worship, the mosque's golden dome dazzles the traveller, even from a distance of several miles. Beneath that dome is an octagonal base of blue and white marble, lavishly inscribed with flowing Arabic script. Yet on the Day of Judgement, tradition teaches that an angel will appear on this spot to blow the trumpet to signal to the world the end of time: the fulfilment of all prophecy:

> Send forth your light and your truth, let them guide me; let
>   them bring me to your holy mountain, to the place where
>   you dwell.
> Then will I go to the altar of God, to God, my joy and my
>   delight. I will praise you with the harp O God, my God.
>   (Psalm 43:3–4)

But although Sinai and Zion have inspired Jewish, Christian and Islamic believers with their auras of ancient wisdom, the highest mountains in the Middle East, Demavend and Ararat command recognition for the ways they also preserve eternal truths. At a height of 18600 feet, the summit of Mount Demavend can be seen from over forty miles away by the citizens of Tehran, capital city of Iran. And at almost 17000 feet, Ararat, in eastern Turkey also towers physically and spiritually above its surrounding landscape. But with their eerie-looking deposits of white and grey ash, and volcanic debris from past eruptive activity, Demavend and Ararat can sometimes appear to mysteriously float among the clouds, high above the surface of the earth, like ancient ghosts or spirits.

Demavend, and in particular, the range of which it is a part, was the Elburz, or Hara Berezaiti of Zoroastrian scripture: the inter-galactic mountain which rose from the centre of the earth to dwarf even the stars themselves. And on the mountainsides, grew the white haoma plant which possessed the elixir of eternal life.

But scholarly debate still continues about whether it was Demavend or Ararat where Noah's ark finally came to rest, bearing among its cargo of flora and fauna the only righteous man on the planet, Noah, along with his family. Both mountain peaks have been considered by academic authorities as sites for the incredible landing of that unique floating ark.

> The water receded steadily from the earth. At the end of the hundred and fifty days the water had gone down, and on the seventeenth day of the seventh month the ark came to rest on the mountains of Ararat. (Genesis 8:3–4)

Ararat: even the name contains a thousand perplexing mysteries. Literally, the word 'Ararat' refers to a whole country, or at the very least a region, a land or a kingdom. Even if further studies of the Bible are made, only two other references to Ararat are found, neither of which identify it more precisely. Ultimately therefore, Ararat remains an enigma which beguiles us with its possibilities and its location. For many scholars and students who have sought Ararat, and its spirit of Biblical wisdom, they must surely have been tempted to echo the searching despair of the 121st Psalm:

> I lift up my eyes to the hills — where does my help come
>   from?
> My help comes from the Lord, the Maker of heaven and
>   earth.
>   (Psalm 121:1)

Despite these frustrations, Ararat is a vital name in Jewish and Christian wisdom as the site of the first of the three covenants, or agreements, between God and his people. The second covenant arose after one of the most terrifying trials any man has ever endured. Upon the summit of Mount Moriah, God commanded Abraham, father of the Jewish nation, to kill his only son as a living sacrifice. Even today, when the story has become familiar to millions of Jews and Christians, it is impossible to imagine the horrors which must have swept and torn through Abraham's tortured mind as he led his innocent young son, Isaac, to the point on which he was to be sacrificed. But as Abraham raised his arm to strike the fatal blow, God intervened, and spoke to Abraham once more:

> I swear by myself, declares the Lord, that because you have done this and have not withheld your son, your only son, I will surely bless you and make your descendants as numerous as the stars in the sky and as the sand on the seashore. Your descendants will take possession of the cities of their enemies, and through your offspring all nations on earth will be blessed, because you have obeyed me. (Genesis 22:16–18)

Abraham's test was over. Isolated and confused, on the bare face of Mount Moriah, Abraham had shown that wherever God led him, he would obey his Lord. A sublime relationship between a man and his God.

But elsewhere, and during more recent times, God has chosen a mountain landscape as the setting for some of the most important events within the Christian faith. The transfiguration of Jesus Christ is one such example, traditionally believed to have been sited on Mount Tabor, near Nazareth:

> After six days Jesus took with him Peter, James and John the brother of James, and led them up a high mountain by themselves. There he was transfigured before them. His face shone like the sun, and his clothes became as white as the light. Just then there appeared before them Moses and Elijah, talking to Jesus. Peter said to Jesus, 'Lord, it is good for us to be here. If you wish, I will put up three shelters — one for you, one for Moses and one for Elijah.' While he was still speaking, a bright cloud enveloped them, and a voice from the cloud said, 'This is my Son, whom I love; with him I am well pleased. Listen to him!' (Matthew 17:1–5)

In reflecting upon all these sacred mountains of the Middle East, the Islamic Sufi mystic, Al-Ghazali, drew all the principal themes of inspiration into a single expression of his own faith and devotion almost nine hundred years ago:

If among the objects of the world of the spirit there is
something fixed and unalterable, great and illimitable,
something from which the beams of revelation, the streams of
knowledge, pour into the mind like water into a valley, it is to
be symbolized by a mountain. If the beings who receive these
revelations are of differing ranks, they are to be symbolized
by a valley; and if the beams of revelation reach the minds of
men, and pass on from mind to mind, then these minds are
likewise to be symbolized by valleys. (Quoted in Skrobucha
1966, 2)

For the modern day Jews, Christians, Muslims and other travellers
to these mountains, the spirits and inspiration which their ancestors
first encountered can still remain as powerful resources of insight, awe
and wonder within their everyday lives. None of these ranges are
either spiritually barren or meaningless. Nor are they simply impass-
able barriers. Rather, they can serve contemporary visitors as an
enticing collection of spiritual paths for their journeys, trials and
revelations. Always a journey. Always a journey with the opportunity
to carry along the way this wisdom and insight born from the sides of
these sacred mountains.

First visits

The mountains of the Middle East have attracted more contributors to
this book than any other range of mountains in the world. For visitors
following one of the Semitic faiths of Judaism, Christianity or Islam,
these mountains are fundamental elements of their spiritual inheritance. For Rudi, Louis and Hannah, three environmental researchers from London University, their first journey to Jebel Musa gave
them an opportunity to compare their experiences on that mountain,
with their experiences previously considered in the Himalayas (see
Chapter 6).

HANNAH:
*My one abiding memory of that first visit to Jebel Musa was when I'd
just woken up on the first day there. And it was only just dawn. And
the deep earthy orange of the mountains was just beginning to be*

picked out by the sun. And that, for me really was an eternal moment ... because if Jebel Musa was actually the site of Mount Sinai, then that was almost the same scene, and colour, and chill of the early morning air which Moses would have felt.

RUDI:

For me, that first dawn was also important because it just proved that you don't need to have studied thousands and thousands of books about Jebel Musa or our faith, or even sacred mountains. Because all you really need to do is to actually go there, and be ready for what God has to show you ... whereas in the Himalayas, your instincts for human survival force you to be more active and less immediately receptive to the divine nature of what you're seeing ... on Jebel Musa you can sit down in greater comfort and just think about what you're seeing all day.

The first and abiding impression which Jebel Musa made on these women was that it is a mountain on which they could contemplate the ancient wisdom and modern meanings of their Jewish faith in a 'calm, collected and contemplative state of mind' (Rudi). But in recognizing this opportunity to reflect on their faith in this way, all these women, as well as other travellers who contributed to this chapter, agreed that contemplation can be an extremely active way of engaging with the contemporary meaning of Jebel Musa. It is an active participation in the most profound mysteries of the mountain. The way it has inspired centuries of monastic devotion. The way it has challenged tens of thousands of visitors, from all over the world, and from almost every faith known to humankind. Active contemplation of Jebel Musa allowed these women to sit as children and learn to be instructed in the wordless immensity of the created universe: of Jebel Musa's place within that universe, and of their place alongside Jebel Musa. These were lessons which were learned in awe and wonder. No text books were necessary. No written tests were taken. This was instruction by inspiration. Instruction by physical presence. And instruction by historical implications.

LOUIS:

I think the three of us spent most of our time sitting around on Jebel Musa, just gazing out to the horizon ... In the Himalayas, we were so busy all the time, we did most of our contemplation about those moun-tains when we'd got home. But on Jebel Musa, we weren't fighting for survival like we did out there (on the Himalayas) so we had the time,

but also the presence of Jebel Musa almost forced us to make that kind
of commitment to the time we had there ...

As these themes of inspiration and contemplation were developed
by these travellers, Gabbi suggested that one of the most profitable
ways in which she contemplated Jebel Musa was 'playfully.'

GABBI:

I'd travelled to Jebel Musa with an Israeli artist friend of mine who has
this strong interest in surrealism and poetry. And her way of seeing
things can turn anything completely upside down ... so for example,
she'd talk about historical figures, like Moses, in terms of them waiting
for us. Instead of us just remembering them. Or she'd almost turn
herself upside down and talk about the rocks being the sky and the sky
being the desert floor ... But in saying all that, there was a point to
what she was doing because none of it was meant to be irreverent. She
was being playful, and bringing the eyes of a child to Jebel Musa to try
and search out new ways of understanding the place.

During that visit, Gabbi and her friend were discovering the joy
which a child-like view on the world can bring. But in understanding
and approaching that playful joy, it is essential to understand the difference between a child-like perception and a childish way of looking.
The former is a view of innocence, playfulness, awe, wonder, discovery, creativity, invention, liberation, revelation and spiritual enlightenment. In contrast, a childish mentality, in this context, is an indifferent,
self-centred way of looking at the mountain. The child-like way of
contemplating Jebel Musa reached out to the mountain. It searched. It
was ready to receive fresh insights. The childish mentality however
would have been almost completely closed to that inspiration.

GABBI:

Even as I think about that time, we weren't running around and laugh-
ing all the time like a couple of kids. But we were definitely playing
around with those images ... And my friend was definitely teaching me
through her example to do that ... and when I look back, that whole
playfulness did bring up some pretty amazing questions.

Instead of looking back, and trying to understand Moses and his
people, these women imagined Moses encouraging his people to look
forward and anticipate Gabbi and her friend developing their Jewish
faith in the late twentieth century as they visited Jebel Musa.

Instead of thinking about the austerity and poverty of the early Christian monks on Jebel Musa, these women talked about the richness of that monastic life. The desert and mountainous colours. The ways in which those colours changed through the course of a day. The ways in which the horizon changed colour from dawn to dusk. The scent of the clear air. The sound of the breeze. The soothing massage of that breeze on their faces as they stood looking out toward the horizon. The touch of Jebel Musa's rock. Touching the same areas of rock as other pilgrims, novices and monks have touched since the first time anyone came to Jebel Musa. In all, the playfulness and joyous innocence which Gabbi brought to the mountain created a set of personal inspirations for her. Something unique which both women took away with them to share with others.

GABBI:

> *If I hadn't met up with my friend, and if I hadn't taken her with me to Jebel Musa, that trip wouldn't have been as amazing as it was ... The idea that God had brought his people together, and had led them out of slavery, and taught them their culture with me in mind was staggeringly wonderful ... And not only did it almost crush me with a feeling of humility and thanksgiving, which I don't often feel, but it also really gave me a big encouragement to carry on with my work (as a feminist journalist and campaigner.)*

The contemplation in which Gabbi and her friend engaged can be considered as a form of extrovert meditation. Instead of sitting quietly, composing themselves, calming their minds and reflecting upon the mountain, both those women were always walking about. Looking round corners. Talking. Thinking. Wondering. Searching onward. Showing each other what they had found. Sharing with each other. Standing in wondrous silence. And then 'skipping on to search for more things to see' (Gabbi).

This playful, spontaneous and child-like way of contemplating Jebel Musa was also adopted by Davey and Joseph, two pan-pipe musicians from Los Angeles, California. As Buddhists, these men came to the mountain with a completely different set of spiritual practices with which they were familiar. However, they were equally aware of the reverence with which Jebel Musa is treated among Jews and Christians:

JOSEPH:

> *I'll tell you what it (Jebel Musa) did for me. And that was to make me*

*find some space on my own, away from the crowds, face the horizon
and play my pipes. And that's what we both did.*

DAVEY:

*It was beautiful. Because some of the time he'd lead the music, and I'd
follow. And then we'd change, and I'd lead.*

The fundamental truth which Joseph and Davey discovered on
Jebel Musa was that spiritual truths do not always have to be expressed either in words or in silence. Those truths can also be sung.
They can be played on musical instruments. Those truths which have
inspired pilgrims across the millennia can be danced, chanted, painted,
sculpted, embroidered, and moulded with clay.

JOSEPH:

*That was really interesting for us being there, and we've talked a lot
about it since ... Jebel Musa is one of the most calming and soothing
mountains I've ever visited. There's an amazing power about that
mountain which builds from all those centuries and centuries of prayer
and study which have gone on there.*

DAVEY:

*... and one of the few sections of the Bible which I know is a part from
Paul's letter to the Ephesians, and while we were playing our music
out there (on Jebel Musa) it actually came back to me, so I tried to
weave the meaning of those words into my own experience of being
there, and to express it in our music ...*

> *For we are God's workmanship,*
> *created in Christ Jesus to do good works,*
> *which God prepared in advance for us to do.*
> *(Ephesians 2: 10)*

DAVEY:

*... and although I don't have the Jewish or the Christian God in my
(Buddhist) spirituality, I can really relate to those words. Because I like
the idea that that moment for the both of us was actually prepared and
made ready. I mean, that makes you feel pretty special. Being on this
amazing mountain where the Bible has been studied for thousands of
years. And in that Bible, there's a teaching that says the moment was
prepared for us ...*

JOSEPH:

It's a moment which you can either grasp hold of, or you can walk way from. You can accept the moment, or you can deny it. You choose.

Other Buddhist travellers were also able to weave their own spirituality alongside other Biblical scriptures as they reflected upon their first visits to Jebel Musa as well as Mount Zion. With Hillary for example, a policewoman from Ohio, USA, both mountains served to inspire her beliefs. But of equal significance, Jebel Musa and Zion also served to form links between Hillary's Zen spirituality, and the Jewish and Christian faiths.

HILLARY:

I wasn't sure what I'd find on those mountains because, as a Buddhist, I was kind of apprehensive about how they'd make me feel. So it was like going into the unknown for me ... But what I discovered was that everywhere I went on those mountains I heard people talk about the ways they were making up their own responses to being there. You know, this means such and such for me. And then someone else would share how they were feeling ... and yet when I've told that to Christian and Jewish friends of mine they've said they hardly ever get a chance to talk that freely in church or in their synagogues.

When Hillary first told her Jewish and Christian friends about those discussions she overheard on Jebel Musa and Zion, those friends frequently found it hard to understand. Having spent all their worshipping lives being told what the scriptures meant, and having been told the accepted interpretation of their respective faiths, neither the Jewish nor the Christian friends to whom Hillary spoke were used to having an opportunity of developing personal and creative interpretations about any aspect of their faiths.

HILLARY:

As a Buddhist, that's what I'm encouraged to do all the time ... and I know there are some Christians and Jews who need to do that too ... But there is one poem which I have to read out which just perfectly captures everything about those times I spent on those mountains because it sums up that whole feeling I had about being anxious about going there. Being worried about the unknown ways it would effect my own beliefs, and then finding this amazing opportunity to sit and think and compare their (Jewish and Christian) faith with mine ... and letting that creative thinking-time go on and on ...

> *Into fog, through the fog*
> *We rowed. Then:*
> *The wide sea — so blue, so bright!*
> *(Shiki)*

That last line is especially important for my feelings about those mountains (Jebel Musa and Zion) because I've enjoyed checking out the Bible and comparing it to my own beliefs ... There are obviously some major differences, but there are also some major similarities too ... Before I flew out to Israel, I brought a Bible with that idea in mind, but I didn't have any idea it would be so wonderful ...

Among the Biblical scriptures which Hillary found as she contemplated Jebel Musa and Mount Zion was the following sentence from the Old Testament Book of Hosea:

> I am like a green pine tree;
> Your fruitfulness comes from me.
> (Hosea 14:8)

HILLARY:

It's like a Zen haiku poem isn't it! It's simple and beautiful and right on the button. And I guess that whatever your faith, you can develop some very close ideas about a place whatever your background ... You can build on the common ground as well as your differences, and develop some wonderful new ways of understanding a mountain, or a piece of poetry or scripture ... the possibilities are endless!

Alongside this woven tapestry of Buddhist poetry, Biblical wisdom, and personal mountain experiences, Alfred, a retired archaeologist from Phoenix, Arizona, identified a further literary reference from the Zen artist Kenji Miyazawa. As was so often the case when Alfred discussed his own mountain experiences for this research, they captured the essence of others within his interview group:

> Everyone should feel as an artist does. Everyone should be free to let his or her inner mind speak to them. And everyone is an artist when they do this. (Miyazawa 1962, 2)

ALFRED:

Unlike a lot of mountains I think we've all visited (in that interview group), Jebel Musa and Zion don't oblige you to fight for survival against the elements ... So I think maybe, it's a little easier to sit and be creative with the moment of being there ...

GLENDA:

But don't you think a lot of people are scared to try that sort of experimentation ... because they've never had that opportunity before?

ALFRED:

That's true. And I think it's criminal the way so many people really have never sat down and been creative with their faith ... But I do know from people I've met that, although you're right, they've felt the need to make the moment of being there their own ... and they've either written poetry, or thought their own new thoughts and really dug deep into themselves, maybe for the first times in their lives, to dig out those personal responses (to those mountains).

The final theme which arose from these first visits showed how some travellers' meditations were able to heal their anxieties. Anxieties about their faith, as well as other anxieties about their everyday lives: who they have become, where they are going, their friends and their family. In offering their contributions on this subject, Lionel and Seb, two American Jews from Miami, Florida exemplified the thoughts and experiences of others:

SEB:

The first time I went out to Jebel Musa and Zion when I was staying in Israel, I felt I was going home ... a feeling of returning to my beginning even though I'd never been to those mountains before ... You know in Homer's Odyssey, when Odysseus returns home, he thinks that's the end of the journey, but it's only the start of a new journey ... and that's exactly the way I felt too.

As he thought about this sense of arriving in the mountains, only to discover that his arrival heralded a new awakening within his spiritual consciousness, Seb found that the healing effects of the mountains, and particularly of Jebel Musa, began to work almost immediately:

SEB:

Right now, within the Jewish faith, there's a big debate over where the faith's going, and about the whole future, and the way a lot of the orthodoxies are being abandoned by young families ... And I think that's been playing on my mind a lot because I've been pretty much

*undecided ... but what I got from going out to Israel was a chance to
get back to the roots of where we (world Jewry) came from. And where
we came from was a mentality of confusion and entrapment. And out
from that chaos, God took Moses to lead the people on, and mould them
into a nation ... So getting back to those mountains as major turning
points in that process of being led by God, by the hand, from confusion
to understanding, with laws, and a promised land, that's the foundation
of where we (world Jewry) are today ... So from being confused and
worried about that debate myself, I think being in the mountains helped
me deal with that anxiety because I've seen with my own two eyes
where we've come from ...*

From his state of personal confusion about the future of Jewish
faith, Seb felt healed by the disarming simplicity of the solution to that
debate which he discovered in the mountains. First and foremost, the
Jewish people believe they are a chosen people. A people chosen by
God and led for untold years until they bore the characteristics of a
nation: a code of laws which everyone could understand, a land of
their own, their own myths and legends, wisdom and literature, their
own heroes and their own leaders. All this simplicity came to Seb as
he sat and walked contemplatively on and around Jebel Musa and
Mount Zion.

In a similar way, Seb's friend Lionel reached a corresponding
conclusion:

LIONEL:
*I'd have to go along with everything (Seb's) been saying because I felt
that being at those mountains, I received a lot of answers to a lot of
questions. Not only about the future of the Jewish faith in general, but
also my own role within that faith ... But the answer's simple. We've
(world Jewry) always been led by God when we've been heading in the
right direction. So now is the time to wait for his leadership to show
the way. Don't get anxious. Don't do anything stupid. Just wait. Have
faith. And be ready to be led.*

When God shows the Jewish people the direction in which he
wants them to proceed, both Seb and Lionel believe that moment will
affirm the distinctive identity which world Jewry embodies. In that
sacred, wondrous moment, these men believe the world will witness
the full meaning of the unique Jewish faith: its laws, its history, its
wisdom and its great contribution for world spirituality.

LIONEL:

When I was out there on Jebel Musa, the words which summed up that need to respond to the simplicity in our faith when God calls us together came from Shakespeare's Hamlet. And as soon as I remembered those words, I knew what Shakespeare'd been saying, and what we (world Jewry) should be saying too:

> *To be, or not to be — that is the question;*
> *Whether 'tis nobler in the mind to suffer*
> *The slings and arrows of outrageous fortune,*
> *Or to take arms against a sea of troubles,*
> *And by opposing end them? To die, to sleep;*
> *No more; and by a sleep to say we end*
> *The heart-ache and the thousand natural shocks*
> *That flesh is heir to, 'tis a consummation*
> *Devoutly to be wished. To die, to sleep;*
> *To sleep: perchance to dream. Ay, there's the rub;*
> *For in that sleep of death what dreams may come,*
> *When we have shuffled off this mortal coil,*
> *Must give us pause.*
>   *(Hamlet III 1:56)*

LIONEL:

You can trace through each line of that speech all the major dilemmas which Jews are currently talking and worrying about. Each line! And yet what I find so amazing is that the answers to each question which we're (world Jewry) asking about can be answered by the very, very simple truths which came to me, and which, I'm sure, come to thousands of others, when they visit Jebel Musa ... Being out there (on Jebel Musa) is an incredibly instructive experience which everyone should try and achieve. And then, they should take home those simple truths which they discover about their own faiths.

Subsequent visits

Among the more experienced travellers who contributed to this chapter, these ideas of a creative response to personal spirituality were developed further, and within the context of a wider set of literary references. The most frequently quoted author was the pioneering psychologist Carl Jung. For Jung, there were an almost infinite variety of ways in which an individual can approach, and understand, his or her spiritual commitment. Some people will prefer to read and talk about their faith. Others will approach insights through their imaginations, meditations and dreams. Many other people find it stimulating to express their faith through painting, pottery and sculpture. In discussing their response to Jung's insights, the experienced travellers to the Middle Eastern sacred mountains described their encounters with spiritual development which were less repressed, less self-conscious and more experimental than many of the travellers who described their first visits to these mountains. The following contribution from Linda, a Christian librarian from Ipswich, England, exemplifies this progression away from what Jung calls spiritual 'cramp,' and what Linda calls simply 'spiritual constipation':

LINDA:
> *As I look back over the (four) times I've been out to Jebel Musa, I can really feel this progressive erosion of my western style of strict, conforming, and constipated way of worshipping and understanding God. So now I'd describe Jebel Musa as my number one place of worship. I go there to breathe in the warm air, and gaze at the landscape ... But what I do now, and which I didn't have the confidence to do previously, and certainly not on my first visit, is to walk away from the crowds, sit down, close my eyes, and be ready to receive. And every time I've done that, opening my mind up in that way, I've always received some wonderful messages: things I should do, people I should see, passages of the Bible I should read ... so I always take a note book with me so I don't forget anything I'm given!*

Throughout Linda's discussion of her developing relationship with Jebel Musa, she concentrated on two themes. First, the mountain has become a place of worship. A place in which she feels most free to offer her thanksgiving to God. But none of this worship is conducted within any chapel on the mountain. It is a form of worship which is conducted outside where Linda engages in the second aspect of her relationship with Jebel Musa: the receipt of wisdom messages from God. A divine wisdom. A wisdom which Linda does not always fully understand. But a wisdom which is tailored to Linda's everyday life, as well as the lives of her friends, family and other people she knows:

LINDA:

When I come back from Jebel Musa with a message for someone I know, I always have to be really diplomatic about the way I try and pass it on to them. I mean, if I just said 'Oh, God told me you've got to do this or that,' I wouldn't get very far at all! So I bring it into the conversation as a question: 'Have you thought about doing this?' or 'I wonder what would happen if you tried that.' And that approach is best ... But whenever I've gone to Jebel Musa, I find I bring back more and more messages like that, and it's a wonderful privilege ... I'd like to think it means that God feels he can trust me to take those messages and deliver them ...

In his book, *Modern Man in Search of a Soul,* Carl Jung stated that everyone's social and emotional problems have a spiritual foundation. From Linda's contributions, and from the other experienced travellers who echoed her continually developing appreciation of Jebel Musa, it is possible to suggest that everyone's life can be fundamentally enriched by building upon their spiritual foundation. For Linda, she has built a sense of confidence in travelling to Jebel Musa, using the place in a way she feels comfortable. Offering her private worship to God. And receiving his instruction, his inspiration, his wisdom, and his messages for others. In a similar way, Jane discussed her relationship with Jebel Musa and her understanding of Jung's prescription for a 'new level of consciousness' within a developing spiritual commitment:

JANE:

Jung's phrase, a 'new level of consciousness' is exactly what it is. The more I spend time just sitting around on Jebel Musa, and soaking it all in, the more I feel in contact with the absolute simplicity of what Jung's on about. It's about a developing relationship between people and their sacred goals: their vision for what spirituality can mean to them. And that's it. But the key word is developing. We've got to allow ourselves to be led into situations, like being on Jebel Musa, where our lives can grow and flourish, and as Jung rightly says, reach a 'new level of consciousness.'

Among these experienced travellers, there was a clear insight into the need for individuals to trust their intuitive and creative response to their faiths. But equally, there was an appreciation of needing to accept the fact that spiritually committed individuals will spend most of their lives not knowing all the answers to their faith. Particularly among the Buddhist contributors to this research, this theme of the adventure of uncertainty was given strong emphasis. In the following illustration for example, Andrea, a colour therapist from Liverpool, England, compared her three journeys to Mount Ararat in eastern Turkey with her growing willingness to accept the uncertainties of her Buddhist faith alongside the other uncertainties of her everyday life:

ANDREA:

... well, for a start, it's uncertain whether Ararat is actually the landing place for Noah's Ark, so that's a good start to accepting uncertainty! But for me, Ararat's got a lot to recommend it because I really respond to colour. And there are basically only a very few colours which you see from the summit of Ararat. But within those colours there is infinite variety. So that's the point which I've learned to appreciate more and more ... Basically, our lives are limited, for all sorts of reasons. So, you can see that as the restricted number of colours. Blues, mauves and whites etcetera. But although our lives are restricted, we can still discover an infinity of richness ... So what I've found is that we can work with our restrictions. Our limitations ... We can get on with life and our faiths ... I've realized that we're never going to know all the answers, so I've given up trying. But I hope I'll never give up developing those parts of my life which I do understand!

Beyond the level of accepting and working with life's uncertainties, other travellers to Ararat found the mountain inspired them to accept their 'lack of abilities' (Jade) which had previously caused them significant anxiety. For Jade, Ararat has become one of the most 'sacred and precious places' to which she has travelled, and in which she has come to terms with many of her 'imperfections':

JADE:

For many years, right the way through my childhood and teenage years, one of the big issues in my life has been a problem of making friends ... for many reasons, I've never really had a close circle of people I can call on ... and it was only when I first travelled right out to Ararat and spent time camping out in those foothills that I realized that maybe that wasn't such a big deal. Maybe my life is meant to be more solitary. And I can remember the first time that thought came to me, I was drinking a beaker of orange squash, and staring out over that amazing landscape, and realizing that I had a huge grin of contentment right across my face! So for me, Ararat will always represent that lesson ... and the more I go back there, the more it's become important to my understanding of who I am, and where I'm going.

Problems which an individual may previously have regarded as personal imperfections can become part of the marvel and joy of developing a spiritual faith. They can be woven into the rich tapestry of a living commitment. They can even become the foundations to sustained themes of spiritual maturity, such as Jade's acceptance of the attractive possibilities within her single life. Whilst others may agonize about that prospect, Jade finds it now rests easy with her, following her inspirational meditations on Ararat:

JADE:

The way I feel about going back to Ararat is that being alone there is definitely an advantage. I can do the climbs at my own pace. I can stop when I want. I can move on when I want. I can camp when I want. And it's complete and utter bliss! ... but because I'm really serious about my Zen beliefs I like to spend a lot of time meditating there, and you really can't do that when you're in a crowd. Well, I couldn't anyway.

As part of her meditations on Ararat, Jade has found that one haiku poem in particular always returns to her attention:

> Lightning flash:
> Still water gleams bright
> Between the dark trees.
>   (Shiki)

JADE:

I look at that poem as being the three parts of my acceptance about all my supposed inadequacies. In the first line, you've got the lightning flash of inspiration when I discovered that being alone isn't such a bad thing after all! Then in the second line, you've got this beautiful word-picture of a pool. And I'll either just imagine that water, sparkling in the sunlight. Or other times, I'll imagine jumping in and splashing about, and really having a great time ... And then in the last line, you've got this idea that the pool and the lightning flash are hidden from a lot of people's views by the tall dark trees. And only if you're on the right track are you going to find the pool and its inspiration.

Another 'Ararat poem' which Jade finds inspirational and instructive, and which also continues to recur within her associations with that mountain, is the following verse by Shiba:

> Happiness:
> Waking, alive again,
> In this grey world of winter rain.
> (Shiba)

JADE:

I'd say that I feel really comfortable, and almost at home, on Ararat these days. You know, when it first comes into view again, something inside me breathes a sigh of relief, and it's like coming home. Or one of my 'homes,' anyway. But this haiku by Shiba is another pure and graceful one. It begins with how I feel when I go back to Ararat. Happiness. Or supreme and complete contentment. And then, from the second line, I feel alive to every moment of being there. And I feel my batteries re-charged enough to face the grey world of routine and work when I go home.

As Jade reflected upon the gradual and stimulating ways in which Ararat has calmed her anxieties, and stimulated her imagination, she suggested the mountain had significantly helped her create the understanding of herself which she now has. In that way, Mount Ararat has acted within Jade's imagination in two ways. First, whether or not the mountain is actually the site of Noah's landing, Ararat carries with it profound resonances of a sacred presence — an aura, an ambience of ancient wisdom which transcends the limitations of Judaism or Christianity.

Second, Ararat is not only located in a relatively isolated region of eastern Turkey, but it also contains a range of visual contrasts including sun-baked rock and snow-covered peaks at the same time. Many of these elements and contrasts have stimulated Jade's imagination and spiritual sensibility. But as she engaged with Ararat's inspirational aura, Jade was determined to avoid the superficiality of a simple day-trip to the mountain. Rather, she camped on the foothills. She spent weeks at a time on the mountain, listening to its voice, witnessing its many moods and displays of natural and spiritual wonder, touching its many textures of rock, smelling its raw, clean, timeless breeze, and relishing the pure mountain snow at its summit. Altogether, a multi-sensual engagement with all that Ararat has to offer to an open-minded and receptive traveller. As Jade jokes, in a parody of the expression attributed to Julius Caesar by the Roman historian Suetonius:

JADE:

I came. I saw. I was inspired!

A further theme which was discussed by experienced Christian travellers to the mountains, developed from the following profound observations by Jesus Christ, recorded in the gospel of Matthew:

By their fruit you will recognize them. Do people pick grapes from thorn bushes, or figs from thistles? Likewise every good tree bears good fruit, but a bad tree bears bad fruit. A good tree cannot bear bad fruit, and a bad tree cannot bear good fruit. (Matthew 6:16–18)

ROBERT:

Through my work and holidays, I've been back to the Middle East seven times. And whenever I can, I always try and take a couple of extra days to visit Jebel Musa, because I find it's teaching me so much about those words (from Matthew's gospel). I think they oblige us to look for opportunities to build upwards from our faith ... to make changes in our lives and in others. And the possibilities for that are almost endless.

Of all the possibilities which have suggested themselves to Robert, two in particular have attracted most of his attention. First, there is the need for more dialogue and more cooperation between individuals from different faiths. Whenever Robert visits Jebel Musa, he is always impressed by the way that mountain attracts travellers from a diversity of spiritual backgrounds. Upon that experience, Robert suggests there should be more projects which bring members of different faiths together. Musical projects. Worship events. Educational initiatives. The possibilities are evident. But the leadership to take up that challenge is rare and lacking in encouragement.

The second possibility which Robert suggested for 'bearing fruit,' as Christ suggests, would involve religious groups cooperating in social welfare projects — projects directed at homeless people, the unemployed, the elderly, addicts, victims of domestic and other forms of violence.

ROBERT:

> *These are all the issues which come to mind whenever I travel to Jebel Musa. Or, these days, even when I think about that mountain ... When I first went there (to Jebel Musa), I was overwhelmed by the beauty of the place. Now, all these years later, I'm overwhelmed by these thoughts of bearing fruit. There's a different kind of beauty. A beautiful sense of the need for justice.*

Robert's practical and personal response to this inspiration from Jebel Musa has been to begin working at weekends for a London charity among homeless people. However, at the time of writing, he is contemplating the possibility of giving up his career as an insurance underwriter, and devoting himself, full time, to that charity work. At present, he finds the prospect of that move to be 'completely daunting.'

ROBERT:

> *In one sense, it seems absolutely inexplicable that a mountain can effect me so profoundly ... I've had similar experiences among the mountains of New Zealand, but they've never pushed me so far as Jebel Musa has in the ways I see my faith now, as well as in the future ...*

Turning points

Denisse and Wanda, from Dallas, Texas, first travelled to Jebel Musa as part of a package vacation in 1988. At that time, both women had been recently divorced and had travelled to Israel for a 'complete break from all our troubles' (Wanda). When they booked the vacation, Denisse and Wanda believed their choice of Israel as a destination had been made almost by chance. Neither of them had travelled to the eastern Mediterranean before, although it had always been a country which attracted them, both for its ancient architecture as well as its natural landscapes, including Israel's accessibility to the Sinai desert. Certainly, the motivation for making that journey was simply as casual tourists, with no significant spiritual curiosity at all. Although both women had been born into Roman Catholic families, they had not maintained any commitment to that faith since the time they left home to attend college for their nursing qualifications.

WANDA:

> *The way we'd have described how we felt with life at that time is to say*
> *we were pissed off with just about everything. Our marriages had gone*
> *down the tubes. Other family problems were going on for us both. And*
> *we were totally out of sympathy with just about everything America*
> *was standing up for at that time.*

Specifically, both women were disillusioned with the frivolity of modern urban society in the United States. To illustrate those concerns, Denisse and Wanda identified an extended list of examples which included 'TV game shows,' 'chat shows,' 'advertising,' 'the state of American education,' 'federal (government) priorities' and 'the complete bankruptcy of our nation, financially and morally.'

DENISSE:

> *... so all that was going on in our minds. And it was a subject we*
> *spoke about every day. Either something we'd see in a newspaper or on*
> *the TV would spark us off ...*

WANDA:

> *And we found a lot of modern Israeli culture is becoming American-*
> *ized. What with their music and movies and stuff ...*

DENISSE:

> *So with all that going on in our minds, we got our first day at Jebel*
> *Musa. It was a huge, long drive, but when we got out of the bus, blam!*
> *We were silenced.*

For the first time in these women's lives, they encountered a personal and profound sense of awe and wonder. At first, neither of them spoke. Neither of them could speak. Their minds were numbed into a state of wordless incredulity.

DENISSE:

> *I was into new territory out there. And so was she (Wanda) ... There's*
> *a powerful presence about Jebel Musa which I can't imagine anyone*
> *ignoring.*

WANDA:

> *As I look back on that moment of first seeing Jebel Musa, I'd say it was*
> *like a re-birth to my Catholic belief. But I'd also have to say that now,*

*my awareness of many other beliefs, particularly native American be-
liefs, are also included into my Catholic beliefs.*

Not only did that first encounter with Jebel Musa stimulate these
women to look again at their Catholic faith, it also served to expand
their appreciation of the potential breadth of Christian spirituality. At
first, this renewal and expansion of Catholic interest caused Denisse
and Wanda to talk about the ways they had been taught at school
about the Christian Trinity: the three-part identity of God as a divine
Father, his incarnation as Jesus Christ, and God's presence among his
people through the Holy Spirit.

WANDA:

*At school, all that stuff just flew over my head. So I just accepted it,
and pretended to understand it like everyone else does ... But even
without thinking about the Trinity on Jebel Musa, the thought came
into my head that with all those people (other tourists) around the
place, it obviously meant a whole lot of things to them all. And then,
suddenly I got this picture in my mind of thousands of rays of light
coming together, and going into a bright centre, like the centre of a
flower. And that centre was God. But not just a few rays of light, but
thousands and millions of them ...*

The picture was so inspiring that Wanda immediately interpreted it
as a way of understanding the numerous contrasts within God's personality and behaviour. But instead of using the vocabulary of the Christian Trinity, which she had been taught at school, Wanda found she
was using her own words to express the meaning of that picture. God
was therefore seen by Wanda as a 'teacher,' 'friend,' 'counsellor,' 'heal-
er,' 'artist,' 'guru,' 'leader,' 'judge,' 'conscience' and 'guide.' Instead of
being composed of three elements, God was seen to comprise a rich
tapestry of 'thousands and millions' of aspects to his divine personality. And in sharing this vision with Denisse, both women agreed that
many of these aspects to God's character were visible at Jebel Musa.

WANDA:

*I guess that's what prompted me to imagine that picture of a flower
with all those rays of light going into it, because, on Jebel Musa, there
must have been millions of Christians, as well as many other people,
who've brought their own special experiences of God to that mountain.
So you go a long way beyond just three school-book parts to God, because there's so much more to him than just three clichés.*

DENISSE:

> *And, for me, as soon as (Wanda) described her picture to me, wham!*
> *That did it for me too! It was like an explosion going off inside my*
> *brain. All at once, I saw so much. And so many things fell into place ...*

Following the inspiration of Wanda's mental picture of a multi-faceted God: a God of an infinitely rich significance, both women have subsequently embarked on private programmes of study and travel, prayer and meditation, which have built upon the foundation of Wanda's picture. In doing so, and having returned to Jebel Musa, together, on three further occasions since their first visit in 1988, both women have discovered and contemplated God's ability to create beauty as well as his ability to destroy. His ability to create harmony across the entire cosmos, as well as his ability to wreak havoc within individual lives, families, communities and entire continents for reasons which still elude precise interpretation.

DENISSE:

> *Apart from finding more to God than the three cliché parts of the Trin-*
> *ity, I think we must have touched base on just about every other part of*
> *his personality ...*

WANDA:

> *But the main thing we've discovered for ourselves is that God can't be*
> *seen as pretty or nice, or convenient, or instant, or superficial, or any*
> *of the other ways that folks want him to be these days. You know,*
> *having an instant God who you can call up, like dialling for a pizza.*
> *He's not like that! And that's pretty tough for a lot of folks to under-*
> *stand. But it's true. Just think about it.*

Having first visited Jebel Musa in a state of personal confusion and frustration, and with a spiritual curiosity which was almost completely consigned to regimented and restricted memories of childhood, Denisse and Wanda have become repeatedly inspired by their response to the mountain. They have discovered a rich and wondrous treasury of sacred inspiration within their current vision of God which they had never previously considered, or even glimpsed. This new vision has emerged through the three-way interaction between these women, Jebel Musa, and the inspiration of God. As such, the mountain has been an active, provocative, challenging and attractive element within this interaction of newly discovered inspiration. Jebel Musa's new role within the lives of Denisse and Wanda has drawn them back to its magnificent heights and ancient meaning. It has calmed them. It has inspired them further. It has been a place where new friendships with other pilgrims have been forged. And it has served both women as a vast, solid proof that a curiosity for sacred inspiration can remain vitally important for each aspect of everyday life in the late twentieth century.

WANDA:

> *I cannot emphasise too much just how much that mountain means to the both of us. Every time we go back, we greet it with a smile ... We're excited about going there. We save for it. We look forward to it. We talk about it, and read up about it, and take off in our studies in all sorts of different directions ... But at the heart of everything, we always know there's that amazing and enormous figure of God using that mountain in our lives. And long may it be so!*

Conclusions

The dominant theme within the interview discussions on the mountains of the Middle East has been the way in which these peaks have almost immediately calmed the minds and sensibilities of these travellers. However, having been calmed, those same travellers have all recalled being inspired to new heights of spiritual insight and wonder, excitement and anticipation.

WANDA:

> *I've enjoyed listening to these stories and memories (in one of the research interview-groups) ... and I'd say they're all about the calm before the storm. You know, everyone seems to have found a real calming, soothing, relaxing way of spending time on these mountains. But once that calm is all under way, bang! Then you get the inspiration or the teaching you need.*

When Wanda made this observation, Robert was also in attendance at that interview meeting, and was able to develop Wanda's thoughts from his personal experience:

ROBERT:

> *That's right. It's precisely the teaching you 'need,' as you (Wanda) said. It's not necessarily the teaching you go looking for, or the teaching you might expect, or feel comfortable with.*

For the Jewish travellers who contributed to this research, this precise form of inspiration was seen as undeniable evidence that their faith, alongside others, remains 'valid and potentially full of life.'

HANNAH:

> *You know, in the Himalayas, the adventure is basically surviving! But in the Sinai, or around Mount Zion, so many people have been telling their stories, in these (research interview) meetings about how they've found out, in their own ways, that these mountains are still alive! And our (Jewish) faith is alive too. It has some big things to offer. Even today! At its heart is the simple, simple truth that we are God's chosen people who he gave a set of simple laws to in the desert. And as long as we all keep our attention on him, and not allow ourselves to be distracted by any in-fighting, we'll last forever.*

At a broader level, Jade suggested that not only do these mountains serve the Semitic monotheistic faiths of Judaism, Christianity and Islam, but they have a distinctive contribution to make in other faiths too:

JADE:

> *What's been interesting for me in listening to everybody (in this interview-group) talking about their own experiences on these mountains has been the way it almost exactly matches a whole lot of other conversations I've had on those same mountains with other people, from all over the world (during Jade's own travels). And what we've confirmed here, and what I've heard on countless other times in my own travels, is that these mountains are fantastically powerful in terms of the raw, basic inspiration they give ... And for New Agers, Hindus, other Buddhists like me, cult members, everybody gets something from those mountains ... And not only that, but I'd also say these mountains are probably the only set of mountains in the world where people get some form of inspiration, even when they don't follow a religion. And you can't always say that about a lot of mountains. But in those (Middle Eastern) countries you can.*

CHAPTER 10

Africa

We need their spirit still ... It is we who shall have lived in vain unless we follow on from where their footprints are covered over by the wind of the moving spirit that travels the ultimate borders of space and time from which they were redeemed by their story. Woven as it is into a pattern of timeless moments, their story may yet help the redeeming moon in us all on the way to a renewal of life that will make now forever.

Van der Post (1993, 229)

Ancient wisdom

African mountains have inspired profound spiritual curiosity and insights ever since the earliest human ancestors evolved almost two million years ago. Within the sedimentary clay and volcanic ash of northern Tanzania's Olduvai Gorge for example, there may have been early traces of this reverence within the lives of *Homo habilis,* one of the most important of all human ancestors. From the faded cave paintings of succeeding generations of prehistoric peoples, including the evolving clans and tribes of *Homo sapiens,* it is clear that mountains have been regarded as objects of mystery, awe and wonder throughout that two million year period. More proof of this ingrained mountain reverence is evident in other cave paintings and inscriptions within the Drakensburg Range of South Africa, the Tsodilo Hills of Botswana, as well as the Saharan desert massifs of Tibesti and Ahaggar. Together, this is a collection of human spiritual expression which is not only unsurpassed anywhere else in the world, but which also continues to elude complete understanding among modern scholars.[1]

Africa's highest peak, the 19340 foot snow-capped dome of Kibo on Kenya's Mount Kilimanjaro, has been of particularly sacred value for the Chagga tribes ever since they sought sanctuary from Masai warriors within the last five hundred years. But even before the Chagga began to live near Kilimanjaro, there is every reason to believe that the original pygmy inhabitants of that region had also developed a sophisticated collection of prayers and legends through which they regarded Kilimanjaro as a sacred mountain. Even among Chagga legends, there are stories of little spirit people: members of a sacred and royal council, who inhabit the paths and rocks of Kibo's summit. Only if they are approached with an appropriate expression of humility and respect, will those spiritual pygmies share their fabulous wealth and herds of fine cattle with the visitor.

Among the Dawamish, Nisqually, Puyallup and Skikomish groups of Chagga people, there are other stories which describe the divine forces which created each of Kilimanjaro's three volcanic peaks: Kibo, Mawenzi and Shira. The legend tells of an arrogant, spiteful malcontent named Tone who lived at a time before the mountains came into being. At one point during his evil life, Tone tricked the supreme Chagga god, Ruwa, to inflict a terrible famine on his people. Angered and vengeful, the tribe sought to capture Tone, and punish him for his stupidity and malevolence. But with his deceptive cunning, Tone escaped, and ran to find safety with an elderly cattle herdsman who agreed to help Tone on one condition. Tone had to guard two prized cows, Tenu and Meru. Under no circumstances whatsoever was Tone to let Tenu and Meru out of his sight. At the beginning of his task, Tone was careful and vigilant. But as time passed, he began to forget his responsibilities. He let his attentions drift, until one day, Tone became so complacent that he left the cattle to wander unattended. In no time at all, Tenu and Meru escaped and were free. As soon as Tone discovered his terrible mistake, his heart pounded like a drum. Desperately, he searched the horizon for the precious cows only to see nothing but dust and sky. Sickened by his own foolishness, and petrified that the elderly herdsman would turn him over to the angry tribe, Tone had no alternative other than to continue his anxious search. But still, the horizon revealed no sign of the cows. Days of more frustration passed until, finally, Tone was at the point of abandoning his search.

Then, suddenly, Tone saw Tenu. Without thinking Tone charged after the cow as fast as he could run. In the blazing heat of the hot day, Tone's lungs almost burst with the effort. But to make Tone's breathless struggle even more exhausting, Tenu mischievously created an enormous hill and threw it straight in Tone's way. Then another hill arrived. And another. And another. The faster and more desperately Tone searched and climbed, Tenu threw more and more hills in his path. Higher hills. And higher. Even higher hills all came soaring through the sky to land before the frustrated and gasping figure of Tone. Each new hill crushed Tone's arrogant and self-serving spirit further into oblivion. At one point, Tenu allowed Tone to believe that he had finally caught her. Then, at the last moment, Tenu grinned triumphantly, created the mighty 19340 foot peak of Kibo and slammed it down in Tone's path. The last anyone saw of the pair was when Tenu ran playfully down into Kibo's volcanic crater, closely pursued by the manic and delirious figure of Tone.

They were never seen again. Only their inspiration remains. The folly of Tone's arrogance. His complacency at leaving the cattle to wander unattended. Tone's eventual understanding that he could never recover from his stupid mistake as he was forced to climb the incalculable mass of mountainous rock and cloud-piercing summits of domes, smoothed edges and pinnacles which Tenu threw in his way. Tone's lessons can therefore be read in the physical and spiritual presence of these rocks. Their towering enormity reminds all who have the eyes to see that Tone's arrogance and laziness are attitudes to be guarded against with care and wisdom.[2]

Two hundred miles to the north of Kilimanjaro, in Kenya, rests the awesome mass of Kere-Nyaga, the Mountain of Brightness, often known by its modern name of Mount Kenya. As the second highest summit in Africa, the peak of Batian stabs at the Kenyan sky to a height of 17058 feet. Adjacent to Batian, as the other two elements of Kere-Nyaga's shattered volcanic core, are the summits of Point Lenana, with an altitude of 16355 feet, and Nelion at a height of 17022 feet. Around these peaks is a jagged landscape of plummeting cliffs, and unearthly glacial tongues of solid ice. Adding to these astonishing shapes, mists and swirling snows frequently obscure the observer's view, and lure foolish travellers toward eternal oblivion.

Among Kenya's largest tribe, the Kikuyu, Kere-Nyaga is the earthly abode of Ngai, the tribal god whose immense presence fills all African skies. But Ngai is also a creator god. According to Kikuyu legend, Ngai created the earth and all the cosmos. Having done so, he then created the first Kikuyu man and led him to the summit of Kere-Nyaga. Before the man and his god was a panorama of the whole world. Groves of magnificent trees. Breathtaking mountains. Cool waters, and meadows carpeted with wild flowers of every colour. As a companion for the man, Ngai created a woman with whom the man fathered nine daughters. From each of those daughters, came the future generations of the Kikuyu tribe's nine clans. Nine families with a single, sacred ancestry, a family tree which can be traced through this legend to a direct association with Kere-Nyaga, and the time when their forefather had been created and shown the world and all its fruits and richness by the awesome god, Ngai. From this enduring self-identity as a divinely chosen people, the Kikuyu have developed a culture of ancient wisdom and rituals which has bound their succeeding generations to Kere-Nyaga's spiritual and practical inspiration.

Probably the most fundamental of all such unions between the Kikuyu people and their mountain has developed within their rituals and prayers for rain: the source of all life.[3] The prayers were spoken whenever the crops needed rain, or when the rains were late in their arrival. A rain-prayer ceremony would begin with the selection of a lamb of uniform colouring. Two children would then lead the little animal toward a sacred tree which had been selected to represent Kere-Nyaga. With a gourd of beer in one hand, and another containing milk in the other, a tribal elder would slowly raise his arms to the heavens and implore Ngai to bring rain. The beer and the milk were offered as initial sacrifices to the great god within whose power it is to choose between life and death for his people. Seven times, the procession of children, lamb and elder would circle the tree. Seven times they would continue in silent prayer: in complete reverent union with the mountain. In union with Ngai. And in union with their blessed ability to talk so directly with the creator of all the universe. After the eighth circuit of the sacred tree, the lamb would be strangled whilst its head faced toward the mountain. When the meat had been roasted and shared among the assembled audience of tribal members, more offerings would be made to Ngai in his earthly abode on Kere-Nyaga.

Another important example of this wisdom which kept the Kikuyu in close empathy with their mountain was expressed during the engagement ceremonies between two young people. A fattened sheep was slaughtered, with its blood sprayed in the direction of the sacred mountain. When the union of man and woman was declared by a tribal elder, the two people were also declared as being united with their mountain's eternal spirit: its mighty strength, its spiritual energy to create, inspire and educate, its ability to challenge enemies, and its further ability to lead future generations of Kikuyu toward richer, more united lives with Ngai's fabulous creation.[4]

In a similar expression of union with Kere-Nyaga, the preparation for circumcision rites began with Kikuyu elders collecting small pieces of white chalk from the highest slopes of their mountain. That chalk was used later, during the ceremony, to mark the faces and bodies of the young initiates with sacred symbols. Again therefore, this is a ritual of ancient wisdom which forms a sacred bond between the circumcised youngsters and Kere-Nyaga. The circumcised initiates will then enter into a tribal practice which has been shared among every generation of Kikuyu since their creation by Ngai. It is a bond of simplicity and eternal value. A union between an ancient wisdom which appreciates the power of Ngai's creation, and the lives of Kikuyu clans at every stage of their history.

Toward the late twentieth century, too much of this ancient wisdom of legend, prayer and ritual has been lost within Kenya's modern urban society. Significantly though, when droughts become particularly oppressive for Kikuyu farmers, many of them purchase lambs of uniform colour, usually red or black. They will then perform the sacrifices and prayers which have served their ancestors so faithfully throughout Kikuyu history. Eventually, the rains come. But it is not uncommon for the wise elders of Kikuyu families to realize that when Ngai was worshipped more regularly, and with greater reverence, rains appeared to come more freely, as if in response to the stronger union of reverence and empathy between the chosen people and their creator god.

For contemporary visitors to African mountains, it is often the strong and historical unity between humankind and sacred inspiration which is of particular fascination. A union between humanity and divinity which has endured for almost two million years from the primordial times when *Homo habilis* first looked upon these mountains, and gazed in silent wonder. Without any distractions from that empathy with the ancient peaks, early peoples lived in complete, rugged unison with the rhythms and moods of their landscape. Theirs is an example, and an inspiration, which modern travellers can only marvel at and envy. With sophisticated, analytical minds, and lives full of technology and pollution, no modern visitor can ever fully recover the union between human and mountain which was so spontaneously experienced by *Homo habilis* and the early *Homo sapiens*. But whilst those barriers remain, the ancient wisdom and empathy can still be admired, wondered at, contemplated and prayed for. We are the heirs of a challenge to re-imagine this precious empathy in the modern world. We need to re-educate ourselves in its profound value. And we need to re-shape our priorities and lifestyles in recognition of its proven grace.

First visits

The volcanic landscapes of Tanzania were the most frequently visited mountain region for travellers who described their first-time visits to Africa. Within those discussions, the areas of northern Tanzania, around Olduvai Gorge for example, were described variously as 'the womb of mankind' (Bethany), 'the cradle of humankind' (Andrea) and 'the Mothering place of all the world's peoples today' (Frances). As one of the most widely known areas of Tanzania where archaeologists have found human remains from the *Homo habilis* peoples, Olduvai had come to the attention of these travellers through television and newspaper coverage which it regularly receives. With Frances for example, a sculptor and practising Buddhist from London, England, the way she described her feelings about standing, for the first time, in Olduvai Gorge, captured the meaning of similar experiences which were also discussed by others:

FRANCES:

> ... *It was like stepping into an enormous womb. This natural, rough, harsh place was the area where we (all humanity) first became suffi-ciently aware, and alive in the sense we are today ... But this almost overwhelming feeling I got of being in a place of incredible birthing created an immense variety of images in my mind almost all at once ... and I cried for as many different reasons as you can think of. I mean, I cried out of pride for all the amazing things we've (humanity) accom-plished. But also for the waste, the viciousness, the conceit ... but Oldu-vai, and places like it, is where it all began.*

Despite her mixed feelings and dilemmas over the developing history of human achievements, as well as the simultaneous history of human savagery, Frances insisted that her experiences at Olduvai left her feeling more optimistic about the world's future than before her visit:

FRANCES:

> *Olduvai Gorge is one of those incredible places which people find for themselves, where they can sit down and contemplate the whole of life. Life in the whole. And that's vital, and everyone should try and do that because it's educational ... I think my Buddhism has made me more of an optimist about the possibilities of that kind of travelling and discov-*

ery because almost in a second, you can find people completely chang-
ing their whole set of priorities and outlook on their lives, and how they
deal with others ... So Olduvai won't always be the most comfortable
place to visit, either physically or spiritually, or even emotionally, but it
will cleanse. And that cleansing of the mind, and soul, is so vitally
important in these superficial times of ours.

These mental images and experiences of giving birth to new spiritual insights, personal discoveries and inspirations were also described
with reference to Biblical Old Testament references by the Jewish
travellers to Olduvai:

HANNAH:

Oh, the first time I looked down into the (Olduvai) gorge, I was totally
stunned! I mean, that was the beginning wasn't it. Or at least one of
the places where we all came from ... but when my mind had calmed
down, I really felt an incredible sense of calm. And it was as if God
was there beside me, proudly showing me where I, personally, had been
born. But that incredible calm feeling, and also the feeling that every-
thing is still in God's hands ... although we're told the world is in a
mess, I felt really reassured there. I wasn't given any great blinding
flashes of understanding, but the calm and the reassurance were really
powerful and clear.

Along with other Jews who visited Olduvai with Hannah, as well
as others who had made independent visits, a short passage from the
Old Testament Book of Isaiah was frequently quoted as the words
which captured both this sense of being calmed by God's divine
hands, as well as being reassured that God remains in control of his
creation:

As a mother comforts her child, so I will comfort you; and
you will be comforted over Jerusalem. When you see this,
your heart will rejoice and you will flourish like grass; the
hand of the Lord will be made known to his servants, but his
fury will be shown to his foes. (Isaiah 66:13–14)

HANNAH:

The pseudo-feminist in me really likes that image of God the mother
figure. The bearer of all humanity. I like that. It's so beautiful.

ROSELLE:

It should be more widely talked about because, you're right, it's a won-
derful image. But when you picture Olduvai, when you read those
words (from the Isaiah passage quoted above), it brings it all home. All
the feminine qualities God has ...

HANNAH:

But they're all there in the Bible!

ROSELLE:

I know! But most people who've been brought up as Jews, and this
goes for Christians too, they've been brought up in a completely male-
dominated world. And male images about God are the only ones they've
been taught to understand ... And that's so incredibly limiting!

HANNAH:

Basically they're too scared of God as a mother, aren't they ... and they
haven't been taught to accept that idea without going crazy!

The gifts and breadth of understanding which Hannah and Roselle
brought to Olduvai from their Jewish background, and which Frances
also brought from her Buddhist faith, all emphasised Olduvai's ability
to inspire fresh, vibrant, strong, relevant and eternal insights. All these
women, along with other travellers who shared their insights, shared
an ability to look beyond Olduvai's clay and volcanic ash, and appreciate the profound spiritual meaning of the gorge alongside its geolog-
ical and physical presence. Olduvai's ancient rocks are therefore
anything but dry and sterile. They are anything but dead. Rather,
these rocks, which saw the first humans struggling for survival, have
also borne witness to these modern travellers who gazed silently about
them, struggling to imagine how it might have been two million years
ago when *Homo habilis* also gazed at those same rock walls. And at the
skies. And at the heavens beyond. For Andrea, a Buddhist and colour
therapist from Liverpool, England, these feminist ideas were extended
into a vision of Olduvai as 'a spiritual garden':

ANDREA:

What I got from my visit to Olduvai was this idea of the place being
full of seeds. Ideas. Inspirations. All popping into my head like pop-
corn. And some of them sparking off all kinds of other ideas ... So
you've got this amazing feeling of this being an ancient landscape
which fed and shaped early mankind. But at the same time you've also

got this incredible idea that the place is still working to shape our minds in 1995! ... and if we're lucky, it'll keep on popping up with these seeds of inspiration for another two million years!

For these, and other, first-time visitors to Tanzania, Kilimanjaro served to inspire further insights in this appreciation of mountain landscapes as a resource for understanding the feminine, creative, playful and benevolent aspects of spiritual awareness. Particularly for those travellers who had first visited Olduvai, and who then made their way to Kilimanjaro, the mountain was unanimously regarded as a 'place for nurturing all these amazing new insights you get from being in Africa ... if you really open your mind to receive ... ' (Kent). For Kent, a Buddhist and school teacher from New York City, Kilimanjaro served as a landscape where he could collect his thoughts from the journey he had made from Cape Town, South Africa:

KENT:
I have to say that I try my best to feel comfortable with these ideas of a feminine side to religious consciousness, because they're coming to the fore in just about every faith in the world. And part of me still feels unsure about it, but the other part says 'Well, why not. Of course it's right!' ... But Kilimanjaro, for me, was a place where I could rest after the trip up from Cape Town, and put all the pieces together in a way which kind of made sense. And having that calming environment wrapped around me, along with the strength of these amazing images from my trip, were like two sacred parents, a mother and a father. One calming and encouraging me, and the other one being strong, and feeding me with all those memories ... and so I actually came back to the idea of feminine spirituality by the back door: I was so much into taking it easy on Kilimanjaro, with all these lessons being learned within my mind, I was living proof that feminine spirituality can work, even before I realized what I was doing!

For two Drama Students from Chelmsford, England, Patrick and Edward, this way of seeing Kilimanjaro as a place which helped develop a broader vision of their Christian faith was described with particular reference to their climbs through the snowfields of Kilimanjaro's highest peak, the 19340 foot Kibo.

PATRICK:
I think we'll probably keep that mental picture all our lives ... At that

stage of our climb, we'd been going for a couple of hours, so we just rested and looked back over where we'd come.

EDWARD:

And we actually looked back on this massive silhouette of the Mawenzi peak (16896 feet), a little bit obscured by some wispy clouds around the crater. But then in the background, a carpet of cloud stretching out into the distance, way below us.

PATRICK:

That's what climbing's all about isn't it. It takes you to completely isolated places, and says, right, sit down, and look, and learn! ... And that's what we did ... In front of that amazing scene, we rested and talked and prayed together, really spontaneously. But that climb put everything we'd seen and done in Africa into a really uplifting experience ... And even then we knew our faith had been inspired and matured by what we'd seen there (on Kibo).

That time of inspiration, rest, prayer and conversation on Kibo's snow fields gave Patrick and Edward an opportunity to recall all the 'fragments' of their African travels and put them into a 'meaningful Christian perspective.' A spiritual whole. A free, liberated and creative way of adding to their Christian experience in a thoroughly spontaneous way, but a way which worked completely for those two individuals. But beyond that spontaneity when they were surrounded by Kibo's snow, Patrick and Edward have continued to think about those African inspirations, and in doing so, were able to discuss two passages from the New Testament gospel of Luke, both of which add further meaning to their memories of those breathtaking times on Kilimanjaro:

And Jesus grew in wisdom and stature, and in favour with God and men. (Luke 2:52)

EDWARD:

Firstly, I'm not saying we suddenly grew in divine wisdom and stature on Kibo! I'm not saying that at all. But I just feel that that time on Kibo was like God talking to us both, and bringing us along in our faith, because that was the time he'd chosen for us. He knows we're really into climbing, so why not make those lessons on that incredible place ... So in a small way, but a way that's right for us, God took the initiative to lead us on in the wisdom and stature which he wanted to share with us. And it was a completely wonderful privilege to have that experience ...

The second passage from Luke's gospel which these men wanted to discuss came from Jesus' teachings in the 'Sermon on the Plain.'

> But love your enemies, do good to them, and lend to them
> without expecting to get anything back. Then your reward
> will be great, and you will be sons of the Most High, because
> he is kind to the ungrateful and wicked. Be merciful, just as
> your Father is merciful. (Luke 6:35–36)

PATRICK:
Compared with the first Luke passage, this one's a lot more practical. But I think it's so right to fit in with our memories of Kibo, and looking back out towards Mawenzi because that whole scene had a combination of God's power, and incredible beauty, and subtlety. And all those things are basically the visual expression of God's love. They're God's love made visible for us to learn from ... God's love for us, which we're taught to share with others, like that second passage (from Luke's gospel) says.

This experience of finding lessons on sacred love and compassion on Kilimanjaro was also discovered and discussed by the Buddhists who visited the mountain. With Frank for example, a writer and photographer from Detroit, Michigan, 'the combined strength and serenity of Kilimanjaro' was the central theme of all his meditations in east Africa:

FRANK:
... part of the whole ethos of modern life seems to be a need for people to express their strength through anger and brutality. You've got it all over Africa, the States. Everywhere. But what I felt from really looking closely at the shapes of Kilimanjaro, from a distance, as well as right close up, was that enormous strength can be exerted quietly. And the word which kept coming back and back into my head was 'serenity.' I felt incredibly calm sitting among that strength and the serenity of Kilimanjaro.

From Frank's notebook of haiku poems, he selected an example which further illustrated the spiritual implications of Kilimanjaro's combined appearance of strength and serenity:

A hundred gourds
Born
From the mind of one vine.
    (Chiyo)

FRANK:

Even by haiku standards, those are few words! But just like the others, this poem by Chiyo is not only economical with its words, but it's precisely on the button too. But, for me, you have to read it from the last line to the first. The vine is this sprawling, spiralling collection of ideas and views you get all over Kilimanjaro. And then, in the middle line, it's enough to say they are born. You know, the event of being born, with all the excitement and hope that brings, is strong enough to be expressed in a single word. All those hundred gourds of wine are born! All this amazing strength of flowing vitality and life and understanding become born ... as they did for me on Kilimanjaro ... And chief of all those gourds of new lessons was this reminder about the possibility of strength with compassion, rather than strength without it.

In a very similar way to Frank's discovery of 'a hundred gourds' of insight on Kilimanjaro, Buster, a teacher and writer from Dublin, Ireland quoted a haiku by Issa which he only fully understood whilst resting on Kilimanjaro's foothills:

Cherry trees:
Contemplating their beauty,
Strangers are like friends.
    (Issa)

BUSTER:

This was a poem I'd never fully got into until my first visit to Kilimanjaro. And then, bang! I got it! Because if you think about a cherry tree in full blossom, what do you see? Hundreds of thousands of petals. All at different angles. Each of them in just a slightly different hue of pigment to the others. They're beautiful as a collection of petals on the tree, as well as when they're on their own. And so, when you've got that picture in your head, of this wonderful beauty which is common to all, and you think of this beautiful flowing wash of ideas and visions and insights which come upon you on that African giant (Kilimanjaro), you can see how I finally understood the final line. Strangers are like friends. The longer you look at a stranger, the more you realize how absolutely fundamental we all are. Strangers and friends all share fears, and worries, and problems, and extraordinary abilities and amazing experiences. They all have strengths and weaknesses. Superficially, yes, everyone's different. But when you dig, and, as the poem says, you contemplate a friend or a stranger, then you start to see the common things.

It is within those common, shared characteristics, that Buster finds the beauty of human beings. And on the basis of that perceived beauty, Buster developed his observations further to accord more closely with Frank's insights into the compassion which Kilimanjaro can teach:

BUSTER:
> *If you find beauty, real beauty, within strangers and friends alike, how can you not be compassionate? The question's as difficult as that.*

Although all these travellers arrived at Kilimanjaro at different stages of development within their chosen faiths, and although they came to that mountain from contrasting social backgrounds, there was a remarkable degree of agreement in the ways they concluded their discussions on Kilimanjaro. Using their memories of Olduvai Gorge as a foundation to these conclusions, every traveller who discussed their first visits to Africa described a strong appreciation of the common ancestry which is shared among all humankind, and which can be traced back, two million years, to the *Homo habilis* peoples. A common ancestry along the same, extended family tree.

Each of the following conclusions are taken from many different discussions, in different interview groups, throughout the research period for this book between 1985–95. However, together, they provide a clear understanding of the shared appreciation of these east African sacred landscapes:

LOUIS:
> *Everything we know and understand builds from them (Homo habilis).*

KENT:
> *We can never see with their eyes, because of all the incredible cultural histories which have taken place over the last two million years. But, if you trace back along the paths of those histories, you'll come back to those first Africans.*

DEE:

> *A lot of racist people will try and blot out that truth about this shared humanity we have with those early peoples. But a family tree which has spread across two million years is kind of difficult to blot out! So they're only deceiving themselves.*

FRANK:

> *All you need to do is add together one plus one. First, you think about this shared lineage we all have back to Africa. Then, you take that incredible huge and overwhelming feeling of the need for compassion which so many people found on Kilimanjaro. And then just put those ideas together. A common ancestry. And the need to be compassionate. And instantly you've got a better way of living ... The only thing is that too many people in power have too many interests in keeping the world divisive.*

HANNAH:

> *The first time I realized that we're all Africans, I cried because I was so happy.*

Subsequent visits

Kere-Nyaga, in Kenya, was the most frequently visited African mountain by the more experienced travellers who contributed to this book. All those people have encountered the profound realization that they share an African ancestry. But beyond that realization, their more mature and considered experiences of Kere-Nyaga led them to talk about practical ways of broadening and deepening their lives, and to consider the problems of living compassionately and in spiritual richness:

WILLIAM:

> *There's a place I've discovered right down by a small lake called Hut Tarn. And if I'm there early in the evening, looking out over the waters to Point John (a peak on Kere-Nyaga), that, for me, is the balance point between being a part of this world and being apart from it. In one way, I still feel a part of the lying and cheating and pollution and cheapness of the world. But, being there, it's also like feeling how the world might*

be. Calmer. Wiser. People having broader perspectives. And people
realizing that to care is the start of all our answers.

When William described those feelings, he had visited that part of
the Hut Tarn shore seven times. On each occasion he found himself
receiving more and more insights which have progressively changed
his way of understanding the world in which he lives.

WILLIAM:

Just by sitting by the water of Hut Tarn, and looking across to Point
John has been an education, because every time I've been out there, the
lessons have been different. But each lesson has built from the last ...
Each lesson has taught me to simplify the way I look at life. The simple
need for love and compassion. And the need to try and learn more of
the world, and make my life more full of the right things.

Among these 'right things' for William has been a fuller appreciation of the ancient wisdom, myths and legends which have been
inspired by Point John, and other personally inspiring mountain
landscapes. Building from that ancient wisdom, William described his
insights into a completely liberated approach to his personal education. It is an educational programme which does not end with college
or university. Rather, it is a continual quest. A pilgrimage. A journey
through life which listens, sees, touches, tastes and smells the full
meaning of every moment.

WILLIAM:

I've even found that those trashy times, like being stuck forever on the
New York subway, can still inspire your imagination because they
show how far wrong we've all taken our lives. And I know, I'm a part
of it, in a big way. But at least I know the mistakes I've made along the
road and I'm learning to put them right.

Along with his partner Bethany, another merchant bank manager,
who has travelled to Kere-Nyana three times with William, there was
a profound regret that they had 'compromised' their spiritual education in favour of the professional banking examinations taken at the
beginning of their careers:

BETHANY:

Being out there on Kere-Nyana has really hammered home to me
my one major regret in life that I totally sold out to professional

Above: Adam's Peak, Sri Lanka.
(Harald Schon/Image Bank)

Right: Wangla Monastery, India. (Nevada Wier/Image Bank)

Above: Chogolisa Mount, Karakoram Range, Pakistan. (John Noble/Tony Stone)

Left: Crossing snow bridge in the Karakoram, Nepal. (Image Colour Library)

Right top: View from Mount Sinai, Egypt. (Image Colour Library)

Right: Sunset over Sinai, Egypt. (Stephen Studd/Tony Stone)

Far right: St Catherine's Monastery, Sinai, Egypt. (Simon McComb/Tony Stone)

Opposite top: Mt
Ararat, Turkey.
(Jung/Image Bank)

Far Left: Mount
Zion, Jerusalem.
(Jeremy Horner/
Tony Stone)

Left: Western
Wall, Jerusalem.
(Image Colour Lib)

Above: Mount
Kilimanjaro
from Kenya.
(Richard Surman/
Tony Stone)

Right: Ice cave
on Mt Kenya.
(Image Colour
Library)

Opposite top: Croagh Patrick, Co. Mayo, Ireland. (Joe Cornish/Tony Stone)

Left: Mount Olympus, Greece. (Guido Alberto Rossi/Image Bank)

Above: Tholos at Delphi, Greece. (Oldrich Karasek/Tony Stone)

Right: Dionissiou monastery, Mount Athos, Greece (Vic Fellas/Tony Stone)

qualifications instead of spending more time on learning about all those amazing myths and stories, because they're the teaching which matter. And each time he's (William) taken me out there, I feel my life has been made so narrow, because I never spent enough time with those important forms of education.

WILLIAM:

All that goes for me too ... And looking back, what I feel is that, like a lot of people, the breadth of my imagination is infinitely smaller than if I'd spent more time out in the mountains. Or if I'd taken courses in those African myths ... They're the things which are worth learning because they've lasted through hundreds of thousands of years.

Arising from this intense frustration, and the lessons which William and Bethany have discovered from their visits to Kere-Nyana, they plan to abandon their banking careers and to open a book, furniture and accessory shop devoted to ancient wisdom and crafts.

BETHANY:

This is a definite plan we both have. And it's something which actually came to us both on our last trip out there (to Kere-Nyana).

WILLIAM:

Yeah, because it's one thing to talk about your regrets, but we both feel we need to do that, and completely make the change ... and what's more it'll be a service to other people who haven't visited these mountains. Maybe it'll inspire them to travel and stimulate their minds too.

In contrast to the regrets of William and Bethany about their neglect of studies in ancient wisdom, art, crafts, stories and rituals, Glenda, a Buddhist and artist from Colchester, England, finds that her repeated visits to Mogongo jo Mugwe, an active 10000 foot volcano in the savannah lands of northern Tanzania continually inspire her. But those visits also build from her teenage and college fascination with east African wisdom and ritual:

GLENDA:

If I'm allowed to be self-righteous for two seconds then I'll tell you just how smug I feel at having resisted everyone's advice to do a 'sensible degree' course at college! ... The number of times I was told how much time I was wasting reading about the Masai was colossal! ... But having stuck to what I believed, and not what other people wanted for me,

Opposite top: The Matterhorn, Switzerland. (Image Colour Library)

Left: Mont Blanc, France. (Paul Chesley/ Tony Stone)

I now find that those legends fall so easily into my painting that it's a perfect union between ancient and modern: what I've learned and read about, and the ways I choose to interpret them as someone living today.

The literal translation of the Sonjo tribal name, Mogongo jo Mugwe is 'Mountain of God.' Within Sonjo wisdom, Mogongo jo Mugwe is the fabled home of Khambegeu, a supernatural spirit who, thousands of years ago, visited the Sonjo tribe and brought them unlimited peace and wealth. Among the pastoral Masai, the mountain is sacred, and is named Ol Doinyo Lengai — the translation for which is also 'Mountain of God' — the earthly abode of the single Masai God, Ngai. In their rituals of sacrifice to Ngai, the Masai slaughter unblemished lambs. Prayers and chants are then repeated, beseeching Ngai to bless the worshippers with larger families and more cattle.

GLENDA:

I like this idea that two peoples, the Sonjo and, of course, the Masai, find something unique as well as something they can both share from that mountain. And at the same time, here I come along, paintbrush in hand, and I find something which works for me too.

Specifically, Glenda has found that Mogongo jo Mugwe has acted as both inspiration as well as a sanctuary for her. Following the sudden death of a close friend in 1987, Glenda could find no way of dealing with her grief other than by returning to the mountain 'in order to paint all the time, and think and cry.'

GLENDA:

We'd been friends since small children, and I was beside myself with the total, complete agony of losing her. I couldn't sleep. I couldn't do anything. And it was only when I was able to briefly get some very light sleep one night that I dreamed about Mogongo jo Mugwe.

On the basis of her dream, Glenda realized where she could find an environment in which she would finally accept her friend's death. Within a week, she had set up her tent on the Mogongo jo Mugwe's foothills. Two weeks later, the effects of the mountain on Glenda's grief were 'frightening at first, then terrifying, then completely bewildering.'

GLENDA:

The only way I can describe it was feeling like a new self was being born inside me. It was a self-emergence of some new creation which was being born, and then breaking out completely inside me. Destroying the old, grieving, nervous wreck I'd become, and bringing new life into my body. So at one and the same time, it was a complete inspiration, as well as a healing, with no boundaries between those two events.

The only way Glenda can reconcile this radical change of emotion is by suggesting that her life-long study of east African wisdom had forged an even stronger empathy with the mountain's capacity for spiritual inspiration than she had ever thought possible. At the end of Glenda's second week on the mountain, her supplies were running dangerously low, obliging her to return reluctantly home.

GLENDA:

But if anyone's in any doubt about the power of those mountains, or any mountain which really moves someone, then I'm happy for my story to be told, because absolutely nothing else on earth could have helped me through that terrible, terrible time than being on that mountain, at that time, doing almost nothing else other than listen to the spirits talk to me ... And that, for me, was the only way of moving away from my anger and bitterness and everything else I was feeling, and growing back towards a way of life which at least tries to understand the grief of others having been there myself ...

Almost 800 miles north west of Mogongo jo Mugwe, on the equatorial border between Uganda and Zaire, is the Rwenzori range, a name meaning 'Rain Mountains.' Covered with luxuriant tropical plants and frequented by miraculously coloured sunbirds and insects, these mountains have been an irresistible magnet for three botanists from San Francisco. With a particular interest in the Lobelias which grow in the extreme temperatures of day-time heat and night-time freeze, those scientists wanted to find, photograph and study Lobelia specimens which are capable of projecting a sky-blue spike of flowers fifteen feet high:

STEVE:

When you've back-packed through all that heat, humidity and flies, and then you see all those Lobelias in that incredible landscape, it moves you big-time! And you become like a delighted little kid. Your science and your training are all forgotten because you're filled with just the most simple and overwhelming joy and relief, and emotion, and total pleasure at being able to see plants like that, especially when they're in full flower.

NEIL:

I find it incredibly instructive to just look at a plant like that, in that completely remote mountain environment. It's like going in search of a precious jewel. And when you find that jewel, for the first time or the twenty-first time, you grow a little in your self.

JESSICA:

Yes. That's right. You do grow. Your spirit grows. And you feel totally at one with plants like that. But you need to have had to work hard at getting to see them. But once you're there, your imagination goes into lift-off because you're totally involved in that moment of being there. Totally focused. And really a part of the plant's beauty.

During the twelve months in which they developed their scientific research within the Rwenzori, Steve, Neil and Jessica found they wanted to spend as much time as possible developing their own creative responses to being among the forests and other flora which cover those mountain slopes. For Steve and Jessica, that creative expression came in sketching, and developing their shared interests in various abstract artistic representations of that tropical mountain environment. In contrast, Neil chose to simply rest and gaze in wonder at the visions before him. The brilliant colours. The uncountable sounds. The numerous fragrances.

NEIL:

I found it really stimulating walking around taking it all in. Sights, sounds, smells, the different surfaces: some variously rough, or smooth. Just receiving. Taking it all in ... But the thing I've taken away from that time, for me, is really a complete impatience with the superficiality which our society has got itself into: where we're not given too many opportunities at school, or later in life, to take time to think about what we see. Or what we hear, or smell or touch or taste. And that superficiality is a major, major loss to our quality of life.

During her five visits to the Virungas, a range of eight volcanic summits on the borders between Uganda, Rwanda and Zaire, Karen, a Christian and an artist from Colchester, England, has reached exactly the same conclusion to Neil. Superficiality impoverishes our lives. Transient style, without enduring substance, cheapens our lives. Intensive farming which produces food without its full, natural, taste reduces our ability to fully appreciate that food. City architecture which is little more than the design of vast boxes, impoverishes social as well as artistic function. All around us, Karen suggested, 'superficiality reigns supreme. And I object to it in every way!'

KAREN:

> *... but as I've got to know, and more fully understand the Virungas, I've become more and more angry at the way modern society has completely and totally turned its back on the idea that our senses should be stimulated. In the Virungas, your senses are bombarded with the most incredible sights, and sounds and smells and feelings to marvel at. All the time ... And we call ourselves 'advanced' and 'superior' when we've actually gone backwards, away from all those marvellous experiences! ... And since we are so arrogantly deprived of those sensual stimulants, our lives are made poor. We're less able to discover something incredible in a modern urban jungle than we are in an ancient tropical jungle. And that is not progress!*

On her most recent visit to these mountains, during November-December 1994, Karen identified another important dimension to the ways in which our lives have become deprived of the multisensual stimulation which is freely available in ancient mountain environments, such as the Virungas:

KAREN:

> *... Why do you never have artists, or writers, or sculptors on the board of directors of companies? You have the various functionaries: accountants, production people etcetera, but never an artist. You never find someone being commissioned to advise those directors on improving the quality of lives for their employees. But just think what a difference it would make! It's exciting to think about, but it's probably a naïve dream because the people who take those decisions have minds completely closed to that sort of initiative ...*

At every stage in her discussion, Karen drew parallels between the lack of sensual stimulation within modern society, compared to the jungles and volcanic Virungas, and the simultaneous lack of spiritual stimulation offered by 'most church leaders':

KAREN:

> *... there's such an appalling narrowness to the ways Christianity is taught in churches these days. When I'm on a mountainside, such as in the Virungas, I've found my Christian experience goes through quantum leaps of development almost every day ... There's such a richness*

to creation in those environments, that you often don't know which
way to look first to take it all in! But again, it gets back to my earlier
point about most modern people being actively prevented from making
discoveries for themselves about how rich their lives can be, and also,
for Christians, how rich their Christianity could be, if only they had the
right stimulation.

Turning points

Alongside Karen's passion for the rich, spiritual and sensual experiences which she discovers among the Virungas, there is a deeper, more intimate reason why she finds so much personal significance in those mountains. In 1982, after a difficult pregnancy, Karen suffered a miscarriage. Having split with her partner during the pregnancy, and having been ignored by her immediate family for five years, Karen had never felt more alone than during the months which followed the miscarriage:

KAREN:

It's not something which can be easily put into words. But the nearest
I've come is to say that the loneliness was like a physical pain. I felt a
failure. I'd start crying over nothing at all. I even found myself crying
as I woke up in the mornings. I felt so thoroughly wretched ...

For six months, Karen lived in virtual isolation. Friends brought in food and other shopping, and tried to console her, but without success. Most of Karen's mail was also left unread until the day a letter arrived with a curious, strangely familiar hand writing on the envelope. Intrigued, Karen read the letter from a former college friend, telling her about a four-week tour she was planning to make to the Virungas, and inviting Karen to accompany her.

KAREN:

At first I threw it on the kitchen table with all the rest of my un-
answered, and mostly unopened, letters. I simply had no reaction to it.
I'd read the words. I knew what they meant. But they had no more
meaning than that ... But after three weeks of it still in the back of my
mind, haunting me, I surprised myself by picking up the phone and

agreeing to go along. I felt completely indifferent to be perfectly honest,
but looking back, that was how God led me ...

Within less than eight weeks, the two women, accompanied by two
Rwandan guides, were exploring the foothills of the highest of the
eight volcanic peaks among the Virungas, the 14782 foot Karisimbi.
Later in the expedition, the group also explored the adjacent slopes of
Muhavura.

KAREN:

It was my first visit to that sort of incredible, overwhelming environ-
ment. But for the first two weeks out there, I was still a zombie. I could
carry my own pack, and help with the various chores, but that was it.
I'd still break down in tears for no reason. And all in all, I was still a
real mess.

On the Sunday morning of the third week, Karen awoke early,
possibly, she suggests, due to the bird calls which surrounded their
camp. With her eyes still closed, the sounds seemed to wash Karen's
mind in the most soothing, sensitive way:

KAREN:

I was just lying there in bed. But there was something so innocent and
beautiful in those sounds. They were incredible. And you couldn't
isolate one bird song from another, because I was hearing everything.
All at once ... And the only way I can describe it is to say it was like
having all my guilt, and my hurt, and my depression being gently
washed and soothed by those sounds. And I lay there for a couple of
hours like that until the others woke up and we started our day again.

For the first time since her miscarriage, Karen found herself needing to sketch. Her friend lent her a pad and some pens which Karen
stored in her backpack before setting off with the others for that day's
hike.

KAREN:

My friend gave me a wink just before we started off, because, I know
now, she'd seen a change in me. And I remember, I walked third in line
with tears streaming down my face, but with the most excited tingle
down my back. And I knew I'd turned the corner ... I kept on having to
wipe away tears all the time, but I looked right up at the trees, and all
around, and tried to bring in as much as possible. And it was like

being a child again, and marvelling at everything I could see and hear and feel and touch.

Karen's recovery had begun. But it was neither instant nor simple. There were relapses. There were days on which Karen woke feeling little better than when she had first agreed to travel to the Virungas. But over the eighteen months following her return from the mountains, Karen's depression finally left her. Inspired by the sketches she had made, Karen also developed a strong interest in the creation spirituality of medieval Christian writers, including Hildegard, St Clare, Mechtild, and the fourteenth century Meister Eckhart:

KAREN:

> *That eighteen months was a time of re-building for me. I eventually found God through my experiences in Africa, and I developed a very personal Christianity by studying those medieval writers because their Christianity was so in tune with my own questions, as well as my art ... So I had my life, my Christianity and my art all as parts of a complete, complementary whole, like different colours on a round ball, rolling in a single direction.*

Conclusions

The African mountains which attracted the curiosity of these travellers have inspired them to consider the full span of human history as well as the vast breadth of human experience. From the earliest groups of *Homo habilis* living almost two million years ago, to their comparison with modern urban societies, African mountains have provoked a distinctive collection of insights and questions for these travellers. Insights into the birthing of new ideas and fresh creations. And questions about humankind's failure to develop societies and institutions which encourage and stimulate imaginations of all ages, from all social backgrounds.

WILLIAM:

> *You don't have to spend too much time in those mountains to realize they're unique. And they're unique because they've been the focus of so much human quest and search for individual meaning.*

BETHANY:

> *But if you ask how those mountains have continued to feature in modern ways of looking at life, you'd have to say very little ... We've neglected them, haven't we. And that's just typical of the way Africa as a continent has either been abused through slavery or colonialism, in its various forms. Or ignored by spiritual leaders as a source of incredible inspiration.*

All the travellers who contributed to this book can be aligned with Bethany's suggestion that Africa, as a continent, has either been abused or ignored by modern, technological societies. For Alfred, a retired archaeologist from Phoenix, Arizona, that 'arrogance and neglect' has significantly contributed to 'the ways western culture has progressively drawn away from nature instead of getting closer to it in new ways':

ALFRED:

> *We live in a modern world which has almost completely failed to build on our African inheritance. Picasso picked up on it. And it revolutionized his art. And a few other artists have done the same. But I'm talking about the institutions of education and work. We haven't learned! ... And whenever I've been out in those (east African) mountains I've felt that neglect more than ever. When I listen to a tribal elder describe their wisdom through their parables, it makes me humble ... and I really do feel impoverished by coming from a supposedly progressive society which hasn't taught me to fully understand the simply beauty of parables like that.*

Among other travellers, the modern failure to fully accept the inspiration of these mountains is simply due to a lack of courage. A lack of courage to change from rampant consumerism toward a more sympathetic and receptive relationship with the created world. Whilst governments and major companies and corporations weave some of those sentiments into their public relations strategies, the commitment which must lay at the foundation to that courage to accept change is not yet in place:

HANNAH:

> *So many times I've sat on the (African) mountains I've visited and prayed for someone to come along with sufficient vision to see a need for change and to do something about it. Because that's how it's going to happen. There'll be someone like Mahatma Gandhi, or a Bob Geldof figure, who'll capture everyone's imagination ...*

For Karen, the move toward a fuller appreciation of Africa's spiritual importance will only diffuse through society with sufficient force when a radically changed school curriculum is adopted:

KAREN:

Why are there no courses for school children on African studies? Why aren't children given the chance to find out about these mountains and all the stories and natural history and art and carving and poetry which has gone with them? They're the questions which should be asked! And it makes me so angry and frustrated to see how future generations of kids are been given a narrow education which is only marginally better than their parents ... We have yet to learn all the lessons there are from Africa ... and we haven't even begun to pass them on to our children in the right ways.

CHAPTER 11

Europe

*In the end the spectacle has something — I don't know
what — of magic, of the supernatural, that ravishes the
spirit and the senses; one forgets everything, one forgets
oneself, one no longer knows where one is.*

Rousseau (1976, 45-46)

Ancient wisdom

Mountains appear in European wisdom cultures in a distinctive diversity of ways. Within the Norse mythology of Scandinavia for example, the place of honour reserved in heaven for courageous heroes of wars and battles was called Valhalla: an ancient name which can be translated as Rock of the Slain.[1] Valhalla was also the magnificent, legendary palace of Odin, the master of all Norse gods, the god of war, and the god of wisdom. From his throne-room, located within the dark cliffs and pinnacles of Valhalla, Odin surveyed the whole world. He saw everything. And with his incalculable wisdom, Odin also understood everything he witnessed at each and every moment.

Another legendary Norse mountain spirit was the mighty Heimdall, a great and holy guardian who resided over the towering monolith of Himinborg: the Mountain of Heaven. According to the fragile and fading pages of the *Eddas,* a collection of Scandinavian medieval chronicles, Heimdall had cultivated a miraculous ability to see across vast distances from his mountain top. And yet he was also able to hear every human and natural whisper. No words were ever unheard. And no evil deed ever went unnoticed, or unpunished.

When Christianity became accepted more widely across the Norse lands, other legends developed in importance to replace the dominance of Odin and his fellow gods. Mountains were regarded increasingly as the domain of giants, elves and the demonic and everchanging trolls.[2] With their hideous appearance, the trolls' strength was weakened only by their remarkable gullibility. But for those victims and prisoners of troll malevolence who did not realize their stupidity, there was often only the promise of a future spent in continual humiliation and servitude among the trolls' freezing mountain hideaways.

Similar stories of evil spirits haunted the forested Harz Mountains of central Germany. When the sun shone from behind a climber, projecting their shadow onto the swirling clouds which engulfed the upper slopes of the Harz, those shadows were often believed to reveal the presence of sinister and malevolent spirits. But as stories became told of these Spectres of the Brocken, as they were often called, a strong reputation developed around the Harz peaks as the principal points of convergence for all European wizards and witches: a terrifying spectacle with ghastly, nightmarish proportions. Choirs of dark spirits would loom high above the mountains, among the restless clouds, to sing and chant evil curses until their voices rasped and died to a snarling contempt toward any human foolish enough to enter their domain.

Along with their Germanic contemporaries, the Celts living in modern day France and Switzerland 2500 years ago considered their mountains to be inhabited with divine spirits and gods.[3] It was therefore completely natural for Celtic legends to become woven around their understanding of British mountains after their westward migration five centuries before the birth of Christ.[4] But with the spreading influence of Christianity, much of that ancient legend became discarded and lost for ever. Only on the outermost reaches of Celtic influence were there scholars sufficiently astute, and dedicated to their wisdom, to record it for future generations. When Christian missionaries, such as Saint Patrick, arrived in Ireland, part of the task they set themselves was to claim for the Church all lands which had been sacred to the Celts. As Patrick journeyed through County Mayo in western Ireland for example, legend describes his ascent up the 2510 feet quartzite pyramid of Croagh Patrick. At the summit, he encountered a fierce brood of snakes and other hideous creatures. Courageously, Patrick stood his ground. And with the resounding echo of a ringing bell, he banished the evil creatures, and claimed the mountain in the name of Jesus Christ. Even in the late twentieth century, Christian pilgrims still interpret Patrick's encounter with demonic forces on the mountain as being a close parallel with Christ's temptation by Satan. In the Bible, Satan is frequently described as an evil snake: a poisonous, unpredictable and vicious creature. In the same way as Christ's experience, Patrick is said to have spent forty days and forty nights on the mountain, wrestling with the Celtic snake spirits before consigning them to oblivion through the strength of his Christian faith.

The European Alps which form an arc from southern France in the west, to Slovenia in the east, contain some of the most photogenic peaks in the world. Among them, the jagged pyramid of the Matterhorn, the Eiger, and the Alp's highest summit, the 15781 foot tall igneous dome of Mont Blanc. According to the sixteenth century scholar, Josias Simmler, it was within Mont Blanc's Great Saint Bernard Pass that the Devil's attempt to crush Saint Bernard's progress through the Alps was completely defeated by the saint's strength of faith.[5] Although Satan caused lightning to flash, and thunder to roll across the skies around Mont Blanc, Saint Bernard and his followers stood firm, and eventually climbed up the rugged pass to exorcize the Devil from his lair. With so many sinister legends like this, Mont Blanc had been avoided until the eighteenth century by local people who named the mountain Mont Maudit, or Mont Maillet, the Cursed Mountain.[6] Only when travellers came to appreciate the sublime power of these towering heights, were Mont Blanc and the other Alpine mountains finally appreciated as a source of enduring spiritual inspiration. For the German poet Johann Wolfgang Goethe for example, his visit to Mont Blanc in 1779 left a profound and lasting impression on his imagination. Seeing Mont Blanc at night, against a clear, star-lit sky, the vision riveted Goethe's attention. Twenty years later, he was still thinking and writing about that overwhelming moment. In his letters, Goethe describes that night on the foothills of Mont Blanc:

> The beauty of this view was quite extraordinary. Shining
> among the stars that surrounded it, glittering not as brightly,
> but with a vaster, more coherent mass, the mountain
> appeared to belong to a higher sphere. (Quoted in
> Schmitz, 1884, 25)

From the beginning of the nineteenth century, European Romantic thought turned increasingly to appreciate the power and importance of spiritual encounters within the Alps. In reaction to the unnaturalness of modern industrial society, travellers, artists and writers found a profoundly natural and satisfying inspiration from the miraculous presence of alpine mountains such as Mont Blanc. For the English poet, Percy Bysshe Shelley, Mont Blanc had its own unique voice. A powerful and undaunted voice which could cleanse the soul of even the most fraudulent and pitifully corrupt individual. Mont Blanc

therefore stood for everything good, redeeming and pure. It was an
enduring, solid and visible symbol of complete serenity:

> Mont Blanc yet gleams on high: — the power is there,
> The still and solemn power of many sights,
> And many sounds, and much of life and death.[7]

Further east, the limestone summits and valleys of Greece, and its
offshore islands, were an inspiration to the earliest European civilizations. Among the Minoans of Crete for example, living between 3500
and 5000 years ago, their worship was almost exclusively conducted
on mountain summits which symbolized the fertility and beauty of
their mother goddess. More recently, starting about 4000 years ago, a
series of invasions from northern Europe and Asia brought new
possibilities to the interpretation of these mountains. Instead of a
single, female deity, masculine gods began to dominate the reverent
ways of seeing these mountains. At their head was Zeus: king of all
gods and unrivalled sovereign of Mount Olympus in northern Greece.
Born on Crete, in a hidden cave on Mount Aegeum, Zeus was later
carried to the adjacent Mount Ida where he grew up in the company
of wise mountain spirits and guardians. Having thoroughly learned
the wisdom of those spirits, Zeus defeated his disreputable father,
Cronus, and thereafter assumed complete power over the entire
universe. From his palace on Mount Olympus, Zeus governed every
moment of human life. With his wife, Hera; their children, Aphrodite,
Apollo, Ares, Artemis, Athena, Hephaestus and Hermes; Zeus's two
brothers, Hades and Poseidon; and his sister Hestia, there was nothing
which escaped either their attention or divine intervention.

As the Greek gods' influence became replaced by Christianity 1500
years ago, hermits and monks sought contemplative sanctuary from
the world of everyday concern. Among these mountain sanctuaries
overlooking the northern Aegean Sea was Athos, a white-cliffed peninsula capped with a 6670 feet mountain of solid marble. Monks began
to arrive on Athos in the ninth century after Peter the Athonite had a
dream that the Virgin Mary told him to sail toward the Aegean.[8]
Although his journey was blessed with a good, steady wind, Peter
was mysteriously unable to sail past Mount Athos. Having heard incredible tales about a host of murderous demons which populated this
remote part of the Greek coast, the sailors lacked Peter's faith and
abandoned him in fear of their lives as soon as he stepped ashore. For
seven years after his arrival on Athos, Peter was continually tormented
by demons. They tempted his mind and badly wounded his body.

They drove him to the limits of his patience and his faith. Eventually he emerged from the harrowing experience, wiser and spiritually victorious. Whilst the demons continued to bring more temptations before him, Peter's battle had already been won. By the middle of the tenth century, Athos was the setting for a growing number of monasteries including the Great Lavra founded by Saint Athanasios. One hundred and fifty years later, Athos was host to over 7000 monks, many of whom had brought Russian Orthodox influences to the peninsula. Even today, with their numbers substantially reduced, monks continue to live in contemplative isolation, protected from the distractions and concerns of twentieth century life, and attracting pilgrims who travel in search of a simple existence devoted to physical labour, meditation and prayer.

First visits

Among the travellers to Europe who contributed to this book, the overwhelming majority of first visits were spent in the Alps.[9] With Amos for example, a Christian and teacher from Philadelphia, Pennsylvania, his first visit to Mont Blanc was part of a three month tour of Europe in 1986. His contributions however, exemplified those of many other travellers who found a stark contrast between the inspiring beauty of the Alps, and other impressions they had formed during earlier stages on their European journeys including 'an absence of any long-term vision for what Europe can offer the world ... Europe seems to be a continent on the slide, in spiritual decline, and there doesn't seem to be any real search for alternative educational patterns which can deal with that slide ' (Amos).

AMOS:

> I look at Mont Blanc and I find it represents a lot of my worries about how European culture has turned its back on mountain spirituality, and just about every idea there is about 'sacred Earth.' From what I can make of it, the whole problem with religion right now in Europe is that everyone still wears a mask of inflexible dogma which doesn't exactly excite anyone's imagination. And Mont Blanc represents that for me. There's no culture anymore in Europe about seeking any kind of a reconciliation with Mont Blanc's deep inspirational

qualities ... So instead, it's all about 'superficialdom': a culture which is purely and completely superficial with no attempt at spiritual substance to it.

The first time Amos saw Mont Blanc it was sunset. The mountain's glaciers were tinted with a gentle peach-coloured light, with their upper surfaces a pastel shade of mauve. And yet alongside that gentle, graceful colouring, Amos was unable to separate that vision from his knowledge of European history during the last three centuries:

AMOS:

For me, I don't think you can just take a mountain and say, yes, that looks good. You have to look a lot deeper than that. And for me, that incredible beauty of Mont Blanc lies there in a real great contrast with the kind of things European powers were doing around the world during the colonial era or during the (world) wars. Mont Blanc represents a simple beauty. A kind of attitude to life which doesn't need to go around shooting and stealing from other countries ... It's a lesson which hasn't been read enough, or learned at all.

During that first visit to Mont Blanc, Amos was reminded of a short passage from the Gospel of Mark which captured the essence of his perceived contrast between the mountain's divinely created grace and the 'ugly and inappropriate behaviour in a lot of recent European history ...'

No-one sews a patch of unshrunk cloth on an old garment. If he does, the new piece will pull away from the old, making the tear worse. And no-one pours new wine into old wineskins. If he does, the wine will burst the skins, and both the wine and the wineskins will be ruined. No, he pours new wine into new wineskins. (Mark 2:21-22)

AMOS:

It's all about appropriate behaviour, isn't it. Learning to do the right thing at the right time in the right way. And for me, I looked at Mont Blanc in all its sunlit glory and I wondered how much consideration was given by the Great Powers to the lessons which that mountain has to offer ... before they all started to carve up the world for themselves ...

Among European visitors, this same point was repeatedly emphasised. Within a continent whose cultural history has been woven around a framework of Christian faith for 2000 years, the absence of widespread contemplative thought which has been devoted to mountains with the inspirational power of Mont Blanc was a cause of sustained debate and frustration among all first-time visitors to the Alpine summits. In the following conversation between two German women, Roselle and Dee, they recall their first memories of Mont Blanc when they were still young children:

ROSELLE:

I was taken to see Mont Blanc by my elder brother when I was about five or six. And I can remember thinking to myself that that's how I'd like to think of Europe: containing God's creation with loads of people all around me, all gazing upwards to the peaks and being inspired by it ... But of course, if the truth is to be told, people just look, but don't see. And they won't allow themselves to be changed by their experiences.

DEE:

That's right. Most people will agree there is a need for major changes in the world. We all need a new heart, and new social frameworks. And what's more we have the inspiration to push us in the right directions! Mont Blanc! How much clearer or bigger or more widely known do you want? Everything's there for us. But hardly anyone will read from places like Mont Blanc the lessons God is surely putting to us.

For all these travellers, there can be no salvation from human turmoil without a clear appreciation of the lessons which are available through God's creation. In a similar way, many of the Buddhists who described their first visit to the Alps were able to align themselves with the idea that spiritual growth, and personal change, cannot fully develop without a profound appreciation of natural landscapes. With Thomas for example, an administrative clerk from Leeds, England, his first visit to the Alps was undertaken only two months after he had begun to pursue a personal commitment toward Buddhism:

THOMAS:

That was an important time for me, and it was interesting to take those very early thoughts about the meaning of Buddhism to places which are so incredibly instructive, like the Alps ... And I'd have to say that it was there, in those mountains and glaciers when the power of meditation really first hit me ...

As an enthusiastic amateur geologist, and hill-walker in the English Pennine mountains, Thomas wanted to find and photograph the glacial evidence of scouring on rocks within the Mont Blanc massif which had left jagged peaks on the Grepon, the Dru, the Aiguille du Midi, and the Grandes Jorasses:

THOMAS:

Nothing I've read since that time from books, or anything else I've been taught, has done as much as that time, among those peaks, for the way I look at the vital importance of meditation ... First and foremost, I see meditation as enormously practical, and that's something which isn't always fully appreciated. There's so much to look at in a mountain area like Mont Blanc that it's just impossible to learn everything from it in one visit. Or maybe even several visits. So it has to be studied. And the only way I know how to study anything, is to sit down, get comfortable and really look ... and if necessary, even take your binoculars out if you want to search out a detail that's too far away to walk.

Another Buddhist, Leon, an engineer from Newark, New Jersey, finds that, alongside all the horrors of twentieth century Europe, the Alps inspire him with the wisdom of one single truth:

LEON:

If the European influence on the world had been more to do with co-operation, and less to do with conquering, the inspiration of those Alps would have been made known to the world ... However, as we all know, European aggression has torn its way through Africa, through Asia, and all over. And honestly, it's as if the whole meaning, the fundamental meaning of those (Alpine) mountains wasn't there at all ... It would have been the same as if, instead of those incredible mountains, there was just an empty wasteland of soot and ash. Uninspiring? Yes. But if people are going to ignore that inspiration when it's so close to everyone, why get upset if the mountains are one day taken away from you?

The final point which these first-time visitors recalled, was expressed most clearly by Jeremy, a Christian and Art Student from Cardiff, Wales.

JEREMY:

I first went to the Alps when I was eleven on a scout camp. And the main memory I have of those three weeks was being woken up at the most incredibly early hour of the morning ... I always remember just how new and fresh those mountains looked whenever I saw them ... And they always made people look, if only for a moment. Even the wildest kids, really seemed to see something otherworldly, and different, and wonderful in those mountains ... And even if some of them hadn't learned very much about the Bible, they seemed to respond to those mountains. As if the mountains inspired them at a higher level than ordinary language. And I think what we were seeing there was quint-essentially pure and God given ...

Among so many travellers, from so many different backgrounds, a single conclusion was accepted. The spiritual inspiration of the European Alps has been almost universally ignored, not only among government organizations, but also among educational and religious institutions. Whilst mountains such as Mont Blanc have been identified by these travellers as offering a wisdom for contemplation, wonder and humility, those lessons have been almost completely set aside in favour of confrontation, commercial exploitation, war and genocide.

Subsequent visits

The themes which first-time travellers evoked regarding their experiences of the Alps were developed by the more experienced mountaineers and walkers. In particular, these experienced travellers sought to concentrate on the future, rather than comparing the inspiration of European mountains with historical events. And within this discussion of the future, some of them were able to employ their gifts for prophecy: gifts which are too easily dismissed within cynical, distrustful, and technological societies. With Agnes, a Buddhist and teacher from Baltimore, Maryland, the gifts of prophecy are not only respected, but she also employs them as part of her appreciation of mountain landscapes:

AGNES:

I've never thought of myself as being particularly gifted as someone who can read the future because it's always come so naturally to me. For me, it's just like having one more sense, which builds on my other five ... But from what I've seen of Europe, and in particular the way people use their mountains as part of their lives, I'd say that within the

*next thirty years, the European Churches will either become so small
that their voice loses all credibility, or there will be a major change of
direction where they'll turn more to the way their natural landscapes
can inspire them ... Personally, I'm sad to say, I foresee them going into
oblivion, because there's not a lot of courage at the moment to make the
sort of changes which are needed.*

Agnes was particularly reminded of her impressions about the
ways 'people use the Alps as a playground' alongside the almost
equally undervalued ways of seeing the Greek mountains of Olympus,
Parnassus and Athos:

AGNES:

*With the Alps, and particularly in winter, most visitors just use it as a
playground. And I've been out there in winter four times now, and on
each occasion I never saw one person taking too much time just to look
at the mountains and to draw in the purity there. So that's the Alps.
But then, when you think about Greece, and whether its the pre-
Christian sacredness of Olympus or Parnassus, or the Christian mean
ing within Athos ... what you find, again, is that although they're not
playgrounds like the Alps are, not enough people have been schooled in
the discipline of looking deeply into what they see ... They're all too
much into superficiality, and that, I'm sure will have its implications.*

For Charles, another Buddhist, and a shop-owner from Oklahoma
City, his prophecies for the future of European spirituality drew more
specifically from his six visits to Greece, and in particular his fascination with Mount Parnassus, eighty miles from Athens. With its labyrinthine collection of ravines and caves, along with groves of trees and
brilliantly coloured wild flowers, Parnassus has attracted the attention
of travellers and poets for almost three thousand years.

CHARLES:

*If you just take one place on Parnassus, say, Delphi. You've got one of
the most beautiful places in Europe where worship and sacred awareness has been practised for most of the last three thousand years. And
yet now, if you watch the people who go there, very, very few of them
take time to just sit down, shut up, and consider all that tranquillity,
and let it change their lives.*

On the basis of those observations, Charles was able to describe his
prophecy for the future of spiritual development in Europe:

CHARLES:

> *It's not so much what I saw on Parnassus, it's what I didn't see, or hear, that got me worried. Because in all my travels through Europe, I don't see too much experimentation in the way folks practise their religion. It's often too much stuck in the past, with not too many ingredients brought in from the nineteen nineties ... So I'd have to say that unless new life and new, deeper ways of appreciating mountains like those in Greece, are introduced into the lives of European believers, of whatever faith, there'll be a massive number of completely fragmented church and synagogue groups, none of which will have a genuine sense of direction ... but all the time, they'll have some of the big answers to all their problems staring them in the face. The mountains! ... That will help so, so much. Go out there. Look at them. See them for what they are! Make my predictions wrong! ... But I'm sad to say that I think I'm going to be right, because I don't want to be right this time.*

Further predictions were offered by James, a Christian, and archaeology student from Cambridge, England. Although James shares the concerns of Agnes and Charles, his own prophecy for the future of European spiritual practices concentrated on the 'failure of European Churches to appreciate the full potential of the faiths they're preaching':

JAMES:

> *There's a very difficult balance which has to be achieved between a sense of continuity with the past, and appreciating the traditions and lessons from the past, and building something new which can be useful in the present. And at the moment, from what I've seen of both eastern as well as western Europe, the balance is too much with the past, and not sufficiently building something credible and relevant to the present ... And I'm afraid I have this terrible prophecy in my head that almost all the organized, institutionalized forms of religion in Europe are simply going to crumble into a dusty irrelevance unless much greater attention is paid to drawing inspiration from landscapes, such as the Alpine mountains, and using them in an educational and inspirational context. And if that challenge isn't accepted then the next thirty years look very, very bleak indeed.*

To illustrate his concerns, James described the mountain shrines devoted to the Virgin Mary, and the ways they are regarded by many contemporary pilgrims and worshippers. In particular, James described his visit to watch the festival of Our Lady of the Snows on the highest pilgrimage destination in the Alps: the 11605 foot summit of Roche Melon:

JAMES:

I wanted to watch what went on up there because I'd actually gone there feeling fairly depressed about the future of Christianity in Europe. And I'd have to say that although the actual ritual felt really moving and reverent, the priests were missing out in the way they seemed to ignore the amazing mountains surrounding them ... The mountains as God's creation are every bit as inspiring as the Virgin Mary, with all she represents, but it was as if the mountains didn't exist! And if ever you're looking for a literal example of blinkered mentality, then that's it!

A clear example of this alignment may be taken from the recollections of Suzannah, a teacher from Manchester, New Hampshire. As a devout Christian, Suzannah visited the Black Madonna in the monastery of Jasna Gora, overlooking Czestochowa in southern Poland:

SUZANNAH:

There was a big lump in my throat as I watched all the little old ladies trooping in to pay their homage to the Black Madonna. And I looked into their faces, and I could see how intensely they were feeling about being there ... It was almost timeless, most of the women were in their black dresses which, I guess, their mothers would have worn forty years ago. But that was the sad thing I came away with. Too much history. And not enough 'now'! And I didn't see too many young people coming in. And those who did come in, did so with a much more blank expression on their faces. You know, it didn't mean all that much too them, and they looked bored.

The final theme discussed was the question of who is served most directly by individuals who are committed to a specific faith. From the observations of these travellers, too much European spiritual faith is overly introspective. 'They seem to be self-serving faiths' (Charles). Too many Christians were regarded as being led by their ministers into spending 'too much time contemplating their salvation, instead of contemplating God's creativity' (James), and the ways in which that divine creativity can inspire the Christian faithful to serve others: to be more compassionate toward others, or to make a courageous stand against social trends which are unjust, racist or sexist. But whilst all drew similar conclusions about European Christianity, and other

European faiths, Simon's concerns were expressed from a Buddhist perspective:

SIMON:

... I've often found myself amazed just how much European Buddhists tend to be so self-conscious about their faith ... And what it comes down to, I think, is the whole way Europe seems to be too tight and rigid about the ideas which can and cannot be accepted as legitimate spirituality. But there's just too much which the European Buddhists haven't discovered ...

But in particular, no-one, Buddhists, Christians, or Jews, seems to have escaped from themselves and developed a way of living with their faith which looks out, towards the need of others ... That's what's missing, even though you have all those mountains, all of which seem to say, slow down, take in the beauty, share it with others. Share your lives with others ... The mountains of Europe need to be studied a lot more closely!

To justify these statements, Simon suggested that all the European Buddhists, 'and other European religious followers' with whom he has spoken have 'too much of a narrow theory of what spirituality is about.' For Simon, a spiritual commitment is essentially an all-embracing and open-ended way of life: a set of moral, aesthetic and psychological values which should accommodate a continually growing wealth of inspiration, knowledge, literature, painting, memories, travel experiences, as well as a 'practical sensitivity' toward the anxieties, social pressures and stresses of others.

SIMON:

There's quite an amusing haiku which sums up this way I see European spirituality as having neglected so much of the amazing inspiration which is all around them:

> *Surprise!*
> *A snail at my feet.*
> *When did he get here!*
> *(Issa)*

I always think of this guy in a clown's costume bursting out of a birthday cake when I read that poem. Surprise! You can almost see his big painted smile! But if you've ever studied the slow intricacy of a snail, it's easy to understand what Issa's on about. The surprise, and delight we can have, if we look hard enough, at finding this tiny little creature at our feet. So think how much more overwhelming and fantastic it can be, again, if you have the eyes to see, the mountains down in Spain, or the Alps, or in eastern Europe. There's no shortage of really great inspiration in Europe. But what's needed are the teachers to show Buddhists and other devotees from other faiths that bigger way of thinking about their various life-commitments.

In an almost exact echo of Simon's observations, Pauline's discussion of European Buddhism, from her 'European perspective,' concentrated on a specific area of neglect which she also found rooted in 'the narrow agenda of Buddhist concern in this country (England) as well as on the (European) continent ... ':

PAULINE:
This is one of the reasons why I enjoy listening to Buddhists from America a lot, or from the Far East, because they've been so much more open to ideas in their commitment than a lot of British Buddhists, or the European Buddhists I've met ... The best example I can quote is the virtually nonexistent European Buddhist contribution to women's rights ... Because surely, if you're out in the mountains, in the Alps somewhere for example, you become more in tune with natural harmony. And natural compatibilities. Balance. The need for care and compassion ... So why haven't European Buddhists taken those thoughts home with them to ask the difficult questions about how women can be accepted more widely in more jobs and across a greater breadth of activities ...

For Pauline, this silence among the European Buddhists she has met arises from not having the vocabulary with which to express these ideas within a distinctively Buddhist manner.

PAULINE:
Most English Buddhists I've met read a very narrowly defined set of books. And they won't stray into finding out how they might build up a way of looking at women's issues ...

As an illustration of neglected literature, Pauline quoted from the American poet, Adrienne Rich with her poetic style and content of verse which can be easily used during meditations. One short passage of Rich's work is of particular relevance to Pauline's memories of the European Alps since it was during a visit to Switzerland that she discovered these poems and found them 'to be in complete accord with the whole way I felt inspired by the mountains all around me.'

> My heart is moved by all I cannot save:
> so much has been destroyed
> I have to cast my lot with those
> who age after age, perversely,
> with no extraordinary power,
> reconstitute the world.
> (Rich 1978, 67)

PAULINE:

Adrienne Rich writes in all her books about women's experience in the late twentieth century. But the first line in that passage, 'My heart is moved by all I cannot save' precisely, precisely matched up with my feelings the moment I read it. And I'm not ashamed to say, I shed a few tears because it was so beautiful and so unexpected to find a writer who came that close to how I felt ... Even though Adrienne Rich wasn't writing directly about mountains, that was how I felt having been overwhelmed by the mountain's I'd been out in.

Among the Europeans, as well as the non-Europeans who contributed to this chapter, their observations on the neglected role of mountains within European spirituality offer an important agenda for thought and further discussion among religious believers as well as their leaders. For example, if the mountains of Europe continue to be ignored as a valuable source of spiritual inspiration, what will be the implications of that neglect? Will the prophecies of Agnes, Charles, and many others, come tragically true? Will European spirituality continue to maintain its reputation as being too narrowly focused? Too stuck in the past? Insufficiently looking forward? Insufficiently struggling to understand contemporary problems, illustrated by Pauline's frustration with the ways European Buddhists have yet to develop a widely influential agenda of responses to the role of women in late twentieth century society? Whilst no single source of inspiration can be reasonably expected to address all these problems, greater attention to the inspirational value of European mountains can, and must, be allowed to make its contribution to the immediate and long-term development of European spiritual awareness.

Turning points

The extreme weather conditions which are frequently encountered in the Alps contributed to one of the most dramatic encounters with spiritual insight among the contributors to this chapter. At the time, Alex was a business manager living in Southampton, England. The climb on the Matterhorn was with four German customers of the company for whom Alex worked. Each climber was experienced, physically fit and well equipped. They were also excited and apprehensive since, with the exception of the youngest German, none of the others had climbed the Matterhorn before. With their route planned, the climb began mid-morning in fine, sunny weather. Three hours later, the mountain was cloaked with heavy cloud. And the wind was beginning to gust.

ALEX:

I actually noticed the wind pick up appreciably when I was just making my way over a ledge. I was pulling myself up when suddenly the most almighty blast of air punched me in the face! Well, that was how it felt ...

A second later, the wind was virtually silent again. Reassured by the gentle breeze, Alex looked up the rock face to his companions, saw they were alright, and continued his climb. With the cloud all around him, and with an experienced appreciation of the wind's ability to gust ferociously around the Matterhorn's rugged pyramid shape, Alex chose to climb slowly and cautiously.

ALEX:

At the back of my mind, I could sense that the wind might start behaving badly again at any moment ...

Without further warning, a blast of freezing air pinned Alex to the mountain side. Instinctively, he gripped the tiny outcrop of rock to which he had been reaching. With every expectation that it was just another irritating gust, which would abate after a few seconds, Alex was not immediately worried. But when the wind dramatically changed angle, almost sucking him off the mountain with even greater force than previously on the climb, his mind became rigid with terror.

ALEX:

> *... Not only was the wind howling and blasting the side of the moun-*
> *tain, but it had literally pulled my legs from under me so I was only*
> *hanging on by my hands, and the ropes leading up to the others. But it*
> *was blind terror, and I'd never been in anything like it before ... I was*
> *completely out of control. And losing all sense of time, so I can't tell*
> *you how long it all lasted. Maybe a few minutes? But when you're at*
> *risk of losing your life at every split second, the old cliché's right!*
> *Those seconds pass like hours!*

With no way of telling how long the frenzied gusting would last, and without being able to regain either of his foot holds, Alex poured all his attention into his hand grips. If they too were lost, Alex would only have the support ropes trailing down from his companions to rely on. And with every confidence that they too were facing similar problems with the wind, Alex's mind focused exclusively on the need for an uncompromising hand grip.

ALEX:

> *... And it was the first time in my life that I actually found myself*
> *praying. It was as if the prayer had been begun by someone else in my*
> *mind, and I only noticed it going on inside me after the first few*
> *words. But all I can remember praying were the words 'dear, precious*
> *Jesus!' And I was praying them while I was looking intently at my*
> *hands, willing them to remain strong ...*

The wind slapped, ripped and punched at Alex's flailing body with even greater intensity. At one moment, Alex felt his left hand weaken, but in numbing desperation he gripped harder, and continued to pray, learning what it is to rely helplessly upon the strength of one's faith. In his state of complete physical exhaustion, a force greater than Alex could imagine held his body against the freezing rock.

ALEX:

> *Looking back on all that incredible experience, I feel honoured and spe-*
> *cial to have this story to share with people, because I really don't think*
> *prayer has the respect it should do. For most people, both within the*
> *Church, as well as others too, it seems to me they often think of prayer*
> *as nothing else but a hot line to God where you can ask him for things.*
> *But prayer has got to be much more than asking. In my case, it was*
> *simply a strengthening of the bond I have with him. Concentrating on*
> *that bond, and bringing that strength to my hands gripping the moun-*

tain ... So the prayer, my whole being, and my hand grips were practically all one and the same ... But if I didn't have the facility of that Christian faith, or the facility to pray so freely, I have no idea how I'd have managed ... Certainly, two of the others, who were on the mountain there with me, and who have no faith of any kind, have refused to climb again because they were affected so badly by the whole ordeal.

Conclusions

For Europeans and non-Europeans alike, these mountains offer a unique set of spiritual lessons, presented in the form of stark, and often disturbing contrasts. Contrasts between the gentle grace of Mont Blanc at sunset, and the crass arrogance of European colonial behaviour. Discordances between the tranquillity afforded by these mountains, and the ways that tranquillity is too easily ignored in favour of noise and aggression. Many of the contributors were able to identify some of the very real implications arising from the neglect of this mountain inspiration:

AGNES:

I know I might be accused of over-generalizing now, but I'd say that what Europe needs is someone to really give it an inspiration. Because, although you have small pockets of energy, it seems like a tired continent. People are gradually waking up to the fact that Asia is where the energy's happening ... But if Europeans want to find that energy and inspiration, then look no further than the mountains! Look at them! ... How can anything so wonderful and amazing be so completely ignored by so many people? It's crazy!

But in addition to the conclusion among these travellers that the inspiration of European mountains is insufficiently alive in modern culture, there was a feeling that the ancient wisdom of the Greeks, Celts and Norse peoples has also been neglected in education and religious teaching.

CHARLES:

In the States, there's much more of a respect for the native American ways of understanding mountains. But I haven't found that respect in

Europe. And that's very noticeable. The people who I've spoken to about this think I'm crazy for asking these questions ... But these folklore stories aren't just stories! They're reminders that, long ago, folks took the time to study these mountains, and to play with the images they got. And out of that play, those old stories emerged. So why can't we have new stories told about these mountains? With new characters. And new lessons in them.

Conclusions

How many are your works, O Lord!
In wisdom you made them all;
The earth is full of your creatures ...
May the glory of the Lord endure forever;
May the Lord rejoice in his works.
He looks at the earth and it trembles;
He touches the mountains, and they smoke.

Psalm 104:24, 31–32

The preceding chapters reveal the extraordinary diversity of experiences, wisdom and insights which have been encountered by the 144 people who contributed to this book. In their individual ways, these travellers have proved that the mountains they visited can inspire a richness of meaning which transcends all boundaries between contrasting spiritual paths. In recalling their memories, and in sharing those stories within the interview groups, they showed a sustained appreciation of each others' spiritual goals, instead of dismissing them with condemnation or derogatory judgement. In doing so, they offer a valuable insight to everyone who reads these words. Difference need not be marginalized. It can be celebrated, cherished, discussed, and learned from.

These travellers' experiences of mountains have also transcended the boundaries between their spiritual awareness and the lives they pursue at work, at home, or with friends and family. In discussing this point, Waylon, a teacher from near Tulsa, Oklahoma, spoke for all the other contributors:

WAYLON:

What I've found sitting here, listening to everyone who's spoken, is that these mountain journeys and experiences are so strong, and so valuable to everyone, that every part of their lives has been touched in some way ... And there's no getting away from that inspiration, because the mountains are with you in your memories whether you're hard at work, or wherever ...

But this all-encompassing inspiration was never passively received. None of these people simply sat or stood beside a mountain and waited to become inspired. Rather, they developed a form of active dialogue with the realities around them. Many of them drew upon all their physical senses as they learned to find the full power of those contemplative moments. They considered carefully what they were seeing. They listened. They breathed in the distinctive mountain air. They thoughtfully ran their finger-tips across differing surfaces of rock, tree-bark, moss, lichen, stream-beds, ice, snow and the dust of mountain paths. They tasted the spray of waterfalls, or dry, crisp air on their tongues. Consequently, their prayers and meditations were rarely, if ever, one-dimensional spiritual experiences. Instead, they were multi-sensual, and therefore multi-dimensional. And through that eclectic range of inspirations which these people developed in the mountains, they developed a passion for being in those remote but stimulating environments. For Jade, a Buddhist, and railway information officer from London, England, this multi-sensual way of meditating is essential to her everyday life, as well as the way she actively seeks inspiration from her mountain journeys:

JADE:

> It just wouldn't occur to me, these days, to restrict myself to a meditation on the things I can hear, when I've got four other senses all waiting to be plugged into! I have five senses. So I use all five ... And sometimes, I use them one at a time, to concentrate on everything in its constituent parts. But it's also interesting to concentrate on grouping my senses together and, say, closing my eyes and just concentrating on the sounds I hear, and the textures on the ground where I'm sitting. That's often an interesting one, actually ... But the main thing is to play with those combinations, so you discover more about where you are ... as a kind of spiritual exploration of yourself and the place where you are.

Beyond the five physical senses, some of these travellers also described their ability to introduce their sixth sense: the gift of prophecy. Among these gifted individuals was Agnes, a Buddhist and teacher from Baltimore, Maryland:

AGNES:

> It's a gift I've always had, so I never have to bring it to mind. It's just there. But how it usually shows itself is whenever I sense something extraordinary: something I've seen, or touched or whatever. And then,

the best way I can describe it is like remembering the future. Everyone can remember the past. But to me, it's as if I'm bringing to mind a memory of something which will happen either in the next few days, or other times something which won't happen for thirty years ... But I must emphasise that this gift doesn't make me special in any way over anyone else. We all have gifts. But I've taken the time to concentrate on mine, and bring it forward a little.

In addition to receiving inspirations from each of their senses, these travellers have learned that they must also search more actively across the mountains for more insights, more inspiration, and more wisdom. Many of these people have therefore climbed, not simply for the achievement of having scaled a particular wall of rock, but in order to gain a clearer view of the summits beyond. Others, who do not climb, have walked, scrambled, slid, skied or rode on horseback across plateaux, boulder mounds, slopes, tracks and rivers to appreciate other aspects of the peaks which surround them. They have also camped out in these environments, endured freezing cold, sweltering heat, storms, accidents and even serious injuries.

NEIL:

The easiest thing in the world is to go out to some of these places, and just say, 'so what?' So you have to make the effort. Get some friends together, and a (back) pack each of supplies, and just head out there, wherever you like. But spend time there. Don't rush through it all too quickly. Pitch your tent and take it all in. And then move on a little. And pitch your tent again. And so on ... You need to be active. Like a detective searching for clues. Piecing that mountain together in your mind until it really means something to you ... So it's never easy. But I've always found it worth making the effort in the end.

The wealth of these travellers' mountain experiences therefore arose from an active, patient search for inspiration, including their willingness to find and compare one mountain landscape with others through which they have travelled. As a consequence of this active search, each contributor has described ways in which mountains have radically influenced and changed their ways of thinking. However, equally importantly, they have also described experiences where their changing personal circumstances have influenced the ways in which the mountains appear to them. Thus, the mountains can change the travellers, but the travellers can also change the ways they read the mountains. With Bethany for example, her experiences in Africa, with her partner William, brought a specific way of seeing Point John, on Kere-Nyaga, in Kenya, which was both personally moving, and radically inspiring:

BETHANY:

One time, I'll never forget. We'd had a terrible few months with a lot of office politics going on all the time. But finally we got away to Kenya. And there's no way of denying that we brought a lot of that tension with us, didn't we?

WILLIAM:

That's right. There was no way we couldn't, because you're the same person in the mountains as you are at work ... But I think all that tension at work made us appreciate Kere-Nyaga a whole lot more than if we'd gone there all mellowed out and relaxed ...

BETHANY:

... and so the practical implication of going there, at that time, feeling the way we did, brought the mountain closer to us as an inspiration for what we want to do with the rest of our lives.

In a similar way, Robert, an insurance underwriter from London, England, brought his specific concerns for homeless people to the way he drew deeply personal meaning from Jebel Musa, in the southern Sinai Desert:

ROBERT:

It's like a two-way conversation. I felt God inspire me through the huge presence of Jebel Musa. But at the same time, yes, of course, I was bringing me into the picture too. My anxieties over homeless people, to name just one example. And even when I wasn't actually thinking about those people, they were deep within my consciousness. So they could still be touched by the mountain ... I was bringing the way I felt about the homeless to that mountain, and the mountain was moulding and shaping me as a person where those thoughts were developing.

Robert's concluding remarks show clearly that it is impossible to isolate this exchange of sacred inspiration and human concerns from wider social, economic and political relationships. Rather, those broader relationships simply add to the dialogue between traveller and mountain, just like other people might occasionally contribute to a conversation between two people. All these travellers have therefore been able to recall memories where social concerns and dilemmas have added to this complex weave of influence and counter-influence. From Brian's recollections of his journeys through Latin America for example, this broadly-based set of exchanges is illustrated clearly:

BRIAN:

If you picture a theatre stage in your imagination, with two main characters exchanging views, sometimes calmly, sometimes dramatically. But at the same time, other characters on stage may also be having their say too ... And that's how I always describe my relationship with the mountains down in Latin America. You can't just talk about me and the mountains without also talking about how angry I always get with all the poverty and disillusionment I see down there in the cities, or out in the farming areas ... So this whole way of forming ideas about mountains draws from a pretty large network of ideas and influences from completely different issues.

Throughout the ten year period of this research, it has been clear that the adolescent travellers have consistently drawn from a far broader set of social influences, and other ideas, than older adults. Consequently, many of the students and other young people in their teens and early twenties described how their interests in music, art, film, television, dance, literature, fashion, and various addictions and obsessions all contributed to the contrasts they drew between mountain inspiration and their everyday lives. However, among the adults, a far more narrow set of influences were used to describe the contrasts between their mountain experiences and their everyday lives. Among the adolescents therefore, there was generally more spontaneity and creativity in the way inspirations became developed from the mountains they visited.

The meaning of sacred mountains clearly arises from an emotional response as well as an intellectual, cerebral interpretation. Indeed, on many occasions during the ten year development of this research, some of the men and women reached frenzied levels of joyous excitement as they described parts of their mountain experiences. Equally, on other occasions, individuals have been convulsed in tears by the weight of contrasting experiences: the death of friends, the discovery of profound insights into spiritual wisdom, or experiences of being emotionally healed by mountain journeys. But for Karen, a Christian and artist from Colchester, England, there was another reason why she has often felt intensely emotional during the interviews to which she contributed:

KAREN:

> *It's been so beautiful to meet with a group of people who accept each other's stories about their mountain travels, and to be genuinely interested in those experiences ... because so often, certainly within the Christian Church, people are never encouraged to discover things for themselves or to do their own thing ...*

Many of the Jews who contributed to this book also described their joy at having been able to listen to others, and talk about their mountain experiences. Dee, an architect from Berlin, Germany, spoke for all these Jews:

DEE:

> *What I've learned from coming along to these interview meetings is that it's so necessary to seek out new and different things on our travels. But second, it's now clear to me that it's also so essential that we all need groups, like this, in our synagogues, but I guess too, among the churches for Christians ... Because none of these meetings have had any agendas, have they? We've just talked, and listened. It sounds too simple to work. But it's been a time when I've cried, and wanted to cry, and when I've also shared in the joy and laughter of other people here too ... More groups like this should be set up and kept going.*

Many of these travellers have struggled to find the right words to describe their experiences in ways which are sufficiently clear for others to understand. But in engaging with those struggles, and in watching others hesitate in their search for clearer ways of explanation, each of the contributors to this book was re-emphasising the remarkable degree of loyalty and ownership they had felt toward this project. This was a project for which it was worth making an effort. It was worth the time they freely volunteered. And it was worth getting right.

It is also important to emphasise that these people's experiences of mountains will not end with the completion of this book. Rather, they will continue to travel. They will continue to discover new, fresh inspiration from the mountains they visit. And they will continue to bring more of their own beliefs, preferences, anxieties and dilemmas to colour those ways of seeing and contemplating. Consequently, this book has really only taken a 'snapshot' across ten years of mountain experiences, all of which will continue to grow and develop in the wealth of insights they contain.

In pursuing their individual and shared mountain journeys, these people are making their experience of sacredness into something which is visible and solid. Sacredness, for them, is therefore neither abstract nor remote. For two pan-pipe musicians from Los Angeles, California, Davey and Joseph, and their friend, Mary, a percussionist, this direct engagement with a form of sacredness to which they can directly relate is essential to them all.

DAVEY:

If I'm able to live the life I want to live, then I'll carry on playing my pipes and travelling through the world's mountains. Because that's the pilgrimage I'm on. It's my journey! And one of the major themes on that journey is to continue drawing into myself as much of the sacred feeling of these mountains that's possible from what I can see, feel and touch.

JOSEPH:

You speak for all of us on that one, brother ... We're all on a journey, or a pilgrimage, which always tries to draw in inspiration. We try and put that inspiration into our music. We play our music on the street, or other places. And then we move on. But it's a way of life which definitely builds as the years pass by.

MARY:

Yes. That's a sign to me that what we're doing is positive. And it carries with it an important momentum ... What you see and feel in the Middle East will draw from the mountains there, as well as other mountains we'll have visited some place in the States. So it's a continuous process of seeing, listening, feeling, and then sharing, and travelling on.

In contrast to Davey, Joseph and Mary, who exemplify the travellers who wish to experience as many mountains as possible, other contributors were satisfied to develop their understanding of sacredness from a single mountain. With Gillian for example, an archaeologist from London, England, she is convinced that her Buddhism will 'find all the nourishment it needs from more visits to Machu Picchu in Peru':

GILLIAN:

I really feel content to learn more and more from Machu Picchu because that place and its surrounding mountains really has a complete hold on the way I feel about the whole sacred and spiritual realm. And for me, my own understanding of sacredness has to be about something I can see, smell, hear, touch and sometimes even taste ... But there's more than enough to discover at Machu Picchu than I'll ever be able to learn in one lifetime, so I'll keep going back as often as I can, for as long as I can!

One of the most consistent themes which has remained evident throughout this research is that these ongoing journeys are not simply paths of personal, spiritual discovery on which these people feel reluctantly obliged to travel. Instead, both the past journeys, as well as those planned for the future, are regarded as being constructive opportunities for a 'really joyous discovery.' For Josie, a Buddhist and English Literature Student from Seattle, Washington, this joyousness is fundamental to her 'passion for the mountains':

JOSIE:

What's the point in carrying on with your faith if it's become boring, sterile and monotonous? ... For me, every time I'm in the mountains, at some point in being there, I'll have at least one 'Wow!' experience! Usually a lot more! But isn't that how spirituality should be? We should all be blown away by living our faiths, because if we're not, there are some pretty major questions which need answering! And by being moved so profoundly like that, that's how we become changed from being in the mountains. It's also how a greater sense of compassion can be brought into society from the mountains.

From a Jewish perspective, Gabbi used precisely the same expression to describe her 'quest of joyous discovery' which she hopes will draw her closer to an understanding of God, but which Gabbi also hopes will enhance her motivation to continue her journalism and campaigning work:

GABBI:

If there were no more books to read, or inspirational tapes to listen to, or scriptures to study, I wouldn't mind, because there'd always be the mountains! And, what I find so wonderful about putting on a (back) pack and walking off, is that you never know what you're going to find. But at the same time, you can be absolutely confident that you'll come away with nuggets of the most amazing sacred experiences ... I always take a notebook into the mountains with me, so I can write down my feelings that night, as I'm looking back over the day.

As Gabbi continued with these concluding observations, she also spoke for all the other travellers who, in various ways, had suggested there are 'some moments in the solitude of those mountains when you leave behind everything there is of this world' (Gabbi):

GABBI:

It's one thing to say that you've got to consider your personal and political circumstances when you're thinking about your own ways of looking at mountains. But when it comes to the mountains' turn to do the talking, and the inspiration they can give you, the individual, then there can be times when you're lifted completely out of the here and now, because the whole experience is so intense.

There was a time during a visit to Uluru, in Australia, when Gabbi became so captivated by her encounter with that monolith that she completely lost all sense of time, as well as her personal identity:

GABBI:

Four hours just vanished for me there on that visit as if they were two seconds. But my mind was so completely overwhelmed by the whole aura of Uluru that, when I was coming down, I got talking to some Australian women, and when we were introducing ourselves, I had to pause for a moment to remember my own name! Because I was still so wrapped up in the mountain ... It had almost taken over my whole mind, and lifted me onto a completely different level of thinking. I was no longer the centre of things. Uluru was. And that really was a deliciously wonderful time to live through.

During rare, intense experiences like this, the influence of the mountains is working at levels within the traveller's imagination almost independently of the individual's consciousness. It is as if the individual has willingly opened his or her mind, like an opened notebook, and invited the mountain to write freely 'on the pages of your selfhood' (Wesley):

WESLEY:

This happened to me in Sri Lanka. Only once though, sadly. But the only way I can describe the feeling was as if the whole, divine, creative spirit of God was able to talk to me, or write in my mind, so directly, and in such a free, uninterrupted way, that my mind was only the blank pages, receiving lessons from that wonderful, completely Godly, transcendent inspiration.

Experiences like these described by Gabbi, Wesley, and others, have virtually no difference to the visions of ancient tribal shamen or the Medieval mystics of Europe. They are all timeless. They all communicate without any reference to historical events or geographical location. They are purely and simply transcendent experiences whose power and energy are impossible to describe fully.

TERESA:

All you can do is to point to the experience, and say that was where it took place, and now I feel like this. And although a lot of us have tried to put those experiences into words, we've all failed, really ... We've groped for the right words, but there aren't any. We've simply been astonishingly lucky to have gone to those mountain places, with a willingness to be moved, and the divine, or God, or the sacredness surrounding us has obliged! ... But although we can't even describe the thing to ourselves, let alone to anyone else, I think those precious times have changed everyone who's been through them.

It was in direct reaction to the roaring silence from their own church leaders that most of the 144 people found their motivation to help develop this book. While their churches, synagogues and temples were considered to be gathering places ideal for receiving instruction and guidance on the spiritual aspects of personal journeys into nature, they felt strongly that those religious communities are being continually starved of such inspiration. At the same time, within the field of television programming, and newspaper and magazine publishing, spiritual topics are segregated by programmers and editors into compartments labelled 'Religion,' while 'Nature' is equally isolated. In reaction to this unnecessary division, many contributors felt that this book was their only opportunity to challenge these unimaginative cultural realities and to help stimulate new and more inspiring initiatives.

I will therefore leave the final words to a selection of those people. Each of the following contributions is taken from different interviews which were held over the last twelve months of the research. Together, they reflect both the consensus as well as the diversity of experiences discussed on the previous pages:

MOISHA:

At a time when it's not always fashionable to be honest about your spiritual experiences, I'd like to think other people will take this book and say, right, I've had enough of leading a boring and sterile faith, now I'm going to do some discovering of my own ...

PETE:

I know many Christians who think that once they've hooked into their idea of evangelical salvation their religious journey is over. But if this book stands for anything, it's to firmly contradict that mistaken opinion, and to show people there are some pretty amazing alternatives out there, just waiting to be found in the mountains.

WESLEY:

What I'd most like to happen is for Church leaders to read through what we've been working on here (in this book) and take this rich, sensual, passionate embrace of Christianity into their own churches ... and build a Christianity which not only gives more to the believers, but which also inspires a greater social concern and compassion to others.

JADE:

From everything I've listened to in the interview sessions, the main conclusion, for me, is that we've shown that all the old boundaries between religions have no real credibility ... And I hope I'm not being too naïve by saying that some of the more open-minded religious leaders might take up the spirit of this book, and use it in their work ... You could have Buddhist teachers taking the sermon in a synagogue or a church. Or rabbis teaching in a church. Or Taoists teaching Jews. Or any combination of teachers and people you can think of.

KAREN:

Of course, some of the most influential teachers in society today are radio and television producers. And what I'd like to see coming from this book is a greater emphasis within the programmes they make on the real, living, late twentieth century kind of inspiration we've all been talking about ... Too often programmes are made which concentrate exclusively on the historical myths and legends. And while they're all important, surely it's equally important to think about the new stories and the new ways of thinking about these mountains as well. So let's have more balance between the ancient and modern meanings in these mountains ...

References

CHAPTER 1
1. Becky, 1982.
2. For an authoritative introduction to the Katahdin legends, see Eckstorm, 1924.
3. The spirituality of Tewa sacred mountain wisdom is clearly introduced in Ortiz, 1969. For Navajo wisdom concerning sacred mountains, see Begay, 1967. But see also Luckert, 1977.
4. A detailed analysis of Hopi cosmography is described in Geertz, 1984.
5. See Nash, 1982; and Turner, 1980.
6. For an excellent explanation of the ways Crow warriors drew inspiration from their local mountains, see Nabokov, 1967.
7. Margolin, 1981 offers a well documented discussion on Indian memories, experiences and stories throughout California.
8. Cohen, 1984 offers a thoroughly researched discussion on the ways John Muir invested his own personality and ambitions in the American wilderness, as well as the ways in which Muir drew fresh inspiration from those landscapes.
9. See De Mallie, 1984; and Neihardt, 1972 for two of the most comprehensive discussions on Black Elk's legacy.
10. Eichorn, 1971.

CHAPTER 2
1. Echevarria, 1979 and 1983.
2. Johan Reinhard offers an excellent range of discussions. See in particular, both of Reinhard's 1985 writings, along with his 1983 discussion in the *American Alpine Journal.*
3. The World in 1995, The Economist Publications p 90.
4. Duran 1975, 255-257.
5. Bastien 1978.
6. Gutierrez offers a clear overview of his work in *The Witness,* April 1977, p.5.
7. Sobrino 1981.
8. Duran 1975, 155.
9. Iyer 1978.

CHAPTER 3
1. Australasia is discussed here as comprising four elements: Australia, and the three island groups of Melanesia, Micronesia and Polynesia.
2. Orbell, 1985, *Hawaiki.*
3. See Layton, 1986 for a comprehensive introduction to the history of Aboriginal reverence for Uluru. But see also Mountford, 1965.
4. Orbell, 1985. *The Natural World of the Maori.*

CHAPTER 4
1. See, for example, Earhart 1970.
2. Basho 1966 is a fine example of his craftsmanship and wisdom as a poet and traveller.
3. One of the most comprehensive discussions of Mount Ontake is presented in Blacker 1975.
4. Tyler, 1981 presents an excellent introduction to the sacred wisdom which has been drawn from Fuji.
5. Hakeda 1972 presents a clear and authoritative account of the spiritual wisdom surrounding Mount Koya with particular reference to the role of Kobo Daishi.
6. Fox 1983 provides a useful introduction to the concept of panentheism.
7. Daitoku 1839 and Hirayama 1984 both provide excellent introductions to the spirituality of the Ohmine mountains.
8. Oda's 1989 and 1993 papers clarify some of the principal elements of the Shugendo devotions within the Ohmine range.

CHAPTER 5
1. For a comprehensive and authoritative introduction to the Himalayas, see Tichy 1970.
2. As a source for further study, Varma (1985) can also be recommended.
3. Van Buitenen, 1973–78.
4. Batchelor, 1987.
5. Kailas has attracted a huge amount of literary interest. Among the most valuable are Allen, 1983; Hamsa, 1986; and Johnson and Moran, 1989.
6. See, for example, Carter 1977; Reichardt and Unsoeld, 1977; and Shipton, 1985.

7. For one of the most evocative references on Annapurna, see Herzog, 1952.
8. For an appreciation of other Himalayan climbing experiences, see Hornbein, 1968.

CHAPTER 6
1. The Shu-ching is a reference to the mountain T'ai Shan, which is sometimes also named Tai Tsung. See Baker 1925.
2. Kroll, 1983.
3. Loewe, 1979.
4. Porter, 1993.
5. Doub, 1979.
6. *ibid.*, 131-134.
7. Han-Shan, 1970.
8. Hotchkis and Mullikan, 1973.
9. Birnbaum, 1983.
10. Hotchkis and Mullikan, 1973.
11. Geil, 1926.
12. Reported in *The Economist* May 20, 1995 p 73.
13. The World in 1995, The Economist Publications p 94.

CHAPTER 7
1. Heine-Geldern 1956.
2. Covarrubias 1946.
3. *Ibid.*, 76.
4. Gomez and Woodward 1981.
5. Paranavitana 1958.

CHAPTER 8
1. For a detailed analysis of the K'un-lun's sacred significance, see Duba, 1942.
2. Although scholars differ in their spellings between Meru and Summeru, Mabbett, 1983, offers a comprehensive overview of the mountain's inspirational significance.
3. See Bernbaum, 1980.
4. Beal, 1968.

5. Rowell, 1983, presents a comprehensive discussion on the exploration devoted to Amneye Machen. But see also J.F. Rock, *The Amnye Machen Range and Adjacent Regions: A Monographic Study*, Serie Orientale Roma 12, Rome: Istituto Italiano per il Medeo ed Estremo Oriente, 1956.

CHAPTER 10
1. Jung 1968 and 1971.
2. Dundas 1968.
3. Kenyatta 1938. See in particular pp. 244-49.
4. *Ibid.*, page 203.

CHAPTER 11
1. Turville-Petre (1975, 55) provides a fuller background explanation to the derivation of Valhalla.
2. Lindow, 1978. See in particular pages 34-35 and 98-99.
3. Loomis, 1963.
4. MacCulloch, 1911.
5. Coolidge, 1904.
6. Mallory, 1918.
7. 'Mont Blanc: Lines Written in the Vale of Chamouni.'
8. Sherrard, 1985. Sherrard's work is widely considered to be one of the most authoritative accounts on the spiritual significance of Athos.
9. De Beer, 1930.

Further Reading

Allen, Charles. *A Mountain in Tibet: The Search for Mount Kailas and the Sources of the Great Rivers of India*. London: Futura, Macdonald, 1983.

Anati, Emmanuel. *The Mountain of God*. New York: Rizzoli, 1986.

Ankelsaria, B.T. (trans.) *Zand-Akasih: Iranian or Greater Bundahishn*. Bombay: Rahnumae Mazdayasnan Sabha, 1956.

Arai, Yusel. *Odaishi-Sama: A Pictorial History of the Life of Kobo Daishi*. Translated by Hiroshi Katayama, Karl Kinoshita and Alberta Freidus. Osaka, Japan: Koyasan Shuppansha, 1973.

Armstrong, Edward A. *Saint Francis: Nature Mystic,* Los Angeles: University of California Press, 1973.

Ashe, Geoffrey. *Avalon Quest*. Fontana, 1984.

Assagioli, Roberto. *Psychosynthesis*. London: Viking Press, 1973.

Atkinson, Edwin T. *Kumaun Hills: Its History, Geography and Anthropology with Reference to Garwhal and Nepal*. Delhi: Cosmo, 1974.

Baker, Dwight Condo. *T'ai Shan: An Account of the Sacred Eastern Peak of China*. Shanghai: Commercial Press, 1925.

Basho, Matsuo. *The Narrow Road to the Deep North*. Translated by Noruyuki Yuasa. London: Penguin, 1966.

Bastien, Joseph W. Mountain of the Condor: Metaphor and Ritual in an Andean Ayllu. *American Ethnological Society Monographs*. No. 64. St Paul: West, 1978.

——. The Human Mountain. In *Mountain People*, edited by Michael Tobias, pp. 45–57. Norman and London: University of Oklahoma Press, 1986.

Batchelor, Stephen. *The Tibet Guide*. London: Wisdom, 1987.

Beal, Samuel, (trans.) *Buddhist Records of the Western World*. 1884. Reprint: New York: Paragon, 1968.

Bechky, Allen. *Adventuring in East Africa: The Sierra Club Travel Guide to the Great Safaris of Kenya, Tanzania, Eastern Zaire, Rwanda and Uganda*. San Francisco: Sierra Club Books, 1989.

Becky, Fred. *Mountains of North America*. San Francisco: Sierra Club Books and American Club, 1982.

Beckwith, Martha Warren. *Hawaiian Mythology*. New Haven: Yale University Press, 1940.

Begay, Harrison. *The Sacred Mountains of the Navajo in Four Paintings* by Harrison Begay. Explanatory Text by Leland C. Wyman. Flagstaff: Museum of Northern Arizona, 1967.

Bernbaum, Edwin. *The Way to Shambhala*. Garden City, New York: Anchor Press/ Doubleday, 1980.

——. *Sacred Mountains of the World*. San Francisco: Sierra Club Books, 1990.

Berry, Wendell. *The Unsettling of America: Culture and Agriculture*. New York: Avon Books, 1977.

Birnbaum, Raoul. Studies on the Mysteries of Manjusri: A Group of East Asian Mandalas and Their Traditional Symbolism. *Society for the Study of Chinese Religions Monograph Series*, No. 2 Boulder, Colorado: Society for the Study of Chinese Religions, 1983.

——. The Manifestation of a Monastery: Shen-ying's Experiences on Mount Wu-T'ai in a T'ang Context. *Journal of the American Oriental Society* 106, No.1 (1986), pp. 119–37.

Blacker, Carmen. *The Catalpa Bow: A Study of Shamanistic Practices in Japan*. London: Allen & Unwin, 1975.

Blofeld, John Eaton Calthorpe. *The Wheel of Life: The Autobiography of a Western Buddhist*. Second Edition. Berkeley: Shambhala, 1972.

Bly, Robert. *The Kabir Book*. Boston: Beacon Press, 1977.

——. *News from the Universe*. San Francisco: Sierra Club Books, 1980.

—— (translator). *Selected Poems of Rainer Maria Rilke*. London: Harper & Row, 1981.

Bohm, David. *Wholeness and The Implicate Order*. London: Ark Paperbacks, 1980.

Boyce, Mary. *A History of Zoroastrianism*. Two volumes. Handbuch der Orientalistik. Leiden, The Netherlands: Brill, 1975-1982.

Capra, Fritjof. *The Tao of Physics*. Berkeley: Shambhala, 1975.

Carter, H. Adams. The Goddess Nanda and Place Names of the Nanda Devi Region. *The American Alpine Journal* 21, No. 51 (1977), pp. 24–29.

Chang, Garma C.C. (trans.) *The Hundred Thousand Songs of Milarepa*. Two volumes. Boston: Shambhala, 1977.

Christ, Carol P. *Diving Deep and Surfacing*. Boston: Beacon Press, 1980.

Clark, Ella E. *Indian Legends of the Northwest*. Berkeley: University of California Press, 1953.

Clark, Kenneth. *Landscape into Art*. New York: Harper & Row, 1976.

Clark, Ronald W. *Men, Myths and Mountains*. New York: Crowell, 1976.

Clifford, Richard J. *The Cosmic Mountain in Canaan and the Old Testament*. Cambridge: Harvard University Press, 1972.

Cohen, Michael P. *The Pathless Way: John Muir and American Wilderness*. Madison: University of Wisconsin Press, 1984.

Cohn, Robert L. The Shape of Sacred Space: Four Biblical Studies. *AAR Studies in Religion*, No. 53 Chico, California: Scholars Press, 1981.

Collcutt, Martin. Mount Fuji as the Realm of Miroku: The Transformation of Maitreya in the Cult of Mount Fuji in Early Modern Japan. In *Maitreya: The Future Buddha*, edited by Helen Hardacre and Alan Sponberg, pp. 248–69. Cambridge University Press, 1988.

Coolidge, W.A.B. *Josias Simler et les origines de l'alpinisme jusqu'en 1600*. Grenoble: Allier Freres, 1904.

Cooper, Adrian. Geographies of Religious Commitment in a Small Coastal Parish. In *Geography of Religions and Belief Systems*, pp. 3–5, 1990.

——. *Geography, Metaphor and Religious Commitment*. Conference Paper, presented to the Association of American Geographers Conference, Miami, Florida, 1991a.

——. *Geography and Religion: Problems and Opportunities.* Discussant Paper, presented to the Association of American Geographers Conference, Miami, Florida, 1991b.

——. Religio-Geographical Research and Public Policy. In *Geography of Religions and Belief Systems,* pp. 3-6, 1991c.

——. *Landscape, Place and Personal Christian Commitment.* Unpublished PhD thesis. Department of Geography, Birkbeck College, University of London, England, 1991d.

——. *Everyday Faith in Ordinary Places.* Radio talk broadcast on BBC World Service and BBC Radio 5, 1992a .

——. New Directions in the Geography of Religion. In *Area,* Vol. 24, pp. 123–29, 1992b.

——. *With The Eyes to See.* Radio talk broadcast on BBC World Service, 1992c.

——. *Landscape, Place and Attitudes Towards Young People.* Conference Paper, presented to the Association of American Geographers Conference, San Diego, California, 1992d.

——. *Other Sides to the City of Angels.* Radio talk broadcast on BBC World Service, 1993.

——. *Ways of Seeing China: Past and Present.* Radio talk broadcast on BBC World Service, 1994a.

——. *Negotiated Dilemmas in the Interpretation of Landscape and Religious Belief.* Conference Paper, presented to the Association of American Geographers Conference, San Francisco, 1994b.

——. Negotiated Dilemmas of Landscape, Place and Christian Commitment in a Suffolk Parish. In *Transactions of the Institute of British Geographers,* NS 19, pp. 202–12, 1994c.

——. Interpretations of Religio-geographical Landscape and Place Meaning Among Adolescents in an English Parish. In *Geography of Religions and Belief Systems,* pp. 1–3, 1994d.

——. Landscape, Place and Personal Pilgrimage Experience. In *Geographia Religionum,* Vol. 8, pp. 81–93, 1994e.

——. *Nature and Christian Faith I-III.* Three meditations broadcast on BBC World Service, 1994f.

——. Adolescent Dilemmas of Landscape, Place and Religious Experience in a Suffolk Parish. In *Environment and Planning D: Society and Space,* Vol. 13, pp. 349–63, 1995.

——. *Discovering sacred wisdom in Chinese landscapes: Shanghai.* Meditation broadcast on BBC World Service, 1996a.

——. *Discovering sacred wisdom in Chinese landscapes: Guangzhou.* Meditation broadcast on BBC World Service, 1996b.

——. *Discovering sacred wisdom in Chinese landscapes: Guilin.* Meditation broadcast on BBC World Service, 1996c.

Corbin, Henry. *Spiritual Body and Celestial Earth: From Mazdean Iran to Shi'ite Iran.* Translated by Nancy Pearson. Princeton University Press, 1977.

Cornell, Joseph Bharat. *Sharing Nature With Children.* London: Ananda Publications, 1979.

Covarrubias, Miguel. *Island of Bali.* New York: Knopf, 1946.

Crausaz, Winston. *Citlaltepetl: A History of Pico de Orizaba Including Exploration, Mountaineering, Natural History, and Geology.* New York: American Alpine Club, 1990.

Daitoku-in. *An Account of Accompanying the Chief Priest on his Mountain Asceticism.* Document held in Tenri Central Library, Tenri University, 1839.

Dass, Ram. *Journey of Awakening.* London: Bantam Books, 1985.

Daumal, René. *Mount Analogue: A Novel of Symbolically Authentic Non-Euclidean Adventures in Mountain Climbing.* Translated by Roger Shattuck. Baltimore: Penguin Books, 1974.

Day, Christopher. *Places of the Soul.* London: The Antiquarian Press, 1990.

Day, Dorothy. *The Long Loneliness: An Autobiography.* New York: Harper & Row, 1952.

De Beer, G.R. *Early Travellers in the Alps.* London: Diswick and Jackson, 1930.

De Laguna, Frederica. Under Mount Saint Elias: The History and Culture of the Yakutat Tlingit, *Smithsonian Contributions to Anthropology,* Vol. 7, Washington DC: Smithsonian Institution Press, 1972.

De Mallie, Raymond J. Lakota Belief and Ritual in the Nineteenth Century. In *Sioux Indian Religion: Tradition and Innovation,* edited by Raymond J. De Mallie and Douglas R. Parks, 25-43, Norman: University of Oklahoma Press, 1987.

——. (ed.) *The Sixth Grandfather: Black Elk's Teachings Given to John G Neihardt.* Lincoln: University of Nebraska Press, 1984.

Dillard, Annie. *Pilgrim at Tinker Creek.* New York: Bantam Books, 1975.

Dixon, Roland. Shasta Myths. In *Journal of American Folklore,* Vol. 23, No. 87 (1910), pp. 8–37.

Dogen. Treasury of the True Dharma Eye: Book XXIX, The Mountains and Rivers Sutra. Translated by Carl Beilefeldt. In *The Mountain Spirit,* edited by Michael Charles Tobias and Harold Drasdo, pp. 41–49. Woodstock: Overlook Press, 1979.

Doub, William. Mountains in Early Taoism. In *The Mountain Spirit,* edited by Michael Charles Tobias and Harold Drasdo, pp. 129–35. Woodstock: Overlook Press, 1979.

Douglas, Anne. *The Feminization of American Culture.* New York: Knopf, 1977.

Downes, David Anthony. *Ruskin's Landscape of Beatitude.* New York: Peter Lang, 1984.

Doyle, Brendan. *Meditations with Julian of Norwich.* Santa Fe: Bear & Company, 1983.

Dubs, Homer C. An Ancient Chinese Mystic Cult. In *Harvard Theological Review,* Vol. 35, No. 4 (1942), pp. 221–40.

Dundas, Charles. *Kilimanjaro and Its People: A History of the Wachagga, Their Laws, Customs and Legends, Together with Some Account of the Highest Mountain in Africa,* 1924. Reprint: London, Frank Cass, 1968.

Duran, Diego. *Book of the Gods and Rites and the Ancient Calendar.* Translated by Fernando Horcasitas and Doris Heyden. Norman: University of Oklahoma Press, 1975.

Earhart, H Brown. *A Religious Study of the Mount Haguro Sect of Shugendo: An Example of Japanese Mountain Religion.* Toyko: Sophia University 1970.

——. Mount Fuji and Shugendo. *Japanese Journal of Religious Studies,* Vol. 16, Nos. 2–3 (1989), pp. 205–26.

Eastcott, Michael. *The Silent Path — An Introduction to Meditation*. London: Rider & Co., 1975.

Echevarria, Evelio. The Inca Mountaineers: 1400-1800. In *The Mountain Spirit*, edited by Michael Charles Tobias and Harold Drasdo, pp. 117–24. Woodstock: Overlook Press, 1979.

——. Legends of the High Andes. In *The Alpine Journal*, Vol. 88, No. 332 (1983), pp. 85–91.

Eck, Diana L. Banaras: *City of Light*. Princeton: Princeton University Press, 1983.

——. Mountains. In *The Encyclopaedia of Religion*, edited by Mircea Eliade, 10: pp. 130–34. New York: Macmillan, 1987.

Eckstorm, Fannie Hardy. The Katahdin Legends. In *Appalachia*, Vol. 16, No.1 (1924), pp. 39–52.

Eichorn, Arthur Francis. *The Mount Shasta Story*. Second edition. Mount Shasta, California: Mount Shasta Herald, 1971.

Eliade, Mircea. *The Myth of the Eternal Return or, Cosmos and History*. Translated by Willard R Trask. Princeton University Press, 1971.

Eliade, Mircea. *Patterns in Comparative Religion*. Translated by Rosemary Sheed. New York: New American Library, 1974.

Eliot, T.S. *The Complete Poems and Plays*. New York: Harcourt Brace Jovanovich, 1952.

Emerson, Nathaniel Bright. Unwritten Literature of Hawaii: The Sacred Songs of the Hula. Smithsonian Institution, *Bureau of American Ethnology Bulletin*, No. 38. Washington: Government Printing Office, 1909.

Evans-Wentz, W.Y. *Cuchama and Sacred Mountains*. Edited by Frank Waters and Charles L Adams. Chicago: Swallow Press; Athens: Ohio University Press, 1981.

Farquhar, Francis Peloubet, and Phoutrides, Aristides E. *Mount Olympus*. San Francisco: Jonck & Seeger, 1929.

Fox, David J. Stewart. *Once a Century: Pura Besakih and the Eka Dasa Rudra Festival*. Jakarta: Penerbit Citra Indonesia, 1982.

Fox, Matthew (editor*) Western Spirituality: Historical Roots, Ecumenical Routes*. Santa Fe: Bear & Company, 1980.

Fox, Matthew. *Original Blessing*. Santa Fe: Bear & Company, 1983.

Galland, China. *Longing for Darkness: Tara and the Black Madonna*. New York: Viking Penguin, 1990.

Gaskin, May. *Spiritual Midwifery*. London: Book Publishing Company, 1978.

Gawain, Shakti. *Creative Visualization*. London: Bantam Books, 1985.

Geertz, Armin W. A Reed Pierced the Sky: Hopi Indian Cosmography on Third Mesa, Arizona. *Numen*, Vol. 31, No. 2 (1984), pp. 216–41.

Geil, William Edgar. *The Sacred 5 of China*. New York: Houghton Mifflin, 1926.

Gersie, Alida. *Earthtales: Storytelling in Times of Change*. London: Greenprint, 1992.

Gomez, Luis O., and Woodward Jr., Hiram W. (eds.) *Barabudur: History and Significance of a Buddhism Monument*, Berkeley Buddhist Studies Series 2, Berkeley: Asian Humanities Press, 1981.

Govinda, Lama Anagarika. *The Way of the White Clouds*. Berkeley: Shambhala, 1970.

Graber, Linda H. Wilderness as Sacred Space. *Association of American Geographers Monograph Series*, No. 8 Washington: Association of American Geographers, 1976.

Grapard, Allan G. Flying Mountains and Walkers of Emptiness: Toward a Definition of Sacred Space in Japanese Religions. In *History of Religions*, Vol. 21, No. 3 (1982), pp. 195–221.

Gribble, Francis. *The Early Mountaineers*. London: T. Fisher Unwin, 1899.

Griffin, Susan. *Women and Nature: The Roaring Inside Her*. New York: Harper Colophon, 1978.

Hakeda, Yoshito S. Kukai: *Major Works*. New York: Columbia University Press, 1972.

Han-Shan. *Cold Mountain: 100 Poems by the T'ang Poet Han-Shan*. Translated by Burton Watson. New York: Columbia University Press, 1970.

Hamsa, Bhagwan Shri. *The Holy Mountain: Manasarovar and the Mount Kailas*. Translated by Shri Purohit Swami. 1934. Reprint: Delhi: Bibliographies Bureau and Balaji Enterprises, 1986.

Hazleton, Lesley. *Where Mountains Roar*. London: Penguin Books, 1981.

Heine-Geldern, Robert. *Conceptions of State and Kingship in Southeast Asia*, Data Papers 13. Ithaca, New York: Southeast Asia Program, Department of Far Eastern Studies, Cornell University Press, 1956.

Hertz, J.H. (editor) *The Pentateuch and Haftorahs*. Second edition. London: Soncino Press, 1961.

Herzog, Maurice. *Annapurna*. Translated by Nea Morin and Janet Adam Smith. New York: Dutton, 1952.

Hirayama, Toshijiro. On an Account of Accompanying the Chief Priest of the Shogo-in Temple on his Mountain Asceticism in 1839. In *Bulletin of the Kashihara Archaeological Institute*, Nara Prefecture, Vol. 7, pp. 343–75 Tokyo: Yoshikawa kobunkan, 1984.

Hori, Ichiro. Mountains and Their Importance for the Idea of the Other World. In *History of Religions*, Vol. 6, No.1 (1966), pp. 1–23.

Hornbein, Thomas F. *Everest: The West Ridge*. San Francisco: Sierra Club Books/Ballantine Books, 1968.

Hotchkis, Anna M., and Mullikan, Mary Augusta. *The Nine Sacred Mountains of China: An Illustrated Record of Pilgrimages Made in the Years 1935–36*. Hong Kong: Vetch and Lee Ltd., 1973.

Hume, Robert Ernest (translator) *The Thirteen Principal Upanishads*. Second revised edition. Oxford University Press, 1931.

Huxley, Anthony (ed.) *Standard Encyclopaedia of the World's Mountains*. New York: Putnam's, 1962.

Hyde, Philip, and Jett, Stephen C. Navajo. *Wildlands*. San Francisco: Sierra Club Books/Ballantine Books, 1969.

Irving, R.L.G. (ed.) *The Mountain Way: An Anthology in Prose and Verse*. New York: Dutton, 1938.

Iyer, Raghavan. *The Moral and Political Thought of Mahatma Gandhi*. Oxford University Press, 1978.

Jacobi, Jolande (ed.) *C.G. Jung: Psychological Reflections, A New Anthology of His Writings*. New York: Harper Colophon, 1978.

Jette, Julius. On Ten'a Folklore. In *Journal of the Royal Anthropological Institute*, Vol. 38 (1908), pp. 312–13.

John the Scot. *Periphyseon: On the Division of Nature*. Indianapolis: Beacon Press, 1976.

Johnson, Russell, and Moran, Kerry. *The Sacred Mountain of Tibet: On Pilgrimage to Mount Kailas*. Rochester: Park Street Press, 1989.

Jung, Carl. *Man and his Symbols*. Garden City, New York: Doubleday and Co., 1968.

———. *The Archetypes and the Collective Unconscious*. Translated by RFC Hull. London: Routledge & Kegan Paul, 1971.

Kalidasa. *Kumarasambhava*. Edited by Kasinath Pandurang Parab. Third edition. Bombay: Nirnayasagara Press, 1893.

Kavanaugh, Kieran. *The Collected Works of St John of the Cross*. Washington DC: Institute of Carmelite Studies, 1973.

Kenyatta, Jomo. *Facing Mount Kenya: The Traditional Life of the Kikuyu*. London: Secker and Warburg, 1938.

Keys, Donald. *Earth at Omega — Passage to Planetization*. London: Branden Press, 1982.

Kong, Lily. Geography and Religion: Trends and Prospects. In *Progress in Human Geography*, Vol. 14, pp. 355–71.

Koyama, Kosuke. *Mount Fuji and Mount Sinai: A Critique of Idols*. Maryknoll: Orbis Books, 1984.

Kroll, Paul W. Verses From on High: The Ascent of T'ai Shan. In *T'oung Pao*. Vol. 69, Nos. 4–5 (1983), pp. 223–60.

Kystal, Phyllis. *Cutting the Ties That Bind*. London: Sawbridge Enterprises, 1986.

Layton, Robert. *Uluru: An Aboriginal History of Ayers Rock*. Canberra: Australian Institute of Aboriginal Studies, 1986.

Lehrman, Frederic. *The Sacred Landscape*. Berkeley: Celestial Arts, 1988.

Levenson, Jon D. *Sinai and Zion: An Entry into the Jewish Bible*. New York: Winston Press, Seabury Books, 1985.

Lindow, John. *Swedish Legends and Folktales*. Berkeley: University of California Press, 1978.

Lipsey, Roger. *An Art of Our Own: The Spiritual in Twentieth Century Art*. Boston: Shambhala, 1988.

Lobell, John. *Between Silence and Light: Spirit in the Architecture of Louis I. Kahn*. Boulder: Augsburg Publishing House, 1979.

Loewe, Michael. *Ways to Paradise: The Chinese Quest for Immortality*. London: George Allen & Unwin, 1979.

Loomis, Roger Sherman. *The Grail: From Celtic Myth to Christian Symbol*. New York: Columbia University Press, 1963.

Lovelock, James. *Gaia — A New Look at Life on Earth*. Oxford University Press, 1982.

Luckert, Karl W. *Navajo Mountain and Rainbow Bridge Religion*. Flagstaff: Museum of Northern Arizona, 1977.

Mabbett, I.W. The Symbolism of Mount Meru. In *History of Religions*, Vol. 23, No.1 (1983), pp. 64–83.

MacCulloch, J.A. *The Religion of the Ancient Celts*. Edinburgh: T. & T. Clark, 1911.

MacDonald, Alexander W. The Lama and the General. In *Kailash*, Vol. 1, No. 3 (1973), pp. 225–33.

Mallory, George. Mont Blanc from the Col du Géant by the Eastern Buttress of Mont Maudit. In *The Alpine Journal,* Vol. 32, No. 218 (1918).

Mao Tse Tung. *Mao Tse Tung Poems.* Beijing: Foreign Languages Press, 1976.

Margolin, Malcolm. *The Way We Lived: California Indian Reminiscences, Stories and Songs.* Berkeley: Heyday Books, 1981.

Maslow, Abraham H. *Religion, Values and Peak-Experiences.* London: Penguin Books, 1987.

Maspero, Henri. *Taoism and Chinese Religion.* Translated by Frank A. Kierman, Jr. Amherst: University of Massachusetts Press, 1981.

Meade, Charles. *High Mountains.* London: Harvill, 1954.

Merton, Thomas. *The Collected Poems of Thomas Merton.* New York: New Directions Publishing Corp., 1977.

Miyazawa, Kenjo. *Life as Art.* Unpublished translation of Miyazawa's 1926 transcript, 1962.

Morrison, Hedda. *Hua Shan: The Taoist Sacred Mountain in West China.* Hong Kong: Vetch and Lee Ltd., 1973.

Moss, Richard. *The Black Butterfly — An Invitation to Radical Aliveness.* London: Celestial Arts, 1987.

Mountford, Charles P. *Ayers Rock: Its People, Their Beliefs and Their Art.* Honolulu: East-West Centre Press, 1965.

Muir, John. Explorations in the Great Tuolumne Canyon. In *Voices for the Earth: A Treasury of the Sierra Club Bulletin,* edited by Ann Gilliam: pp. 4–8. San Francisco: Sierra Club Books, 1979.

Muir, John. *The Mountains of California.* 1894. Reprint. San Francisco: Sierra Club Books, 1988.

Muir, John. *The Yosemite.* 1914. Reprint. San Francisco: Sierra Club Books, 1988.

Muriithi, Kiboi, and Ndoria, Perter. *War in the Forest: The Autobiography of a Mau Mau Leader.* Nairobi: East African Publishing House, 1971.

Murray, W.H. *The Scottish Himalayan Expedition.* London: J.M. Dent & Sons, 1951.

Nabokov, Pèter. *Two Leggings: The Making of a Crow Warrior.* New York: Crowell, 1967.

Nash, Roderick. *Wilderness and the American Mind.* Third Edition. London: Yale University Press, 1982.

Neihardt, John G. *Black Elk Speaks.* 1932. Reprint. New York: Pocket Books, 1972.

Nelson, Richard K. *Make Prayers to the Raven: A Koyukon View of the Northern Forest.* Chicago: University of Chicago Press, 1983.

Nimmo, H. Arlo. Pele, Ancient Goddess of Contemporary Hawaii. In *Pacific Studies,* Vol. 9, No. 2 (1986), pp. 121–79.

Nimmo, H. Arlo. Pele's Journey to Hawaii: An Analysis of the Myths. In *Pacific Studies,* Vol. 11, No.1 (1987), pp. 1–42.

O'Flaherty, Wendy (translator) *The Rig Veda: An Anthology.* New York: Penguin Books, 1981.

Oda, Masayasu. The Formation and its Meaning of the 75-sacred-place View in the Ohmine Sacred Mountain Area. In *Human Geography,* Vol. 41, 6 (1989), pp. 24–40.

Oda, Masayasu. Geographical perspectives on a Japanese Mountain Religion, Shugendo: with special reference to the Ohmine Mountains. In *Dossier de la revue de Géographie Alpine*, No.11 (1993), pp. 135–40.

Orbell, Margaret. *Hawaiki: A New Approach to Maori Tradition*. Christchurch: University of Canterbury, 1985.

——. *The Natural World of the Maori*. Auckland: Collins/Bateman, 1985.

Ortiz, Alfonso. *The Tewa World: Space, Time, Being and Becoming in a Pueblo Society*. London: University of Chicago Press, 1969.

Otto, Rudolf. *The Idea of the Holy*. Translated by John W Harvey. Oxford University Press, 1950.

Pallis, Marco. *The Way and the Mountain*. London: P. Owen, 1960.

Paranavatana, Senerat. *The God of Adam's Peak*. Ascona, Switzerland: Artibus Asiae Publishers, 1958.

Porter, William. *Road to Heaven: Encounters with Chinese Hermits*. San Francisco: Mercury House, 1993.

Powell, Father Peter John. *People of the Sacred Mountain*. Two volumes. San Francisco: Harper & Row, 1981.

Reichardt, Louis F., and Unsoeld, William F. Nanda Devi from the North. In *The American Alpine Journal*, Vol. 21, No. 51 (1977), pp. 1–23.

Reinhard, Johan. Chavin and Tiahuanaco: A New Look at Two Andean Ceremonial Centres. In *National Geographic Research*, Vol. 1, No. 3 (1985), pp. 395–422.

——. High Altitude Archaeology and Andean Mountain Gods. In *The American Alpine Journal*, Vol. 25, No. 57 (1983), pp. 54–67.

——. Sacred Mountains: An Ethno-archaeological Study of High Andean Ruins. In *Mountain Research and Development*, Vol. 5, No. 4 (1985), pp. 299–317.

Rey, Guido. *The Matterhorn*. Translated by JEC Eaton. Oxford: Basil Blackwell, 1946.

Rich, Adrienne. *The Dream of a Common Language*. New York: W.W. Norton & Co, 1978.

Robinson, Doug: The Climber as Visionary. In *Voices for the Earth: A Treasury of the Sierra Club Bulletin*, edited by Ann Gilliam, pp. 289–93. San Francisco: Sierra Club Books, 1979.

Rousseau, Jean-Jacques. *Julie ou la Nouvelle Héloise*. Paris: Garnier-Flammarion, 1976.

Roth, Gabrielle. *Maps to Ecstasy*. London: Crucible/The Antiquarian Press, 1989.

Rowell, Galen. *Mountains of the Middle Kingdom*. San Francisco: Sierra Club Books, 1983.

Ruskin, John. *Modern Painters*. Second Edition. Five volumes. New York: Wiley, 1883.

Ruskin, John. *Praeterita*. Boston: Estes, 1895.

Sahtouris, Elisabet. *Gaia — The Human Journey from Chaos to Cosmos*. New York: Pocket Books, 1989.

Samuels, Marwyn. Individual and Landscape: Thoughts on China and the Tao of Mao. In *Humanistic Geography: Prospects and Problems*, edited by David Ley and Marwyn Samuels, pp. 283–96. Chicago: Maaroufa Press, 1978.

Schmitz, L. Dora (ed.) *Miscellaneous Travels of J.W Goethe*. Translated by A.J.W. Morrison. London:: George Bell and Sons, 1884.

Sharma, Man Mohan. *Through the Valley of Gods: Travels in the Central Himalayas*. Second edition. New Delhi: Vision Books, 1978.

Sherrard, Philip. *Athos: The Holy Mountain*. Woodstock: Overlook Press, 1985.

Shipton, Eric. Nanda Devi. In *The Six Mountain-Travel Books*, edited by Jim Perrin, pp. 15–151. 1936. Reprint. Seattle: The Mountaineers, 1985.

Skrobucha, Heinz. *Sinai*. Translated by Geoffrey Hunt. Oxford University Press, 1966.

Snow, Chief John. *These Mountains Are Our Sacred Places: The Story of the Stoney People*. Toronto: Samuel Stevens, 1977.

Sobrino, Jon. The Witness of the Church in Latin America. In *The Challenge of Basic Christian Communities*, edited by Sergio Torres and John Eagleson. Maryknoll: Orbis, 1981.

Sri Ramana Maharshi (translator) *Five Hymns to Sri Arunachala*. Third edition. Sri Ramanasramam: Niranjananda, 1946.

Starhawk. *Dreaming the Dark: Magic, Sex and Politics*. Boston: Beacon Press, 1982.

——. *The Spiral Dance: A Rebirth of the Ancient Religion of the Great Goddess*. London: Harper & Row, 1989.

Stevens, Stan. Sacred and Profane Himalayas. In *Natural History*, Vol. 97, No.1 (1988), pp. 26–35.

Swift, Hugh. *Trekking in Nepal, West Tibet and Bhutan*. San Francisco: Sierra Club Books, 1989.

——. *Trekking in Pakistan and India*. San Francisco: Sierra Club Books, 1990.

Thoreau, Henry David. *The Maine Woods*. 1848. Reprint. New York: Bramhall House, 1950.

——. *Walden*. Edited by J. Lyndon Shanley. Princeton University Press, 1971.

Tichy, Herbert. *Himalaya*. Translated by Richard Rickett and David Streatfeild. New York: Putnam's, 1970.

Tobias, Michael. (editor) *Mountain People*. London: University of Oklahoma Press, 1986.

Tuan, Yi-Fu. *Topophilia: A Study of Environmental Perception, Attitudes and Values*. Englewood Cliffs: Prentice-Hall, 1974a.

——. Space and place: Humanistic perspective. In *Progress in Geography*, Vol. 6 (1974b), pp. 212–52.

——. Humanistic geography. In *Annals of the Association of American Geographers*, Vol. 66, No. 2 (1976), pp. 266–75.

——. Sacred Space: explorations of an idea. In *Dimensions of Human Geography: Essays on Some Familiar and Neglected Themes*, edited by KW Butzer. University of Chicago, Department of Geography Research Paper 186 (1978), pp. 84–99.

——. *Landscapes of Fear*. New York: Pantheon Books, 1979.

——. *Morality and Imagination: Paradoxes and Progress*. Madison: University of Wisconsin Press, 1989.

Turner, Frederick. *Beyond Geography: The Western Spirit Against the Wilderness*. London: Viking Press, 1980.

Turville-Petre, E.O.G. *Myth and Religion of the North: The Religion of Ancient Scandinavia*. Westport, Conn.: Greenwood Press, 1975.

Uhlein, Gabrielle. *Meditations with Hildegard of Bingen*. Santa Fe: Bear & Co, 1983.

Van Buitenen, JAB., (editor and translator) *The Mahabharata*. Three volumes. University of Chicago Press, 1973-78.

van der Post, Laurens. *The Voice of the Thunder*. London: Penguin Books, 1993.

Varma, Rommel and Sadhana. *The Himalaya: Kailasa-Manasarovar*. Geneva: Lotus Books, 1985.

von Rad, Gerhard. *Wisdom in Israel*. Abingdon: Abingdon Press, 1974.

Wales, H.G. *The Universe around Them: Cosmology and Cosmic Renewal in Indianized Southeast Asia*. London: Arthur Probsthain, 1977.

Waley, Arthur (translator) *A Hundred and Seventy Chinese Poems*. New York: Knopf, 1919.

Warren, Edward. *Freedom and Spiritual Activity*. London: Temple Lodge, 1994.

Webster, Peter. *Rua and the Maori Millennium*. Wellington: Victoria University, 1979.

Wenkam, Robert. *The Edge of Fire: Volcano and Earthquake Country in Western North America and Hawaii*. San Francisco: Sierra Club Books, 1987.

Westermann, Claus. *Blessing in the Bible and the Life of the Church*. London: Fortress, 1978.

Whitehead, Alfred North. *Science and the Modern World*. London: Macmillan, 1927.

Whymper, Edward. *Scrambles Amongst the Alps in the Years 1860–69*. Fifth edition. London: John Murray, 1900.

Winthrop, Theodore. Tacoma and the Indian Legend of Hamitchou. In *Mount Rainier: A Record of Exploration*, edited by Edmond S. Meany. New York: Macmillan, 1916.

Woodruff, Susan. *Meditations with Mechtild of Magdeburg*. Santa Fe: Bear & Co, 1982.

Wordsworth, William. *Poetical Works*. Edited by Thomas Hutchinson. Oxford University Press, 1967.

Wyman, Leland C. *Blessingway*. Tucson: University of Arizona Press, 1970.

Appendix

The contributors to this research

Among the 144 contributors listed below, seven had helped me with a number of academic projects in which I had interviewed them about their attitudes toward religious commitment and the places and landscapes which helped shape those attitudes. The interviews for each element of that work included one-to-one meetings, as well as small group sessions, all of which I tape-recorded and transcribed. But even before I had fully planned this book, many of the remaining 137 people variously contacted me having heard, directly or otherwise, about my academic work and its involvement with landscape, place and faith. Consequently, I have never had to advertise for contributors. All the 144 interviewees are volunteers: people who share my interest in exploring the meaning of spiritual commitment, landscape and place in the latter years of the twentieth century. A great advantage of working with such volunteers was their enthusiasm and commitment to this project in helping to define it, and develop its present form. Right from the start, when I explained the aims of the project at its inception in August 1985, I felt a spirit of shared ownership for the work. The contributors are all individuals who share a strong commitment to exploring the ancient and modern meaning of mountains as a profound stimulation to their spiritual quests. In the preceding chapters, they discuss how ancient wisdom inspires them, and how they also develop new meaning and fresh insights from those sacred, mountain landscapes.

As the list shows, the 144 contributors are drawn from a wide range of spiritual, geographical and professional experience. However, they fall broadly into three groups. First, there are the parishioners from the parish of St Peter and St Paul, St Andrew and St Nicholas in Felixstowe with whom I have developed my other academic work. Second, there are representatives of the United States Air Force based in Mildenhall, Suffolk, along with other volunteers who are drawn from the families and friends of those representatives. Finally, from the University of Essex in Colchester and the University of London, there are contributors drawn from the academic and administrative staff, undergraduate and post-graduate students, and other volunteers who are friends and family members of this third group. In all cases, interviews with these people were arranged informally. No long-term time-table of meetings was ever developed. Instead, the next interview session was only arranged at the end of its immediate predecessor. By this informal strategy, I attempted to remove any sense of obligation to the project which some individuals may have felt. An added element of informality was maintained by arranging our meetings in places where the individuals felt most at ease: in their own homes, favourite pubs, hotel bars, cafeterias, student common-rooms and on town and country walks. Again, this selection of interview places was a conscious attempt to keep the contributors at their ease so they could talk and think comfortably. Despite the order placed on the material in this book, many of the responses were generated in a less structured manner. Through this emphasis on informality, spontaneity became an essential medium for the expression of ideas.

But alongside my attempts to maintain an informality in these interview meetings, it is also important to record that, as with all passionately expressed discussions, the control over some interviews was sometimes taken over by the interviewees. For both the one-to-one sessions, as well as the small-group meetings, some themes of discussion, as well as the ways they were expressed, frequently provoked some of the contributors to question and explore the intervention from others, and to more fully describe and clarify their own discussions. Since I was content to allow these stimulating debates to continue, and for other occasional exchanges of challenge and enquiry to take place, it has remained the case that this project is not simply the product of one man's collaboration with 144 receptive interviewees. Rather, the truth has been more complex, and lively! Many of our meetings followed on from the previous one where contributors continued to discuss personally significant themes, and literary and artistic references, which they had introduced for debate, and developed amongst themselves. In such circumstances, my own role was simply to record those exchanges and to clarify any areas of ambiguity where I felt I did not completely understand a point being made. I also sought to ensure that all present were given a chance to finish expressing their opinions.

Given the energy and enthusiasm from my contributors, I have felt greatly responsible for these individuals' integrity in recording their personal expressions of faith. Their transcripts remain confidential, and have only been used for publication with their consent and following their extensive involvement in drafting the manuscript of this book. For confidentiality, each person has been given a pseudonym.

Whilst these people's stories of intense realization were always provocative and valuable to the development of this research, they occasionally caused significant problems. Some were initially reluctant to share so much of themselves with an interview group of strangers. Others were also initially reluctant to describe their profound experiences within our one-to-one meetings. However, as bonds of trust and loyalty grew between myself and them, as well as between the travellers themselves, many of those with profoundly personal stories learned that they could share as much of those recollections as they felt appropriate, in the full knowledge that their words would be received sensitively and with compassion. And, on many occasions, I felt it necessary to reassure contributors that none of their experiences would be published without their permission. As a consequence, not all their recollections and discussions have been printed here. However, it was never my intention to produce a sensationalist piece of research, but rather, one which grew out of empathy and sympathy with the people with whom I worked.

Although my ethical responsibilities have therefore restricted the amount of data which was available to the final published book, I nevertheless believe that this finished work offers a richer, more responsive and more stimulating discussion than if I had restricted my research method to questionnaire surveys or once-only interviews. Not only are such alternatives almost totally superficial and unsatisfying, but they also impose such a rigid structure on the questions which are asked by researchers, and on the answers provided by their respondents. Questionnaires and once-only interviews would therefore have been a blatant insult to the diverse experiences of the travellers who contributed to this book. Those techniques would have stifled the memories of these people, and would not have attracted either the enthusiasm or the loyalty and patience which each of the interviewees showed as they continued to give of themselves so freely. I also remain convinced that all the most interesting questions which were considered within these interviews were asked directly by the contributors themselves toward other travellers in their interview groups. Alternatively, other questions were inspired directly by remarks and observations offered by these individuals. Consequently, this book is a work of active collaboration and team-work between travellers, most of whom had never met each other before.

List of the contributors

Place of residence and occupation as at time of writing, August 1995. Some interviewees requested that their place of residence should be withheld.

Pseudonym	Year of Birth	Faith	Place of Residence	Occupation
Adam	1943	Taoist	New York City	Artist
Agnes	1948	Buddhist	Baltimore, Maryland	Teacher
Alan	1970	Christian	Anchorage, Alaska	Teacher
Alex	1941	Christian	Southampton, England	Business partner
Alfred	1925	Buddhist	Phoenix, Arizona	Retired archaeologist
Amos	1950	Christian	Philadelphia, Penn.	Teacher
Amy	1956	Christian	New York City	Public relations consultant
Andrea	1958	Buddhist	Liverpool, UK	Colour therapist
Andy	1960	Freethinker	Lincoln, Nebraska	Flight technician
Arnie	1947	Christian	Dallas, Texas	Truck driver
Basil	1951	Christian	Chicago, Illinois	Business manager
Ben	1975	Jew	Chicago, Illinois	Botany student
Bethany	1966	New Age	New York City	Merchant bank manager
Bill	1942	Christian	Southampton, UK	Business partner
Bob	1960	Freethinker	Macon, Georgia	Flight technician
Bret	1966	New Age	New York City	Merchant bank manager
Brian	1949	Christian	Savannah, Georgia	Civil engineer
Buster	1940	Buddhist	Dublin, Ireland	Zen teacher and writer
Carla	1968	Christian	Columbus, Ohio	Driver
Carol	1968	Buddhist	Birmingham, UK	Software designer
Casey	1942	Buddhist	Europe	Business Manager
Charles	1952	Buddhist	Oklahoma City	Shop owner
Chester	1952	Taoist	Austin, Texas	Teacher
Clare	1970	Buddhist	San Bernardino, Calif.	Administration supervisor

Clive	1970	Christian	Anchorage, Alaska	Teacher
Cybil	1950	Taoist	Miami, Florida	Shop owner
Dale	1965	Taoist	Felixstowe, UK	Administration clerk
Danny	1976	Christian	Los Angeles, Calif.	Apprentice mechanic
Davey	1971	Buddhist	Los Angeles, Calif.	Pan-pipe musician
David	1929	Christian	Colchester, UK	Retired Landscape Architect
Dee	1970	Jew	Berlin, Germany	Architect
Denisse	1967	Christian	Dallas, Texas	Nurse
Derek	1951	Christian	Reading, UK	Director
Dianne	1961	Christian	London, UK	Unemployed
Don	1958	Buddhist	Felixstowe, UK	Clerk
Duncan	1959	Buddhist	San Diego, Calif.	Musician
Eddie	1976	New Age	Springfield, Miss.	Communications student
Edward	1974	Christian	Exeter, UK	Drama student
Elizabeth	1975	Jew	Chicago, Illinois	Botany student
Eric	1971	Freethinker	Vancouver, Canada	Designer
Eve	1945	Christian	Montreal, Canada	Shop assistant
Frances	1944	Buddhist	London, UK	Sculptor
Frank	1951	Buddhist	Detroit, Michigan	Writer and photographer
Freddy	1954	Buddhist	Winchester, UK	Engineer
Gabbi	1957	Jew	London, UK	Journalist and campaigner
Gary	1975	Christian	Birmingham, UK	Maths student
Gavin	1964	Taoist	Felixstowe, UK	Administration clerk
Gene	1958	Christian	Tacoma, Washington	Military policeman
Geoff	1958	Christian	Denver, Colorado	Naturalist
George	1956	Christian	Blackburn, UK	Building inspector
Georgia	1960	Christian	San Francisco, Calif.	Art lecturer
Giles	1973	Christian	Cambridge, UK	Archaeology student
Gillian	1958	Buddhist	London, UK	Archaeologist
Glen	1948	Buddhist	Vancouver, Canada	Design consultant
Glenda	1945	Buddhist	Colchester, UK	Artist
Gordon	1937	Christian	London, UK	Marketing executive
Grace	1976	Christian	Norwich, UK	Post-graduate chemist
Gregory	1975	Christian	New Orleans, Louis.	History student
Guy	1957	Buddhist	Glasgow, Scotland	Carpenter and cabinet-maker

Hannah	1973	Jew	Hamburg, Germany	Environmental researcher
Hariette	1951	Christian	London, UK	Journalist
Hillary	1953	Buddhist	Ohio	Policewoman
Hugo	1949	Buddhist	Vancouver, Canada	Design consultant
Ian	1957	Buddhist	Dayton, Ohio	Photographer
Iris	1951	Buddhist	Colchester, UK	Personnel assistant
Jade	1957	Buddhist	London, UK	Railway information officer
Jake	1942	Christian	Chicago, Illinois	Computing lecturer
James	1973	Christian	Cambridge, UK	Archaeology student
Jane	1945	Buddhist	Los Angeles, Calif.	Personnel manager
Janice	1951	Taoist	London, UK	Social worker
Jed	1976	Christian	Los Angeles, Calif.	Apprentice mechanic
Jeff	1952	Buddhist	Colchester, UK	Personnel assistant
Jennifer	1969	Buddhist	Birmingham, UK	Software designer
Jeremy	1970	Christian	Cardiff, Wales	Art student
Jessica	1961	Buddhist	San Francisco, Calif.	Botanist
Joan	1947	Taoist	Toronto, Canada	Linguistic translator
Joe	1976	Buddhist	Felixstowe, UK	History student
Joseph	1969	Buddhist	Los Angeles, Calif.	Pan-pipe musician
Joshua	1962	Buddhist	Sacramento, Calif.	Pianist
Josie	1969	Buddhist	Seattle, Washington	English lit. Student
Julia	1953	Buddhist	Colchester, UK	Personnel manager
Julian	1976	Buddhist	Felixstowe, UK	History student
Karen	1944	Christian	Colchester, UK	Artist
Kathy	1960	Buddhist	Felixstowe, UK	Administration clerk
Keith	1957	Buddhist	Newark, New Jersey	Engineer
Kent	1951	Buddhist	New York City	Teacher
Kyle	1963	Jew	Washington DC	Researcher
Larry	1956	Buddhist	Newark, New Jersey	Engineer
Leon	1954	Buddhist	Newark, New Jersey	Engineer
Lesley	1963	Buddhist	London, UK	History student
Lincoln	1973	Christian	Cambridge, UK	Archaeology student
Linda	1961	Christian	Ipswich, UK	Librarian
Lindsey	1963	Buddhist	London, UK	History student
Lionel	1952	Jew	Miami, Florida	Textile cutter
Lizzie	1973	Buddhist	Bristol, UK	Biology student
Louis	1973	Jew	Munich, Germany	Environmental researcher

Lucy	1953	Buddhist	Jacksonville, Florida	Kitchen assistant
Mabel	1930	Christian	Cheyenne, Wyoming	Retired clerk
Malcolm	1970	Christian	Anchorage, Alaska	Teacher
Margaret	1944	Christian	Colchester, UK	Administration clerk
Marsha	1968	Buddhist	Birmingham, UK	Software designer
Martina	1959	Taoist	Billings, Montana	Pollution controller
Mary	1972	Buddhist	Los Angeles, Calif.	Percussionist/singer
Maurice	1960	Freethinker	Cheyenne, Wyoming	Flight technician
Michael	1954	Christian	London, UK	Systems analyst
Miriam	1970	Jew	Berlin, Germany	Architect
Moisha	1936	Jew	London, UK	Journalist
Nancy	1950	Taoist	Miami, Florida	Shop owner
Neil	1960	Buddhist	San Francisco, Calif.	Botanist
Pamela	1954	Christian	Ipswich, UK	Secretary
Patrick	1974	Christian	Chelmsford, UK	Drama student
Paula	1954	Christian	Felixstowe, UK	Housewife
Pauline	1973	Buddhist	Newcastle, UK	Biology student
Perry	1947	Taoist	Toronto, Canada	Linguistic translator
Pete	1975	Christian	New Orleans, Louisiana	History student
Phillip	1957	Christian	New Orleans, Louisiana	Military policeman
Philippa	1943	Christian	Washington DC	Journalist
Quentin	1959	Taoist	Atlanta, Georgia	Freelance lecturer and writer
Rachel	1975	Jew	Chicago, Illinois	Botany student
Ralph	1956	Buddhist	Los Angeles, Calif.	Zen teacher
Robert	1958	Christian	London, UK	Insurance underwriter
Rosamund	1959	Buddhist	San Diego, Calif.	Musician
Roselle	1970	Jew	Dortmund, Germany	Architect
Roy	1975	Christian	Birmingham, UK	Maths student
Rudi	1973	Jew	Frankfurt, Germany	Environmental researcher
Sally	1976	Christian	Bristol, UK	Post-graduate chemist
Seb	1952	Jew	Miami, Florida	Textile cutter
Shaughn	1951	Christian	Dublin, Ireland	Business manager
Simon	1967	Buddhist	San Francisco, Calif.	Law student
Stan	1941	Christian	Southampton, UK	Business partner
Steve	1961	Buddhist	San Francisco, Calif.	Botanist
Suzannah	1952	Christian	Manchester, NH	Teacher

Teresa	1954	Buddhist	Aberdeen, Scotland	Writer and photo-grapher
Thomas	1957	Buddhist	Leeds, UK	Administration clerk
Tim	1970	Christian	Anchorage, Alaska	Teacher
Tom	1951	Christian	Baltimore, Maryland	Technical sergeant
Toni	1973	Jew	London, UK	Photography student
Tracy	1943	Christian	Southampton, UK	Business partner
Trevor	1975	Christian	Birmingham, UK	Maths student
Tye	1957	Sceptic	San Diego, Calif.	Accountant
Wanda	1967	Christian	Dallas, Texas	Nurse
Waylon	1946	Taoist	Tulsa, Oklahoma	Teacher
Wesley	1973	Christian	Cambridge, UK	Archaeology student
William	1967	New Age	New York City	Merchant bank manager